THE
FOUNDATION
OF ROME

THE
FOUNDATION
OF ROME

Myth and History

Alexandre Grandazzi

Translated by Jane Marie Todd

CORNELL UNIVERSITY PRESS

ITHACA AND LONDON

The publisher gratefully acknowledges the financial assistance of the French Ministry of Culture in defraying part of the cost of translation.

Originally published as *La fondation de Rome: Réflexion sur l'histoire.* © Les Belles Lettres, 1991.

First published 1997 by Cornell University Press.
First printing, Cornell Paperbacks, 1997.

Printed in the United States of America.
Design and composition by Rohani Design, Edmonds, Washington.

Library of Congress Cataloging-in-Publication Data
Grandazzi, Alexandre.
    [Foundation de Rome. English]
    The foundation of Rome : myth and history / Alexandre Grandazzi ; translated by Jane Marie Todd.
        p.   cm.
    Includes bibliographical references and index.
    ISBN 0-8014-3114-X (alk. paper).—ISBN 0-8014-8247-X (pbk. :alk. paper)
    1. Rome (Italy)—History—To 476. 2. Rome—History—To 510 B.C.—Historiography. 3. Mythology, Roman. 4. Archaeology and history—Italy—Rome. 5. Rome (Italy)—Antiquities. 6. Excavations (Archaeology)—Italy—Rome. 7. Archaeology in literature.
    I. Title.
    DG65.G7313   1997
    937—dc21   97-17341

Cornell University Press strives to utilize environmentally responsible suppliers and materials to the fullest extent possible in the publishing of its books. Such materials include vegetable-based, low-VOC inks and acid-free papers that are also either recycled, totally chlorine-free, or partly composed of nonwood fibers.

Cloth printing   10 9 8 7 6 5 4 3 2 1
Paperback printing   10 9 8 7 6 5 4 3 2 1

To Sophie, sine qua non

CONTENTS

PREFACE

Pierre Grimal
Institut de France

T HERE IS USUALLY some ulterior motive behind any discussion of
Rome's beginnings. It is quite probable that Louis de Beaufort, in writing his famous *Dissertation* (which will be considered at length in this
book), was not sorry to bring the tradition of the imperial city—and by virtue
of it, the pontifical city as well—back down to earth, to amputate it from the
supernatural. Do bad intentions make for "good" history? Beaufort's intentions
did not; rather, in virtually repeating what Livy had already said in his preface
to *Ab urbe condita libri*, Beaufort destroyed the history we thought we knew.
Livy was more subtle.

And Alexandre Grandazzi is infinitely more circumspect. When he had read
everything that has been written on the origins of Rome, he looked at the object
of that inquiry and saw it was possible to imagine the most diverse responses.
Only one fixed point remains: the very existence of a city, established on the
left bank of the Tiber, in a place that seems not to be a matter of indifference.
But how was it chosen? Did it occur by chance? Or did a man of genius found
it as Cicero claimed, a man that he, along with everyone else at the time, called
Romulus? Or perhaps it was the result of the kind of fatality that historians liked
to invoke in the past: conditions favorable for production and preservation, and
for traffic in all sorts of resources, from the most commonplace to the most
rare—salt from the sea as well as porphyry and marble. Discussion of the origins
of Rome disrupts all our ways of conceiving of history and casts doubt on the
very existence of the past that history claims to grasp. The subject matter exerts
an irresistible fascination. Everything is or can be called into question, including
what the ancients have told us, though such questioning entails a certain pre-
sumptuousness on the part of moderns. The people of the "Enlightenment,"
harboring a secret desire to reduce the universe to something within reach of
individual reason, wished to believe that anything outside their reach was lies.
Thus they came to imagine that the Romans, beginning at the (inaccessible!)
origin, had told one another fables, explanatory myths. Romulus was said to have
a brother because the consulate was occupied by two men simultaneously. Quite
an astonishing explanation, since one brother supposedly killed the other!
Similarly, the fact that tradition asserted that Romulus's men had ravished the
Sabines' daughters meant that, in ancient times, marriage began with violence.

And historians went on to cite customs practiced among various peoples, none of whom had had the slightest contact with the Romans.

The author of this book abandons nearly every aspect of the theories that have won credence until now. He can do so, first, because the very notion of origin, or, as he prefers to write, primordia (a term that does not exclude the idea of continuous development and does not imply creation ex nihilo), has been diluted. It is now easy to imagine that a religious and spiritual pre-Rome eventually took shape on the banks of the Tiber. And we no longer believe that a city has to be founded in a space devoid of human presence. To make his point, Grandazzi introduces the contributions of archeology. He knows them well, knows that in themselves they are not sufficient to provide the solutions to all problems but are merely one element in the great reconstruction desired. He knows there is a great distance, an abyss, between Livy's account—itself a synthesis of diverse and contradictory traditions—and the brute facts revealed by excavations. The bridge between the two fields, that linking the shard, the wall, or the traces of piles—driven into the soil three thousand years ago—to the texts that tell us the nature of the pomerium, is obviously precarious and perilous. It is always dangerous to infer one sort of reality based on another. Nonetheless, the risk must be assumed. As Grandazzi observes, history abhors a vacuum.

This study of the primordia of Rome begins with ruins: the ruins of theories, which appeared simultaneously or one after the other nearly two hundred years ago, designed to explain the presence of the city of Rome—in a place where it was solidly rooted—and the forces that assured its cohesion from the earliest times, its existence as a spiritual entity, a settlement, and already a nation. Beginning as early as the tenth century B.C.E., there existed many Romes "in germ" throughout the territory of Latium, villages and townships spread out between the sea and the Apennines and the hills. Only one held its ground. This book seeks to discover why, with so many throws of the dice, there was only one winner.

Through the problems raised by the nature of Rome's origin, Grandazzi provides a reflection on what historical method ought to be. He will not confuse in a single category of knowledge objects of different orders, will not totalize, by simply adding up texts and shards, well-attested facts—the existence of rituals and cults, legal concepts valid for a particular period—and generalizations that are grounded in modern and anachronistic presuppositions. It is quite certain that human beings have an irresistible tendency to reconstruct their own past endlessly, to color it in ever-changing hues. No object, no human memory, is immutable, nor is it acquired once and for all. History is a category of the mind; it is living and cannot be objective. History is by its very nature a creator of myths. That may be the most profound lesson of this book: from the very moment of birth, Rome in its beginnings has continued to be rethought. Hence hypercriticism is no longer destructive. On the contrary, it valorizes the very things it was designed to condemn, makes them into what they always were, moments in a history, which, in the end, exists only in human memory.

THE
FOUNDATION
OF ROME

This was the order of human things: first the forests, after that the huts, thence the villages, next the cities, and finally the academies.

Giambattista Vico, *The New Science*, 65.239

INTRODUCTION

I T MAY BE SURPRISING to see an entire book devoted to the foundation of Rome: for a long time, a discussion of that event served only as
a brief but obligatory preamble to any account of Roman history or, at
best, as a somewhat marginal chapter supplementing the study of Etruscan civilization. Beyond question, the apparent disproportion of this book deserves
some explanation.

Most obviously, there are the facts themselves. Like any modern capital, contemporary Rome is the heart of a vast urban agglomeration that is becoming
more densely populated every year. In archaic times, the Etruscan city of Veii, situated about twenty kilometers from the center of Rome, was that city's principal
rival; today, it is nothing more than a distant suburb. Elsewhere, concrete buildings are closing in on sites where the ancients took pleasure in finding the traces
of Aeneas, sites that, even at the beginning of the twentieth century, had not
changed since Virgil's time. Urbanization, which accelerated considerably during
the 1970s, has led to a proliferation of excavations, and therefore, of scientific
discoveries and scholarly discussions.

But the obvious explanation is somewhat deceiving in this case. The increase
in archeological operations cannot fully explain why research on the origins of
Rome has recently taken on such importance. In several key instances, in fact,
interest in the primordia has led to the decision to go out into the field, rather
than being a consequence of it. And if it were merely a matter of data, then the
hut-urns of Castel Gandolfo, revealed nearly two centuries ago, or the archaic
vestiges of the Forum, exhumed at the dawn of the 1900s, would have had a similar effect on scholarship. But the passionate interest these discoveries elicited in
their time did not last long. Therefore, something else must be at the root of current developments.

In a word (and we are, of course, simplifying a great deal), the flourishing we
are witnessing does not stem merely from the quantitative growth in material
(material that, until recently, was left to prehistorians and Etruscologists). More
fundamentally, it is the result of a change in the very idea historians have formed
of their discipline. Through a process whose effects are far from complete, historians have adopted new instruments of measure, new methods, and new questions.

Explored with the tools of political history and the history of events, the earliest days of Rome had little to offer us; revisited in the light of innovative approaches in a discipline that is continually expanding into new territories, they have only begun to reveal their secrets.

Nonetheless, there are numerous obstacles and difficulties to be overcome in the analysis of this unique phenomenon, the birth of Rome as a city. The ancient texts that refer to it were written several centuries after the first appearance of the city. For a long time, criticism used that chronological gap as a justification for denying the slightest value to the texts, in accordance with a method that provided nineteenth-century historical scholarship with some of its most widely accepted parameters and techniques of analysis. This was the golden age of triumphant hypercriticism, to which, in fact, we owe many fundamental works.

Gradually, at the insistence of Etruscologists in particular, historians have become more aware of the existing material vestiges of Rome and Latium from the sixth and seventh centuries B.C.E. They have finally been led to concede that the tradition's account of the last kings of Rome contains at least a kernel of historical truth. Using the few documents and indexes they possess and moving carefully from one deduction to the next, they have succeeded in erecting a model of sixth-century Rome that, in its main lines, corroborates the literary tradition. Less than thirty years ago, the Hungarian scholar Andreas Alföldi, in arguing Rome's weakness during the fifth century B.C.E., denied all historical value to the tradition. Whatever the indisputable and dazzling merits of his study, it now looks more like the swan song of hypercriticism than the starting point for what followed. The vitalist model was not the right one. Today, we readily concede that Rome was already powerful at the time of the Tarquins; the undeniable weakness of the city in the fifth century B.C.E. is no argument against its influence in the sixth, when the Phocaeans, on their way to found Marseilles, went up the Tiber and formed an alliance with Rome.

In the past, the scholarly exegesis of Rome's beginnings systematically argued the reverse position of the written sources. Are we now entering an age when it must again follow them to the letter, as the contemporaries of Petrarch and Dante did? Could the law of eternal return be the last word in the development of historical scholarship? Undoubtedly not: this return to the texts remains prudent and partial. Above all, it has not yet called into question the clear and firm boundary line that Barthold Georg Niebuhr established at the beginning of the nineteenth century (and that Georges Dumézil redrew on other grounds), between the reign of the Etruscans, to which a kernel of historical truth is attributed, and that of the Latin rulers—Romulus, Numa, Tullus Hostilius, and Ancus Marcius—which is still lost in the netherworld of legend. If, unlike those of the nineteenth century, modern historians now concede that Rome did not surge up from the void when it victoriously opposed its great rival Carthage in the third century B.C.E., they do so only to shift the boundary line between history and legend, truth and error, not to abolish it. Before the arrival of the Etruscans, there is still nothing but the shadow of fable; and of course, the very foundation of Rome, situated by tradition in the eighth century B.C.E., still disappears into the fog of myth.

Contemporary research, then, displaying a somewhat contradictory attitude and a sometimes palpable malaise, ends up validating the narrative of origins for the "terminal" phase, even while it maintains the line of demarcation for the very beginnings of the *urbs*.

In astronomy, the farther away the stars, the longer their light takes to reach us. Archeology is similar in that respect: developments in research, and especially refinements in excavation techniques, make visible today what was invisible yesterday. Thus the period stretching from the eleventh and tenth centuries to the eighth century B.C.E. has been increasingly explored in the last few years, and the opportunities for comparing the written sources to recent discoveries are multiplying. Nonetheless, scholars have not been led to question the division of tasks that gradually took root among them: those of archeologists (specialists in "protohistory") and those of historians of sixth-century Rome (who are authorized to make use of the portion of legend that might just be deformed history). Until now, the two fields of study have remained all the more distinct in that their separation itself resulted from developments in scholarship. Yet archeologists have moved forward from prehistoric times, arriving at the eighth and seventh centuries; and historians, who started out from the years when the Republic was first established in Rome, have pushed their investigations farther and farther back.

It now happens that in Rome, at the Palatine (that is, on the site of the legendary foundation of the city), archeologists have discovered vestiges, some dating to the eighth century B.C.E., which may give scholars from the two disciplines the opportunity to confront one another and even perhaps to converge in their research. Such a possibility has far-reaching consequences. A disconcerting breach is opening in the wall, patiently erected by scholarship for nearly two centuries, between the implausible and the probable, between myth and reality, between what lies in the province of reason and knowledge and what can be abandoned to the dream world.

These discoveries, and all those that can be linked to them, will be the subject of this book. They are not merely astonishing but represent a real challenge to assumptions about what can be known and what has to remain unknown. It is our hope that if we cannot definitively answer the challenge, we can at least attempt to measure its scope, with the help of results already obtained by the eminent scholars who have gone before us and led the way.

The reader will constantly find archeological discoveries set against literary sources, despite differences in the nature of the material and in their date. Far from seeking to erase these differences, we have attempted to appreciate them at their true value. Like many others before us, we felt we could make use of both stones and texts in a rational manner, provided we respect certain indispensable rules of method. In fact, this procedure was not only possible but even necessary for our subject.

Needless to say, we will have to refrain from establishing a hasty or superficial link, since we are dealing with two very distinct categories of data. Each set provides a specific type of response, and we obviously cannot ask each the same questions. The analysis must be conducted autonomously for each order of facts and the conclusions rigorously limited to the field considered. Only after all these steps have been taken can we move on to a comparison between the two series of conclusions (and not to an arbitrary combination of their elements). From there, the only conclusions that can be validly applied to both fields are those that were first established separately.

The reader will excuse the clumsiness of these formulations: for an investigation of this kind, the principles of method are essential. It goes without saying, however, that it would be just as misleading *not* to draw the necessary conclusions resulting from a well-founded and progressive comparison of sources as it would be to proceed to a superficial (and rightly condemnable) assimilation. We have made every effort to avoid both pitfalls, by always presenting "the order of causes" proper to each series of data before setting out the results we believe are warranted.

Are we to believe in the tradition or not? Such is the old dilemma of historical criticism. With respect to the legendary narrative of the origins of Rome, historians can be divided into two camps: the believers and the skeptics. We will try to show that, to a great extent, their debate itself is false and ought to be abandoned: the astronomer who observes the sky with ancient instruments will have no chance of detecting the existence of quasars. The historian's optical instruments are the concepts he uses. In studying the primordia, we have found that a number of concepts, all the more powerful because they remain implicit, are the product of a given historiographical context and can only lead to a certain type of conclusion, in this case negative and hypercritical. For the distant times we are considering (and for the others as well, in fact), nothing is visible to the naked eye, and what we see depends on the tools of measurement used. That is why we have taken care to evaluate the characteristics and limitations of these tools in every case. Of course, it would be a mistake to separate historical theory (supposedly changing and open to dispute) and archeological practice (credited a priori with an objectivity that is denied to theory). In analyzing the progressive emergence of an archeological knowledge of the *primordia Romana*, we were able to see to what extent this very knowledge carried within it implicit theories and presuppositions. And these too are not without consequences.

Let us turn, then, to the time of the foundation of Rome, which provides the Roman world with a spatiotemporal reference point. For several years now, Rome—like Egypt, Mesopotamia, and Greece (with the decipherment of Linear B)— has been rediscovering its most ancient historical past with each new archeological find. To make this past understandable, we shall often refer to other sites in Latium that evolved in a similar manner. (The literary sources often have nothing to say about such sites. Conversely, the archeological remains for the most ancient periods of Rome itself are obviously very rare.) It is increasingly clear that numerous classical sources dealing with the origins of Rome provide an extraordinary basis for comparison and are an excellent tool for evaluating archeological discoveries. They can lead us to a general comprehension of this phenomenon, the birth of the city, which until now has remained imperfectly understood in many of its aspects.

Because the foundation of Rome has once more acquired a place within history, we will also need to situate it in relation to what preceded and to what followed. Villages and leagues existed on the site where Rome later emerged; and, in a certain manner, the foundation of Rome was repeated during the age of Servius Tullius.

These discussions will lead us, finally, to the old problem of the transmission of the tradition and the value of literary texts as documents. It seems to us that the discoveries of recent years open new perspectives on this question.

By definition, history cannot repeat the experiences it analyzes, and some have claimed that historical conclusions are devoid of all validity as a result. But what scientist fails to make the broadest use of hypotheses? What astrophysicist has ever been able to verify theories about the origin of the world through experimentation? For each, the only conceivable verification is what the philosopher Karl Popper calls "falsification," the testing of all possible counterhypotheses. Such is the approach we attempt to follow throughout this book.

Thus the foundation of Rome is in no way a preestablished truth that lies beyond doubt: it is only a hypothesis. It is simply that in considering the dossier as a whole, we have come to believe that the hypothesis is necessary.

PRELUDE

WHY WRITE ANOTHER history of Rome's origins?[1] Didn't Livy say it all at the beginning of his monumental book, when, with a weariness that was not entirely feigned, he described the subject as "old and hackneyed"?[2] Since the golden age of humanism and the birth of historical criticism, we have heard, in counterpoint to the majestic roar of Livy's book, the obstinate murmur of patient and fastidious scholarly surveys, now shored up and refurbished by the contributions of archeology. Relentlessly, this perpetual commentary (to use a traditional designation of classical philology, but in a different sense)[3] came to be grafted onto the canonical texts, in order to fill in the voids and to elucidate, ever more subtly, their meaning. For such distant times, there is no hope of reaching the human, carnal dimension of a history that has become almost mythic, simply by dint of being endlessly repeated. On a stage decorated in trompe-l'oeil scenery, disincarnated actors tirelessly perform an outdated play, to a house filled only with professionals. That Rome is not of flesh but of marble, and like marble, it seems cold and dead.

That is why, at a time when history, delivered from the totalizing interpretations of the past, is rediscovering with delight the long-forbidden pleasures of biography (a literary genre, let us note in passing, invented and abundantly practiced in antiquity), the narrative of the origins of Rome seems more than ever to justify the ironic nonchalance of Stendhal, who, summarizing the times of the first kings in his *Promenades dans Rome*, invited his readers to "skip five or six pages."[4] There is so much more passion in the *Chroniques italiennes*! But

---

[1] In the following pages, I use the word "history" not only in the relatively precise and "scientific" sense it ordinarily has, but also in the more general sense of "knowledge of the past." This is a sign of the times: in the nineteenth century, it was the word "philology" that benefited from such an extension in meaning.

[2] "Quippe qui cum veterem tum volgatam esse rem videam" (Livy *Ab urbe condita libri*, praefatio, 1). [Unless otherwise noted, quoted passages from ancient authors and modern scholars are my translations—trans.]

[3] Normally, a "perpetual commentary" is a continuous commentary that explains a text from beginning to end.

[4] "The following facts, which it is my duty to recount to my friends, are hardly less proven or more fantastic than everything schoolboys commonly believe about the history of France. Nonetheless, I invite most readers to skip five or six pages" (Stendhal, *Promenades dans Rome*, ed. V. del Litto [Paris, 1973], 657).

Stendhal was seeking something in Livy that is not there. To be more precise, like most of his contemporaries under the sway of the Enlightenment, he was persuaded that the tradition of the beginnings of Rome was only obscurity and uncertainty; hence he was seeking nothing at all. Once more, Rome reflected the viewer's own image.

PART 1

PROLEGOMENA FOR ANY
FUTURE HISTORY OF THE ORIGINS
OF ROME CLAIMING TO BE A SCIENCE

CHAPTER 1

THE AGE
OF PHILOLOGY

B
Y THE MIDDLE AGES, the times of Romulus had taken on the charms of the supernatural, and countless manuscripts, today dispersed throughout all the libraries of Europe, recount the arrival on the banks of the Tiber of the patriarch Noah, associated for the occasion either with Janus or with Saturn.[1] Noah thus came to replace, or even to accompany, the legendary Trojan hero Aeneas, whom the Romans of antiquity had made their national hero.

Then came the Renaissance, when ancient texts were once more diffused, read, and commented upon. Even though the medieval habit of combining biblical and Roman history continued, it was now done with historicist ends unknown to earlier ages, in a more or less successful attempt to purify the tradition of its artificial additions. There appeared for the first time manifestations of the two opposing currents, conservative and skeptic, which would increasingly characterize the study of the origins of Rome.[2] For the conservatives, it was a matter of finding in the legend traces of a very ancient history (hence theirs is sometimes called a historicist point of view); for the skeptics, the narrative of origins was not historical at all and stemmed entirely from fiction (in the nineteenth century, this type of analysis found its most perfect expression in what is called hypercriticism, associated with the Italian historian Ettore Pais). As different as they were, these interpretations had in common the concern to appeal to the testimony of the ancient texts themselves and, as a supplementary refinement, to compare them with one another, in order to draw out the authentic and true version. Or so it was believed: a method of combinatorial analysis was at the foundation of philology, the new science of texts, and assured it its initial accomplishments. During the same period, Machiavelli was deciphering the precepts of Livy's art of governing, based on the First Decade.[3]

---

[1] On these aspects, see A. Graf's classic and indispensable *Roma nella memoria e nelle immaginazioni del Medio Evo* (Turin, 1882), especially 1: 78–108. On Noah and Janus, see also P. Vidal-Naquet, *La démocratie grecque vue d'ailleurs* (Paris, 1990), 146.

[2] On this period in the historiography of Rome's origins, see by H. J. Erasmus, *The Origins of Rome in the Historiography from Petrarch to Perizonius* (Leiden, 1962). See also A. Momigliano's book review in his *Terzo contributo alla storia degli studi classici e del mondo antico* (Rome, 1966), 2: 769–74.

[3] N. Machiavelli, *Discorsi sopra la prima deca di Tito Livio* (1532).

In the early seventeenth century, and even at the end of the sixteenth, examination of the legendary traditions concerning the birth of the Eternal City became the explicit and restrained version of another, much more burning debate, which remained to a large extent implicit: that bearing on the veracity of the biblical tradition. When doubt was cast on Romulus's historicity, exegetes could question the historicity of Noah and the Bible, but with fewer risks. Thus the beginnings of Rome served as a testing ground for a historical Pyrrhonism that was still going forward masked,[4] a hidden but guiding thread for a controversy in which the two adversaries did not say what they were thinking, and both thought something other than what they said.

Thus everything began to shift: the outside air seemed to be circulating in the solemn edifice.

At the beginning of the eighteenth century, after a few skirmishes among learned abbots before the Académie des Inscriptions et Belles-Lettres, a little book arrived from the nation of freedom of thought, the United Provinces, a book that was to set the tone for a long time: Louis de Beaufort's *Dissertation sur l'incertitude des cinq premiers siècles de l'histoire romaine* (Dissertation on the uncertainty of the first five centuries of Roman history), published in Utrecht in 1738. Although the author was not the first to examine with a skeptical eye the traditional account of the earliest times of Rome (Saint-Evremond, for example, had already brought his moral criticism to bear on it), Beaufort's argument, historical in nature, was entirely new (if we except Pierre Bayle's rapid notations). "It will not be surprising," wrote Beaufort, "that we are so little enlightened about the origin of Rome and the times close to it, since Rome was for five hundred years without historians, since the first it had were inexact, and since almost all the monuments that could have supplemented the historians' failings and recorded the principal events were lost in the fire that consumed the city after it was taken by the Gauls."[5]

Thus we find summarized in a few lines the major epistemological obstacles to any future knowledge of the beginnings of Rome: first, the existence of a chronological gap of at least five centuries between the times of the foundation and the appearance of the first historians; and second, the fire in Rome set by the Gauls led by Brennus. According to the ancients themselves, that fire led to the destruction of most earlier documents.

Nearly every historical study from the following century began from the perspective elegantly outlined in Beaufort's dissertation, whether, as was most frequently the case, to support and specify its conclusions, or rather to attempt

---

[4] See the famous essay by A. Momigliano, "Ancient History and the Antiquarian," *Journal of the Warburg and Courtauld Institutes* 13 (1950): 285–315.

[5] Louis de Beaufort, *Dissertation sur l'incertitude des cinq premiers siècles de l'histoire romaine* (Utrecht, 1738), 4. In December 1722, Abbot de Pouilly had already developed his thoughts on "the uncertainty of the first four centuries of Rome" before the Académie Royale des Inscriptions.

to attenuate its destructive rigor at least, but without ever truly calling it into question. From then on, there seemed nothing more to add, and the major problem was not to reject an apparently irrefutable analysis, but to learn how to reconstruct the ruined edifice of Roman history. For a long time, nothing appeared more serious, more justified by the very declarations of the ancient authors, and, in the end, more "scientific"—to use a word that appeared precisely in that sense at the end of the seventeenth century—than that radical (in the strong sense of the term) doubt Beaufort cast on the earliest history of Rome.

Wasn't that the approach recommended by Descartes himself in the search for truth? "In order that our knowledge be accompanied by some certainty," proclaimed Beaufort, "we must doubt what is doubtful."[6] As a result of a reasoned and systematic practice of doubt, imposed, in the case of the most ancient Rome, by the very nature of the sources, history was slowly coming into being, progressively moving away from its traditional ties to rhetoric. It was also experiencing a certain vertigo, as a result of a form of erudition that led it to negate its own validity. Why seek to know, since nothing could be known? Like Socrates, the novice historians of the primordia now knew only one thing: they knew that they knew nothing, and they had only to recount again, one more time, simply showing here and there by a few signs that they were no dupes, the "fable" with which Livy too had had to be satisfied, for lack of anything better.

As a result, the paths of "antiquarian" (today we would say "specialized") research, particularly topography and numismatics (called the art of medals) seemed more certain and more positive. They respected the methodological necessity articulated by Descartes, both to "divide each of the difficulties" examined "into as many parcels as is possible and requisite for best solving them" and to "everywhere make full enumerations" and "general surveys."

Under these conditions, it is clear why Giambattista Vico's writings, unclassifiable in many regards, did not receive the reception we now feel they deserved. In appearance, the constant mixing of times and places in Vico's works, where, from one line to the next, the reader moves from the biblical East to Roman antiquity, and from Egyptians and Phoenicians to Greeks, seemed to manifest all the signs of a complete return to precritical times. In contrast, the exact division of subject matter was one of the major concerns of the new man of science. Above all, when Vico, a Neapolitan philosopher whose contemporaries considered him essentially a jurist, turned to purely poetic intuition to understand the most ancient eras of humanity, he could only disrupt the efforts of Enlightenment rationalism. Today, we admire Vico's acute awareness of the limitations that the search for abstractly defined universals imposes on history, admire his attempt to apprehend as a totality the different aspects of the life of the most ancient societies, and, more fundamentally, his enormous effort to historicize philosophy and to make history philosophical. The truth is that his

6 Beaufort, *Dissertation*, 19.

contemporaries, when they did not simply ignore him, often saw his dense works as merely undigested hodgepodge. Jules Michelet, G. W. F. Hegel, and Benedetto Croce would have to intervene to give a meaning and a future to Vico, who even today has much to teach us.

At the end of the eighteenth century, the revolutionaries' school memories concerning early Rome, which provided them with a prestigious example of a republic succeeding a fallen monarchy, fueled the enthusiasm for those ancient times.[7] But the true renewal of the critical study of Rome's origins came somewhat later, from a Dane who had gone over to the service of Prussia (which he represented in Rome from 1816 to 1822). A specialist in public finance, Barthold Georg Niebuhr, whose *Römische Geschichte* (History of Rome) was published in 1811–1812 and reissued many times, inaugurated the triumphant period of *Altertumswissenschaft*, the German science of antiquity. Even today, this science is apparent in many irreplaceable catalogs and encyclopedic works. Readers of Niebuhr's history, which was quickly made available in translation to the entire educated public of Europe, had the impression that the gulf discovered by Beaufort and his followers could finally be bridged. They were witnessing the birth of a new discipline. Not content to remain at the preliminary stage of criticizing the tradition, the stage at which the ironic stance of the preceding century had bogged down, the new science assigned itself the task of also offering a new and consolidated historical framework, with the help of the brand new instruments of textual criticism (Niebuhr was a reader of manuscripts, a paleographer as renowned as he was audacious).

In that sense, Niebuhr's oeuvre belongs to his time, when the study of the past was thought to entail a large share of restoration. Think, for example, of the neo-Gothic creations of the time, which were then called the troubadour style. Eugène-Emmanuel Viollet-Le-Duc later justified them with a rigorously deductive logic, but they always remained the expression of a passionate quest for origins. Similarly, during their stays at the Villa Medicis, the highly prized architects of Rome were obliged to draw or paint ruined monuments in their "present state," and then to execute what was called a restitution.[8] Thus Niebuhr's work suggested to his readers, beyond the description of the ruins left by the ravages of time and the intentional deformations of ancient historians, the restored image of the "true" face of primitive Rome. In the reconstructed account of these classical times—the slow and difficult emergence of the Roman plebs in the face of the old aristocracy's arrogance, the irresistible rise to power of the young Roman state—the contemporaries of Napoleon and the Holy Alliance recog-

---

[7] See J. Bouineau, *Les toges du pouvoir, 1789–1799, ou la révolution de droit antique* (Toulouse, 1986). Bouineau demonstrates that the revolutionaries were especially interested in the fall of Tarquinius Superbus and the figure of Brutus.

[8] See the exhibition catalog *Roma antiqua: Envois des architectes français (1788–1924)* (Rome, 1986).

nized the distant prelude to the social antagonisms of their own century. They came away with the certainty that, from the apparent chaos and upheaval of the old order, which they saw disappearing before their eyes, the triumph of the new forces of the Europe of nations would one day soon arise. The reports of the time and Niebuhr's correspondence prove in abundance that such associations were not merely an academic point. (Niebuhr died soon after the Revolution of 1830, which he had followed without sympathy but with great attention.) In the preface to *Römische Geschichte*, in which he manifests strong nationalist sentiments, Niebuhr declares: "When a historian is reviving former times, his interest in them and sympathy with them will be the deeper, the greater the events he has witnessed with a bleeding or a rejoicing heart."[9] Despite the lucidity that accompanied it, such personal involvement, common at the beginning of the nineteenth century (think of Michelet, whose project to "resuscitate the ages" bears some similarity to Niebuhr's project to "live with the Romans as with men of our own flesh and blood"),[10] necessarily granted to restitution and intuition (for which Niebuhr outlined a veritable theory) a share that was quickly judged too great. New documents, now relentlessly sought out, classified, and analyzed, increased the mass of material on which historians worked, and gave them a growing sense (and illusion) of the objectivity and infallibility of their art. In 1816, in a very harsh criticism, A. W. Schlegel showed the fragility of the foundations on which Niebuhr had built his edifice; Niebuhr never responded.[11]

In was on the ruins of that edifice that Theodor Mommsen, the unmatched Titan of studies of Roman antiquity, built his own *Römische Geschichte*, published in the wake of the mid-century revolutions. In reality, he did not stop at the hypotheses formulated by his predecessor: spurning what his French translator called "the too often chimerical conjectures dared by scholars of genius such as Vico and Niebuhr,"[12] he hastened to get to the account of the republican era, giving only a rapid overview of the more ancient periods. The epigraph he chose for the first book of his oeuvre, a reflection by Thucydides on the obscurity of legendary times,[13] shows that he had very consciously given up the idea of

---

[9] B. G. Niebuhr, *The History of Rome*, trans. J. C. Hare and C. Thirlwall (Cambridge, 1831), 1: xiii.

[10] This line can be found in the article in M. Michaud's *Biographie universelle* (Paris, 1854–65) devoted to Niebuhr (30: 597).

[11] A. W. Schlegel, *Werke* (Leipzig, 1846–47), 12: 444–512. See also the famous book by G. C. Lewis, published much later, *An Inquiry into the Credibility of the Early Roman History* (London, 1855). For reasons relating to the political history of Great Britain, the English historians (George Grote, William Mitford, and Connop Thirlwall) turned their attention more toward Greek history, however, which gave them the opportunity to reflect on the notion of liberty.

[12] C. Alexandre, "Avant-propos du traducteur," in T. Mommsen, *Histoire romaine*, ed. C. Nicolet (Paris, 1985), 1.

[13] Thuc. 1.1: "As for the most ancient facts, they could not be exactly known to us from this distance in time. Nonetheless, having looked as far as possible, and in judging by the most trustworthy indications, I did not find any great events, acts of war or otherwise."

spending too much time on eras where he could find neither "facts" nor "great events." His was a very positivist conception of history, lagging clearly behind even his own work as an epigraphist, linguist, and jurist. His interest in the traditional account of the origins of Rome lay not in its immediate historicity, since as a historical account he considered it mere invention and propaganda, but in its value as a representation of the categories of Roman law.[14] It was thus principally in his legal works that we find his exegesis of the legends of origins, or at least those that present the essential schemata of Roman legal thought. But since he conceived of history as merely a set of events and facts, he had to renounce giving an account of the beginnings of Rome. Once more, the study of origins seemed to lead to an impasse, to a choice between an almost ritual repetition of the Livian tradition and an open-ended study of the sources, a study ontologically condemned to be always only preliminary, never to lead to conclusions.

At the same date as Niebuhr, the Italian historian Giovanni Micali proposed to write a history of the peninsula before the Roman influence. But the very absence of archeological documentation of any real scope and the apparent fragility of the philological foundations to which he found himself obliged to resort (fragile because drawn from classical texts that were suspect for two reasons, because of their Romanocentric viewpoint and because of their relatively late date) long limited his influence to the circle of those then called specialists. Indeed, how could he write a history of Italy before Rome, when he had to begin with sources that were, for the most part, Roman in inspiration? The paradox was more concealed than overcome in this anticipatory work, which led a contemporary (Sismondi) to write: "One feels more than ever in reading this book that the center of the entire history of Italy is Rome, and that center remains outside the book."[15] In fact, postulating a radical caesura throughout his survey between the Italic history of the peninsula and the time of Roman domination, Micali placed the very process of the formation of Rome outside his analysis. It is clear from the French commentator's almost continual reprobation, in the notes he added to Micali's text in 1824,[16] that such an anti-Roman point of view shocked readers, who were little disposed to accept it, especially since to many of them it seemed contrary to the contemporary aspirations of Italian liberalism in the formation of a united state. And methodologically, Micali's efforts were grounded on principle in the new desire to make philology auxiliary to archeology, thus reversing the relation of dependence between the two disciplines. But the still rudimentary state of archeology too often left it the humble servant of

[14] "The entire history of the origins of Rome has its foundation in the political institutions from the beginning of the fifth century" (T. Mommsen, *Römische Staatsrecht* [Leipzig, 1887–88], 190 n. 2).

[15] This judgment is recorded in the chapter devoted to Micali in P. Treves, *Lo studio dell'antichità classica nell'ottocento* (Milan, 1962), 294.

[16] The commentator is R. Rochette, author of "notes and historical clarifications" to G. Micali, *L'Italie avant la domination des Romains*, translated into French by P. L. Joly and C. Fauriel.

history, and Micali's book could not escape a grave internal contradiction, which only the subsequent increase in archeological documentation would resolve, at least in part. In any case, Micali bequeathed this problem to the future: although the problem—the coordination between literary sources and archeological data—was major, it was almost unperceived at the time and would not be taken up again before the end of the nineteenth century.

In the decades that followed, apart from Mommsen's survey, there was a striking absence of basic work dealing with the *primordia Romana*. The attention of the scholarly community turned to other periods of Roman antiquity and to other disciplines as well: philology, then the collection and commentary of inscriptions from the republican and imperial eras.

Almost a hundred years before other areas of historical research, ancient history experienced an explosion of different disciplines and a fragmentation of problematics, as a result of the inundation of masses of documents and relentlessly pursued improvements, new methods for deciphering and exploiting sources (manuscripts, papyri, inscriptions), which rapidly led to techniques requiring a high degree of specialization. Enormous surveys, most often (but not always) the result of collective efforts, were able once again to create the illusion of totality and unity, though only for a brief period of time.

In appearance at least, the Rome of origins, of which neither inscriptions nor monuments were yet known, remained apart from this veritable epic of new knowledge. In reality, however, that period in Rome's history was where the new principles of analysis found a kind of negative confirmation, a proof a contrario. As the great edifices of knowledge were erected, a critical labor was at work in the lower depths, on the letter of the tradition. Conducted on exclusively philological foundations, it led to a total "deconstruction" of the narrative of origins. Among the mass of detailed studies published in the scholarly reviews (especially German ones) of the period, Mommsen's memorable articles, beginning in 1870, devoted to the legends of Remus, Tatius, Acca Larentia, and Coriolanus, and to the great mythical figures of the beginnings of the Roman Republic (Spurius Cassius, Manlius, and Maelius), particularly stand out.

In another field, which the works of Georges Dumézil occupy in our own century, comparative mythology saw the appearance of a few valuable studies, notably those of the German scholar Ludwig Preller.[17] It is nevertheless surprising that the archeological discoveries that appeared by chance in the Alban Hills at the beginning of the nineteenth century,[18] which made known for the first time material vestiges contemporary with the earliest times of Rome, were abandoned to the care of "antiquarians" (for topography studies) and especially to the care of paleontologists. One of the essential reasons for this lack of interest on the

---

[17] L. Preller, *Römische Mythologie* (Berlin, 1865).

[18] The find goes back to 1816 and was related by E. Visconti in an essay dated 1817 and published in 1823. It was not until the 1860s that scholars once more became interested in it.

part of historians and philologists was the excessively remote chronology assigned to these funerary urns from the first civilization of Latium. In the absence of any point of reference, they were relegated to the most distant prehistory.

The renewal of interest in the origins of Rome, which characterized the end of the nineteenth century, can be attributed to one of Mommsen's students, the Italian Ettore Pais, who had attended his seminar in Berlin for two years. The circumstances were favorable for this reawakening: finally established on the banks of the Tiber in 1870, the young Italian state was piously bowing to the most ancient past of its new capital and felt a desire not to neglect any part of it. But it became clear that that fervor was not without its dangers, since in the area of the primordia, nationalism, as touchy in the field of scholarship as in other areas, often tipped the scales in favor of a very prudent and conservative interpretation of the classical tradition.

Nonetheless, the history of ideas and of historiography cannot be reduced to the expression of a simplistic causality. During these years, Pais wrote his *Storia di Roma* (it was first published in Turin in 1898 and 1899), which remains to this day the most lasting monument of what is called hypercriticism. The term means "an excess of criticism" and was meant to be pejorative; the defenders of the tradition used it to indicate the problematic Pais had adopted.

How did this perspective differ from skepticism, which, as we have seen, was long professed by an entire current of the scholarly tradition concerning the beginnings of Rome? First, and this can be easily verified, it differed in its concern, now considered an obligation, to shore up the slightest assertion with copious footnotes. What the "gentleman" Beaufort had not for an instant dreamed of doing, what Niebuhr had wished to avoid by proposing his own restitutions, what Mommsen, too eager to move in other directions, had disdained to do, Pais undertook methodically, systematically, fastidiously. One after another, the Roman legends—even the most beautiful, the best known, those that were still being learned by heart in all the schools of Europe—were subjected to the test of a merciless analysis, prodigiously ingenious and ineluctably destructive, as a function of a postulate expressed at the beginning of the work: "In the first lines of this book, we can assert that a great part of what claims to be the most ancient Roman history is only the fruit of belated literary speculations and even deliberate falsifications."[19]

The sacrilege was of great scope, as were the scandals and polemics elicited by the book. Pais's compatriots accused him of importing ideas from Germany, and some even criticized him "for not adequately taking into account the psychology of Romulus"! Beaufort's condemnation of the tradition of Rome's origins had, through its generality and vagueness, allowed for many possibilities of accommodation with a reading that more or less wanted to retain its faith in

[19] E. Pais, *Storia di Roma* (Turin, 1898), 1: 2.

the tradition. To suppose that, because of the loss of documents, a large part of the most ancient history had been forgotten and that the account of the origins was thus characterized by "uncertainty" did not in any way prevent people—this was very clear in Niebuhr—from hoping to rediscover, through analysis and historical induction, the truth of those obscure times. It was something else again to show, in a detailed argument using all the resources of the most masterful erudition, that the beautiful legends of origin could be explained as premeditated fabrications, invented to serve the propaganda needs of the great patrician families and the ambitions of the Roman Republic. In the end, people always prefer to acknowledge their ignorance rather than admit they have been deceived. Pais's adversaries indignantly (but not inaccurately) pointed out that the undertaking, despite the author's explicit adherence to an extremely nationalist credo and to a pedagogical and moralistic valorization of the most ancient Roman history, led to the annihilation of the very possibility of history's existence as such. How was it possible to write about ages for which documents either no longer existed or existed only as fakes? What has so often been termed Pais's failure lies in this dilemma, which he never managed to escape, and in the dual and correlative impossibility of writing history to which it led.

Thus, at the end of the nineteenth century, confronted with an archeological discovery on the very soil of Rome that finally gave substance to the legendary accounts, torn between his nationalism and his rationalism, Pais sought the support that his critical method could not give him in a grandiloquent rhetoric, which was to make him an official intellectual by the end of the interwar period. In the course of its various editions, his *Storia di Roma* tempered the principles that had constituted its originality and greatness. He gave the work a new title, *Storia critica di Roma*,[20] out of faithfulness to himself, and probably also in deliberate opposition to his great rival Gaetano de Sanctis. But it was no use: the slow metamorphosis that led him to rally behind what he had formerly combated, and his almost involuntary recantation, which was not without its pathos, even today reveal the theoretical fragility of his critical postulates. And they also show that historians cannot escape their own history.

Was all that effort expended in vain? And are we to believe, as is generally done, that since Pais's conclusions have been invalidated by the progress of archeology, his efforts are null and void? Certainly not. First, through its indisputable public success, his work obliged the traditionalist camp—those who had faith in the texts (we might call them hypocritical, but, to avoid all confusion, we prefer to term them fideists)—to sharpen their weapons, purify their problematics, nuance their adherence to the tradition, and above all, attempt to justify it. In that sense, the "tempered criticism" set in place at the beginning of this century by de Sanctis, in the first volumes of his *Storia dei Romani*, is inconceivable

---

[20] Id., *Storia critica di Roma*, 4 vols. (Turin, 1913–20), dedicated to Victor Emmanuel III, king of Italy, and reprinted several times.

without Pais's work. But, more than anything else, the publication of Pais's book made the return to determinism, so dear to the entire nineteenth century, difficult. Having been weighed, dismantled, dismembered, and x-rayed as it were, in the accumulation of an inextricable jumble of analyses, the earliest times of Rome and the legends relating to them dissolved into a thousand and one causalities and lost their authenticity, their chronology, and their meaning. How much care and prudence would de Sanctis need then to attempt to propose a reading of the history of Rome in the light of the conflict between freedom and unity! And even so, the author of *Storia dei Romani* is always more convincing in his denunciation of Pais's failings than in his own exegeses.

Until that time, writing the history of the primordia had meant substituting one sort of determinism for another, since it was always implicit that history, even that history, had some meaning: the greatness of Rome in Livy, the emergence of the patricio-plebeian state in Niebuhr. In dispersing his analysis into an infinite number of parts (and not without great disorder; there are few works as dense as the *Storia di Roma*), in multiplying and particularizing a whole series of fragmentary causes, in rejecting any unitary perspective, Pais called into question (a bit in spite of himself, as we have seen) the very principle of a determinist reading of the primordia, that is, a reading ordered along the axis of a chronology implicitly validated as causality. Therein lies the continued vitality of his book even today.

Another merit, which in my opinion is not emphasized enough, falls to that work: it restored the concrete substance and chronological density of the legends of Rome's origins—in short, it made them truly historical objects. In the case of Beaufort, these legends were viewed only negatively, as factors of uncertainty, by virtue of the fact that they were legends. For Vico and Niebuhr, such legends supposedly translated "the souls of vanished peoples" (in a lovely expression we borrow from Jean Bayet),[21] but, because they had come from the fount of ages, they slipped away from any possibility of precise analysis, and their interpretation was most often reduced to the bombastic exaltation of their value. For Pais, in contrast, they were linked to precise circumstances and times. Critics have often and quite rightly insisted on the major fault of his interpretation, which did not take into account the very fact of the tradition's existence and confined itself to detailing the reasons for its use and its survival. Roman history seemed to surge forth from an indistinct fog and to begin only three or four centuries before the Common Era. But the idea that the legend was not conserved "for nothing," that the discourse on the legendary past was, in antiquity, always a discourse about the present, a symbolic and sublimated translation as it were, was altogether new and productive. In believing that legends came into being as a result of the motives for which they were used at one moment or another, Pais

---

[21] J. Bayet, "Les origins de l'arcadisme romain," *Mélanges d'Archéologie et d'Histoire* 38 (1920): 63.

certainly made the mistake of confusing cause and effect, but he opened a new field of investigation for the historian of the primordia. And the attention to topography and religious ritual, as means of explaining the legends, also allowed historians to move decisively beyond Mommsen's legal schematism.

Accompanying the beginnings of unified Italy, the writings of Karl Julius Beloch, a German historian at the University of Rome beginning in 1879 and generally considered the founder of the Italian school of historical science, were primarily devoted to the study of classical Rome. In addition to his monumental *Griechische Geschichte* (History of Greece), which included documentation of exceptional richness, Beloch devoted two monographs to the Italian peninsula and took up and developed the results in a Roman history that ended with the First Punic War.[22] There he attempted an original approach, writing the history of earliest Rome without returning to the condemnation of his predecessors regarding the fallacious character of the literary tradition. He undertook to analyze the cadres in Italy and classical Rome, in a history that was predominantly institutional, economic, and structural. In particular, he manifested a concern for quantitative history, which made him, beginning with his authoritative book of 1886, the pioneer of the historical demography of antiquity, and, let us not forget, of historical demography generally. But these new preoccupations depended on the unchanged postulate of the falseness of the tradition, to which he granted as little confidence as had Mommsen or Pais, and which in any case he did not intend to take literally. Thus he did not hesitate even on essential points to disrupt the classical chronology, to suppress a name here, add another there, in the list of Roman magistrates, to modify numerical data transmitted through the texts, in short, to manhandle the tradition, which was nonetheless his obligatory reference point. This fundamental contradiction constitutes the weakness of the book, in which one sometimes also discerns a concern for originality at any price. When it appeared in 1926, his *Römische Geschichte bis zum Beginn der punischen Kriege* (Roman history up to the beginning of the Punic War) did not receive the attention it deserved, since it went against the dominant tendency of the time, the return to a "fideist" reading of the tradition, more than twenty years after the spectacular discoveries in the Forum. But much more than that historical dissonance, it is the overall viewpoint adopted by Beloch that has to be questioned. He deliberately focused on structures rather than on events. According to him, the reality of events lay beyond analysis, since the events recounted in the texts could be the result only of deformations or falsifications. And that allowed him to escape the impasse to which Pais's hypercriticism had led, without falling back into a pure and simple repetition of the traditional account. By thus eliminating the account of events in favor of economic or

---

[22] J. Beloch, *Römische Geschichte bis zum Beginn der punischen Kriege* (Berlin, 1926). A. Momigliano was the author of the entry on Beloch in the *Dizionario biografico degli Italiani* (Rome, 1966), vol. 8.

(above all) institutional structures, preferring the substantial to the accidental, he eventually chose the abstract at the expense of the concrete, the continuous over the discontinuous, tracing the lines of a history without duration, without contingency, without movement: a nonhistorical (because atemporal) history, a history without life.

Beloch's disciple de Sanctis sought that life with a troubled passion that was not satisfied either with the demolition carried out by Pais or with the cold blueprint so meticulously drawn by Beloch. In response to the empty history of one and the motionless history of the other, he criticized the absence of a sense of the sacred, which had obviously marked the Roman world very strongly. For de Sanctis, Beloch's goal of writing a history without representation ("Geschichte ohne Darstellung") amounted to writing a history without history ("Geschichte ohne Geschichte"). His attention to the religious aspect, which his Christian faith suggested to him, and his concern for the human aspect, thus made de Sanctis the apostle of a reasoned return to the tradition, in accordance with a method he himself called "tempered criticism." He undertook to combine the narrative and critical points of view, that is, to verify the tradition using the methods of scientific history.

In reading the first volume of de Sanctis's *Storia dei Romani* today[23] (it appeared in 1907; a second edition prepared by the author was never published), we often have the impression of a superimposition of different tones rather than a harmonious and unified whole. Nonetheless, his project continues to be pursued by his successors. He began by reconstructing the two columns of the temple that Pais's hypercriticism had knocked down, reestablishing the validity and historicity of both the law of the Twelve Tables and the Fasti Consulares, the annual lists of Roman consuls, two points on which recent research has proved him absolutely right. Nonetheless, the undertaking was not without ambiguity, since, in de Sanctis's mind, it could only be accompanied by a return to determinism, though one conducted with prudence. For him, the historian's task was to give a sense to "primordial" history, but without falling back into the excessive generalizations of the preceding century. And archeology increasingly provided confirmation that it *was* history. Indeed, with the beginning of the twentieth century, a new actor took the stage and gradually attracted everyone's attention: the archeologist.

[23] G. de Sanctis, *Storia dei Romani* (Turin, 1907); republished in 1980, with an introduction by S. Accame.

CHAPTER 2

THE TRIUMPH
OF ARCHEOLOGY?

T HE REASONS FOR archeology's emergence are certainly complex, but it is certain that it was greatly favored by the extraordinary developments in the territory of present-day Tuscany. First discovered by chance during agricultural work and then pursued with passion, an inexhaustible fodder of tombs, jewels, and objects of all kinds, found in the soil of ancient Etruria, gradually made it possible to establish series and typologies, an entire system of classification through which a new space of knowledge was delimited and defined. As a result, the archeologist gradually replaced the "antiquarian" of the past.[1] Thus, when Rome became the capital of the Italian state and a new urbanism began to transform its structure and appearance, systematic excavations were decided upon. They pursued on a larger scale projects begun at the beginning of the century, especially in the center of the city of Rome.

Between 1870 and 1898, archeologists encountered republican and imperial structures in the western sector of the Forum. After Giacomo Boni was named director of the Forum excavations in 1898,[2] they began to dig up archaic vestiges situated at a great depth. On the morning of 25 January 1899, at the foot of the Arch of Septimius Severus in the Forum, the excavators directed by Boni watched as a little rectangular paving stone appeared under their picks. It was black, which contrasted sharply and strangely with the white of the other flagstones. Under this paving stone, they soon exposed an assortment of blocks of different sizes, probably traces of a consecrated enclosure; these included a cippus, broken at the top and covered on all four sides with engraved characters. They had just discovered the most ancient Roman inscription.[3]

Even though the inscription was incomplete, it was clear it had been written in Latin, in an archaic language remote from classical usage, which nonetheless clearly displayed a word that was legible from the outset: *rex* (king). As a result,

---

[1] See P. Grimal, *Italie retrouvée* (Paris, 1979), 231–76.

[2] On Boni (1859–1925), see the entry devoted to him in *Dizionario biografico degli Italiani* (Rome, 1970), 12: 75–77 (by P. Romanelli).

[3] The account of the discovery and the initial publication of the inscription appears in *Notizie degli Scavi di Antichità* (1899), 155–200, signed by L. Ceci. Since 1871, this has been the official publication for archeological operations on the peninsula. For an examination of the different interpretations of the inscription, see F. Coarelli, *Il foro romano* (Rome, 1983), 1: 178–88.

the entire Livian tradition concerning royal Rome seemed to leave the realm of legend and enter that of history. That history was indisputable because based on epigraphy, which at the time was the most developed, the most "scientific," form of the knowledge of antiquity. Of course, adversaries of the hypercritical reading of the tradition, which had been in fashion since Pais, did not let such a wonderful opportunity pass them by. The inscription on the Lapis Niger (Black Stone) thus initiated a public polemic in the popular press, whose scope and vigor very quickly relegated to the background the scientific aspects of the exceptional discovery. And that discovery was soon followed by many others. In 1902, Boni's teams began to discover, near the temple of Antoninus and Faustina, the traces of a necropolis; it was immediately obvious that it was extremely old. Then, urns of dark-colored terra-cotta, clearly made to resemble the huts of the deceased whose ashes they still contained, emerged from the depths where they had been buried for so many centuries. And with them, the times of the foundation seemed to emerge from the shadows, to take on an increasingly tangible reality and materiality with each new discovered object. As ambiguous and as difficult to interpret as they later turned out to be, at the time these major discoveries imposed, with all the illusory force of archeological evidence, the idea of a decisive and definitive confirmation of the tradition. When de Sanctis wrote his Roman history, he drew support from them to dispute the hypercriticism of his predecessors and to propose a reasoned return to the great texts.[4] Boni's excavations, carried out at other points in the Forum and on the Palatine until the eve of World War I, furnished the new tendency, which soon became dominant, with a choice of arguments. Archeology was granted the status and utility of a "science auxiliary to history"; its support of history was esteemed all the more in that archeology seemed to be completely objective and irrefutable. In the end, it all seemed very simple: the tradition had told the truth, and archeology proved it. As a result, historians less subtle and less informed than de Sanctis returned in force to what we have called the fideist school, which found a particularly favorable echo in the cultural and political circumstances of the interwar period.

After World War I, however, Boni did not return to his excavations to any great extent, and the archeological investigation of earliest Rome gradually came to a total end. That development, apparently so surprising, seems to be due less to the chance events of individual destinies (Boni returned from the war very gravely ill) than to the profound logic and fundamental ambiguities in the return to the tradition that had occurred at the beginning of the century. Since arche-

---

[4] In France itself, the movement was illustrated by the theses of A. Piganiol, *Essai sur les origines de Rome* (Paris, 1917); and J. Carcopino, *Virgile et les origines d'Ostie* (Paris, 1919). At the beginning of his book, Piganiol declared that "the archeological discoveries restore the true colors of Rome's past and allow us to go back in time" (p. 5). Carcopino, though his work was deeply marked by Pais's theories, nonetheless placed his own writings within a perspective that revalorized the tradition. It is noteworthy that Boni's discovery, sometime after that of the Lapis Niger, of an archaic shard at the Regia bearing the inscription REX also reinforced the return to the tradition.

ology only confirmed the value of literary sources, once the time of major dis-coveries—possible only at prestigious sites such as the Forum—was ended, archeology gradually became less and less "useful." Did not the Lapis Niger, the necropolis by the temple of Antoninus, and the votive repository of Vesta obvi-ously confirm the historicity of the tradition of origins *as a whole*? Thus the great question bequeathed by Micali to the future, that of coordinating philology and archeology, was reduced to the expression of a mere relation of dependence and to a conception of history as the site where the two disciplines came together and lent each other mutual support. From then on, writing the history of the origins involved adding to an account grounded in the tradition and legitimated by archeology the inevitable contributions occasioned by the flow of new discover-ies, which fortunately, were still rather modest. It was a Sisyphean task, never ending and always begun again.

Despite these difficulties and ambiguities, however, it is important not to forget how decisive the contribution of archeology to the knowledge of the pri-mordia turned out to be. In demonstrating the substantial validity of the tradition on certain key points (let us not forget that the hypercritical school went so far as to deny the very existence of a regal period in Rome), and in thus allowing historians to go beyond the skeptics' non liquet, archeology decisively neutralized the debate about the prejudicial and ontological character of the sources of the most ancient Roman history. The question was no longer whether, in the absence of sources contemporary with the time of the foundation, the history of origins could be truly known; it was rather a matter of understanding how the tradition had managed to conserve the memory of such distant ages. Nonetheless, the weight of scholarly protocol was so great that, despite appear-ances, it was a long time before historians took these considerations into account. Yet archeology eventually provided a veritable Archimedean lever to remove what had for so long been an unsurmountable epistemological obstacle. That is why I have placed my reflections on the sources not at the beginning of this book, as is ordinarily done, but at the end.[5] We must first explore how the paths blazed by Boni were again followed in the wake of World War II, through research directed not only toward Rome but also, under the pressure of urbanization, toward the territory of Latium as a whole: the Palatine, the Forum Boarium at the foot of the Capitol, Gabii, Castel di Decimi, Lavinium, and many other sites as well. At a rate that has increased tenfold in the last three decades, archeology has altered and sometimes transformed from top to bottom the entire scientific landscape of the primordia.

Around the mid-century mark, this "auxiliary science" of the past, already rich in acquisitions and more certain of its methods, freed itself from the guardianship of history and philology. Boni's compatriots rarely followed their

[5] See below, chap. 11.

precursor, more technical than literary in his training, into the field; nor did specialists from southern Europe generally. The revival of archeology came from the Swedish school. In addition to his own work as an excavator, Einar Gjerstad, following in Karl Hanell's footsteps, wrote a survey that gathered together all the archeological data available on archaic Rome. These were published in six volumes under the title *Early Rome*.[6] A few years later, Gjerstad's student P. G. Gierow produced an equivalent survey for part of Latium.[7]

In the last volume of Gjerstad's monumental work, which he terms a "historical survey,"[8] one thing is clear. Even as archeology was asserting its mastery and autonomy as a result of more exhaustive techniques, more precise dating, and more refined typologies, even as it was convincing itself that it was bringing the old debates to a definitive end, it was in fact fanning the flames of past conflicts.

Far from being extinguished, the old quarrel between the fideists and the hypercritics was, in fact, fueled by the new material. By virtue of the sensational discoveries in the Forum, the very heart of the Romulean tradition, at its seemingly most fragile and inaccessible, has taken on life and substance before our very eyes. At the foot of the Palatine, between the Arch of Titus and the House of Vestals, an archeologist recently discovered what may be nothing less than the famous pomerium. According to Plutarch, Romulus himself traced this sacred limit of urban territory, this primordial furrow that started it all.[9]

More generally, the new discoveries that have been occurring at a rapid rate for several decades provide a more precise image of the ancient history of central Italy. In its main lines, the development of Latium since the eleventh century B.C.E. is incomparably better known than it was even twenty years ago. Yet the written sources available to the historian have not increased by a single major item and remain, with a few minor exceptions, almost the same as those available to scholars of the last century. The only truly new documents are the inscriptions that have been dug up, but they date only from the eighth century, are few in number, and, where they exist, provide only select information. They are, moreover, always extremely difficult to interpret accurately. Thus, between written sources compiled at the earliest in the fourth and third centuries B.C.E. (and even that is a hypothesis) and the events they are supposed to relate, not only is there a chronological gap, but it is widening. While the archeologist is moving farther and farther back in time with each discovery, the philologist and the historian are simply running in place.

Under these conditions, archeologists find it very tempting to reassert the specificity of their methods and the autonomy of their approach. The develop-

---

[6] E. Gjerstad, *Early Rome*, vols. 1–6 (Lund, 1953–73).

[7] P. G. Gierow, *The Iron Age Culture of Latium*, 2 vols. (Lund, 1964 and 1966).

[8] Gjerstad, *Early Rome*, vol. 6, *Historical Survey* (Lund, 1973).

[9] The discoveries were made by A. Carandini. Information concerning the excavations comes from two lectures delivered on 16 February 1989 at the Collège de France, and on 18 February 1989 before the Société Française d'Archéologie Classique. See also below, chap. 10.

ment of sharper techniques and the widening of the database made possible by computers allow them to establish their own parameters, their own criteria for truth, with less reliance on historians and philologists. For the latter, the path to be taken raises something of a dilemma: either they must argue from a few spectacular discoveries, such as the Lapis Niger or what is presumed to be the pomerium, in order to reach the general postulate of the validity and historicity of the tradition as a whole; or, in acknowledging once and for all the characteristics proper to archeology and its irreducibility to any other science, they must renounce the universalism of the past by radically dissociating these reciprocal spheres of activity and competence.

The first of these tendencies seems to be imposed by the facts themselves, by an archeological reality of inexhaustible richness. That is why, in the field of the most ancient history of Rome, there is a return to an increasingly marked fideism. The tradition offers proof simply by being the tradition.

The second tendency, which is the modern version of hypercriticism,[10] seems at first glance to accommodate better the fragmentation of techniques and knowledge that characterizes our time, in Roman history as in other disciplines. But this multiplication of centrifugal forces, in the form of scientific specializations ever more independent from one another, only invigorates and reinforces the longtime imperative that fideism serve as the federative principle of a "discursive practice," whose unity would otherwise be compromised. Of course, that is not the only reason for the success that the fideist interpretation of the tradition currently enjoys. As every year, every month almost, a booming archeology delivers its load of discoveries, some of which shed direct light on the tradition, hypercriticism finds itself caught in its own trap. The systematic suspension of judgment, the critical prudence erected into an end in itself, which were a strength in an age when only texts were available and the inventiveness of philologists produced reconstructions as audacious as they were risky, have now led to a theoretical impasse. In fact, because it detaches archeology entirely from the literary tradition and because, at the same time, it insists on the fragility and artificiality of that tradition (and with some accuracy in both cases), hypercriticism proves to be incapable of taking recent discoveries into account. Either it considers the two series of data (those of the tradition and those of archeology) as possibly coincident but radically different in nature (which is true in a certain sense), and therefore refuses to place them in relation to each other; or, when it can no longer deny certain associations, it concedes ground to the proponents of the tradition.

In other words, as a philosophy, hypercriticism is now reduced to a waiting game. Entrenched in the certainty of its uncertainty, it watches as discoveries appear on the horizon, taking them as so many (felicitous? infelicitous?) excep-

---

[10] The best representative of this tendency is currently J. Poucet, who has summarized his views in *Les origines de Rome: Tradition et histoire* (Brussels, 1985).

tions to its own system. In short, the refusal, however justified and legitimate it might be, to cede to the realist mirage created by archeology paradoxically ends in a scholarly practice that is completely dependent on archeological reality. Of course, factually, no one can predict discoveries with precision, since they are in great part due to the chance events of urbanization. I am speaking here only of the theoretical armature that makes the new finds conceivable or inconceivable. On the occasion of all the major discoveries revealed by archeology, the hyper-critical school has consistently practiced a tactic of "elasticity." What will historians who so recently insisted on the "somewhat disturbing absence of true archeological confirmation" say of the evidence recently revealed in the Forum and on the Palatine?[11]

Indisputably, these same discoveries seem, at least initially, much easier to explain from the fideist viewpoint, for which they provide solid support. At the beginning of the twentieth century, the Lapis Niger displayed the reality of a regal period in archaic Rome during the sixth century; as we now approach the year 2000, it is Romulus's rediscovered pomerium that imbues legendary times with historical reality. Curiously, Boni, who preceded modern archeologists at the site, seems to have rapidly given up the idea of pursuing his research,[12] which promised to be as complex as it was productive. But in relation to their predecessor, today's archeologists have the experience of a century of unin-terrupted "coincidences" between archeological data and literary data. They therefore methodically and decisively seek the deepest, and hence the most ancient, levels of the Forum. Nothing appears to stand in the way of the triumph of archeology, and we must not underestimate all the knowledge of the most ancient history of Rome that we owe to it. In the first place, Roman history has acquired the chronological background that Greek history achieved at the end of the last century, with Heinrich Schliemann's discoveries at Hissarlik and Mycenae (and later, with the decipherment of Linear B by Michael Ventris in 1952),[13] but that Rome had lacked until that time. The darkness that had long hung over the ages before the fourth century B.C.E. has gradually dissipated with each new find. Second, these same discoveries have allowed historians for the first time to ground their research in a sure chronology independent of the literary tradition. That major achievement came about only recently and not without difficulty. And third, by that very fact, archeology has provided the study of the primordia with new data, also independent of the written sources (which does not mean they are foreign to them). The progress made in excavation techniques and the process of urbanization lead us to hope for continued discoveries of this kind.

In other words, the two gaps that Arnaldo Momigliano not long ago recog-nized as the major obstacles to the progress of knowledge in the area of the

---

[11] Poucet, *Origines de Rome*, 160.

[12] This information comes from Carandini, lecture of 16 February 1989, Collège de France.

[13] See J. Chadwick, *The Decipherment of Linear B* (New York, 1959).

primordia—namely, the absence of a sure chronology and of new sources[14]—have been in great part filled in by archeologists' picks.

Nevertheless, the ambiguities arising from the continuing excavations in Rome and Latium are equal to the hopes to which the finds have given rise. Nothing better demonstrates the illusions of a certain archeological realism and of the fideist reading of the tradition than the way that archeology, since the beginning of the century, has been placed in the service of the history of earliest Rome. Indeed, it is easy to see that, in the last hundred years, there is not a philologist or a historian who has not in good faith believed that he had found in the archeological data the proof for the interpretations he was presenting. Stones always say what is expected of them, and when historians turn to archeology, they often act like ventriloquists who do not even know they are ventriloquists. Among many other possible examples, we might cite two scholars who have proposed very different, even opposing, readings of the primordia: Andreas Alföldi and Arnaldo Momigliano.

For Alföldi, primitive Roman society was originally organized in terms of two poles, in accordance with a model found in the steppes of Central Asia. For Momigliano, more classically, that civilization was the product of long experience and of a process that led to the clear division between patricians and plebeians only after an already extensive history. But both historians depend on the evidence of archeology, particularly for the question of the role and composition of the cavalry in archaic Rome.

At the beginning of the 1960s, some historians also appealed to the "irrefutable" evidence of archeology to displace by more than fifty years the traditional date of the foundation of the Roman Republic (450 B.C.E. instead of 509).

That is why, in the face of so many contradictory associations, interpretations, and conclusions, the hypercritical approach retains its heuristic value, as long as it does not transform itself into a system in its turn. It is altogether true that doubt remains a useful and necessary stage for all scholarly reasoning worthy of the name.

I am not simply proposing to divide up the territory: To get to the root of the many difficulties encountered by the historian of Rome's origins, it is not sufficient to define, however exactly, the proper use of archeology by the disciplines of history and philology. In reality, in its very ambition to constitute itself as an autonomous field of knowledge, in its movement toward a state of epistemological autarky, contemporary archeology, whatever the developments in its techniques and the refinements in its classifications, has clearly fallen prey to the illusions of a new positivism. Momigliano asked the question as early as 1963:[15] What would we know of archaic Rome if we possessed only the meager evidence exhumed by the archeologists? Not very much, to tell the truth.

[14] See, for example, A. Momigliani, "An Interim Report on the Origins of Rome," *Journal of Roman Studies* 53 (1963): 95–121; reprinted in his *Roma arcaica* (Florence, 1989), 78–100.
[15] Momigliani, "Origins of Rome," 107.

It is not enough to say that the texts guide the archeologist in interpreting the stones once they heve been dug up. When Roman archeologists undertook the exploration of the Forum in 1870, they found the guiding thread for their search in the literary sources. The Comitium had been identified in 1844 by Mommsen and K. O. Müller before it was uncovered by Boni at the end of the century.[16]

It is also not enough to say that, especially in archaic history, the gaps in documentation alone oblige historians (let us use the word in a very broad sense to designate all those who, whatever their specific competence, take on the task of speaking at length about the past) to multiply the hypotheses. Such a statement, as accurate as it is banal, does not in any way suffice to illuminate a process that is far more complex than it first appears. In reality, it is grounded in a reassuring division between a hypothesis—conceived as a kind of makeshift solution made necessary by the gaps in the documentation and defined as the conclusion of a demonstration—and the document, whose material solidity and objective presence supposedly stand in contrast to the changeable immateriality of the theories elaborated by philologists and historians.

We must not forget that a hypothesis is not only the end of research but also—as contemporary epistemology is well aware—its initial condition. Moreover, hypotheses are to be found at every stage of scholarly activity. Like everyone else, archeologists find only what they are looking for. Before he began to dig up the flagstones in the Forum—largely unexplored at the time—near the Arch of Septimius Severus, Boni had reread the classical texts that detailed the function of the Comitium and the location of the Lapis Niger. Of course—and luckily!—when an archeological operation does not lead to the goal envisioned, it guides the excavator toward questions that were not noticed at first. But then, once more, other hypotheses, which are quite often only the first hypothesis transformed and adapted to the requirements of the field, intervene to fuel and shore up the investigation. There is therefore no inert archeology, just as there is no inert philology or history.

And if it is true that scientists find only what they are looking for, the entire history of the archeology of the primordia (to speak only of this field) shows in abundance that the proposition must also be understood in its most restricted sense: they do not find anything except what they are looking for, and, the obligatory corollary, they do not find what they are not looking for. As Momigliano has shown,[17] even before they began their excavations in the Forum, the teams of the Swedish archeologist Einar Gjerstad expected to find confirmation for the theory elaborated by their compatriot Hanell in his 1946 study, *Das altrömische*

---

[16] See A. Fraschetti, "Karl Otfried Müller e gli 'antiquari,'" *Annali della Scuola Normale Superiore di Pisa*, 1984.
[17] Ibid., 103.

eponyme Amt, with the chronological displacement it implied in the dating of the episodes linked to the end of the monarchy in Rome. In other words, their excavation was guided by an initial hypothesis, which, moreover, itself depended on a rereading of the literary sources. And the remains they uncovered seemed to prove them right, so much so that, against the advocates of the traditional remote chronology (which dates the beginning of the Republic at 509 B.C.E.), Gjerstad proposed to place the end of the monarchy only in about 450 and to date the foundation of Rome properly speaking at about 575 B.C.E. It was only after several years of intense polemic and assiduous rereading of the evidence cited that it became clear that this new chronology relied on inadequate criteria of evaluation, forced conclusions, and, in the end, skewed postulates.

Such a phenomenon had been known since Beaufort, but few examples show it so clearly: in the history of the earliest times of Rome, there are few notions as tricky to deal with as those of "fact" and "event." Well before the Annales school of contemporary historiography called them into question, these notions had disintegrated in the laboratory where, since Niebuhr, the history of the Rome of origins has evolved. That does not mean, as a certain historiographical fashion would suggest, that historians fabricate altogether the object they study, by choosing certain events and certain documents at the expense of others that they set aside. That is merely a pointless truism.

To return to our example, we cannot say that Gjerstad neglected important evidence. Such neglect is inconceivable for periods where the material is so rare and where the most insignificant document deserves to be examined exhaustively. While historians of modern times must know how to choose documents from an enormous mass of various materials, historians of ancient societies, and a fortiori those of archaic times, must integrate all the available sources into their reflections. The first group seeks above all to choose data that are unknown because new, while the second seeks to shed new light on already known data. Thus, properly speaking, Gjerstad's opponents did not have any material elements to support their thesis other than those of the Swedish archeologist, nor did they redo the excavation already carried out by their colleague. They simply showed that what Gjerstad considered the decisive parameter for determining the moment of Rome's foundation had neither the status nor the meaning nor even the date he had attributed to it. By in effect making a paving stone in the Forum the tangible and unique sign of the foundation of Rome, at the expense of many other undoubtedly more convincing indexes, and by supposing that the founding of the city had a clear material corollary (a claim that cannot be accepted without demonstration), Gjerstad revealed above all the desire to rediscover in the field confirmation for a chronology he had already adopted even before beginning the excavation.

It is in this sense that we can say that the document is itself only a hypothesis. To be more precise, the document is the index (whether material or not) that an epistemological decision, grounded in one or several hypotheses, leads

researchers to grant the value of a sign or of a parameter, as a function of a definite problematic.

This process can be verified for all the recent excavations of the Forum at the
foot of the Palatine. What the excavators uncovered, to focus merely on the
materiality of the discovery, was an alignment of small cavities in the soil and,
parallel to them, blocks of stones arranged in a line. A first decision was required
to interpret these alignments as the remains of fortifications and walls, and not
as the traces of huts or houses. The latter interpretation seems to be excluded in
fact, given the rigorously rectilinear character of the structures observed. A
second decision was required to postulate that this wall was none other than the
pomerium, whose creation the literary tradition assigns to Romulus. Anyone
who feels, as I do, any interest whatever in the origins of the city that captured
the world's imagination for so long will not fail to be filled with hope at the
thought that someone may have rediscovered the traces of the first Romans. But
to arrive at such a conclusion (which in any case is not confined to simply regis-
tering a material piece of data), we must proceed through a chain of hypotheses
and must remain aware of them. In other words, the document is not a thing in
itself, and the truth does not emerge fully armed from the soil turned up by
archeologists. Thus, between the hypothesis and the document, there is not the
difference in nature that scientistic positivism would like to establish. Nor,
despite appearances, does there exist any intrinsic difference between a history of
archaic periods, which, because it has few documents, supposedly needs to have
many hypotheses, and the history of more recent and fortunate periods, which
can supposedly do without hypotheses because it has a wealth of documents. In
reality, the epistemological process is more or less the same for both; it is simply
more visible in one case than in the other.

Since scientists do not find what they are not looking for, sometimes they
even destroy it. There exists, for example, a type of edifice to which recent
studies have attracted attention.[18] It is a terrace in the form of a quadrilateral,
located at the summit of the citadel in every ancient city. The augur used to
climb up onto it to observe the auspices of the city; for that reason, it was called
an *auguraculum*. The first example identified was in the town of Cosa in central Italy, at the end of the 1960s. Since then, with every new excavation carried
out at the summit of an ancient citadel (*arx*), archeologists have carefully examined the ruins, in the hope of recognizing them as traces of these small
constructions that still have much to tell us about augury among the Romans.
But in reading the account of earlier excavations (those undertaken, for

---

[18] See especially M. Torelli's essay in *Rendiconti della Classe di Scienze Moral, Storiche, et Filogiche
dell'Accademia Lincei*, 1966; and A. Magdelain's essay in *Revue des Etudes Latines*, 1969. See also
the bibliography to my article "Le roi et l'augure: A propos des auguracula de Rome," in *Table
ronde internationale du CNRS sur la divination dans le monde étrusco-italique* 3 (Paris, 1986):
122–53.

instance, in the middle of the last century in Marzabotto, not far from Bologna, where the Etruscans founded an important colony in the sixth century B.C.E.), we realize that in 1856 archeologists—judging it without interest—destroyed a structure situated at the highest point of the acropolis, rectangular in design and with three steps down one side, a structure we can today recognize after the fact as just such an *auguraculum*.[19]

In other words, excavators effaced forever the traces of one of the very rare augural terraces that might still have existed in the Etruscan world, because they did not recognize it; and they did not recognize it because they were not looking for it.

It is thus vain to hope that the history of the primordia can be reduced to the progress of archeological investigation. However diverse they may be in their methodological options, the hypercritical exegesis and the fideist interpretation of the tradition come together in a shared hope and, by common agreement, leave the foremost role to the archeologist, from whom they each expect confirmation for their theses. For the hypercritical school, in fact, which embraced Pais's claim that nothing is known of the earliest times of Rome, all that can now be known comes from archeology, because, on careful reading, the tradition says everything and its opposite. According to this school, historians must not fail to appreciate the specificity of archeology, must allow it to elaborate its own parameters, and must listen to it speak the truth on the origins of Rome, even if it is a fragmented and insignificant truth.

For its defenders, in contrast, the tradition's value and historicity have already been proved, obviously and in abundance, by many discoveries. According to them, historians need only await the discoveries yet to be made, in order to see, day by day, that the tradition speaks the truth about Rome's origins.

The autonomous development sought by archeology and by every scientific discipline can only find comfort in these expectations. But in both cases they rest on an identical illusion, which submits the whole of the research on the primordia to a single question, always identical but given a different inflection depending on the nature of the document considered. It is the question of truth. Yet the archeological documents very often prove only what historians want them to prove. It will be easy, I think, for the hypercritical school to raise well-founded and well-supported doubts about the true nature of the recent discovery of the pomerium. Did we really expect to find in the reality of Roman soil the ultimate definition of what was in the first place a religious notion, and about which the literary tradition contains a wealth of diverse and complex texts? Are we to confine ourselves to saying that the traces of a fence and of walls have been found at the foot of the Palatine? Or are we to consider the question of the pomerium resolved and simply erase the various shadings and ambivalence of the tradition in the name of historicity?

[19] This fact is reported in the exhibition catalog *Santuari d'Etruria* (Siena, 1985), 91–92.

While archeologists may expect everything from documents whose episte-mological status remains uncertain, philologists and historians often consider the literary sources as so many documents whose historicity archeology illus-trates. Among both groups, the same illusion about the document persists. In analyzing the tradition—which in the interest of simplifying matters they call literary, even though it includes very different fields of knowledge—only from the angle of that supposed documentary value, both groups run a great risk of misapprehending its essential aspects. Contrary to what happens in our modern societies, where the concern for memory is very keen, in ancient societies the memory of the past was not cultivated for itself, but always in explicit or implicit reference to the practices, circumstances, and expediency of the present. Even among Roman erudites at the end of the Republic and during the Principate, that utilitarianism had not disappeared. The preoccupations of Varro, for exam-ple, the most famous and prolific of these erudites, prefigured in certain ways those of modern scholarship. In addition, as the hypercritical school has clearly shown, the tradition in a sense fed on itself. It evolved from one author to the next by means of additions and variants, in accordance with specific rules that no longer owed anything to the historical referent.

If, for example, we were to consider the traditional writings on the pomerium as merely documentary texts, we would be led to ignore the very clear ideological dimension that is present most of the time. The entire first century B.C.E. and the Principate of Augustus were permeated by a nostalgia for origins; and beginning with the age of Sulla, that nostalgia prompted every ambitious *imperator* to lay claim to Romulus. It is thus possible to speak of a "Romulean ideology." Since most sources on the pomerium go back to that period, with more or fewer intermediaries, it is clear they cannot be interro-gated for their truth content without the taking of certain precautions. To place, as the fideists do, the general and systematic postulate of the historicity of the tradition at the foundation of any history of earliest Rome is to take the tradition for what it claims to be—in other words, to no longer conceive of it as a historical object—in short, to confuse it with history. It is for that reason that so many exegeses of the primordia repeat with different inflections, as so many variations on a theme, the statement "So said Livy." But, in that case, Stendhal was right, and it would be better, if not to go our own way, then at least to return to the original!

CHAPTER 3

GEORGES DUMÉZIL'S HERMENEUTICS

C ONSCIOUS OF THE need to escape the "unmediated" reading of the literary tradition concerning Rome's origins, whether performed in a hypercritical or in a fideist sense, other scholars have explored a kind of third path, which could be called hermeneutic, seeking to discover the *hidden* sense of the accounts and legends transmitted by the tradition. Mommsen had considered the traditional accounts to be pseudohistorical illustrations of the principal schemata of Roman legal thought. This was a new and productive conception, but, as de Sanctis showed, it could account for only part of the legendary heritage of Rome.

Thus the hermeneutic interpretation turned toward history and myth rather than law. It is the historical perspective that is closest to the classical view: the revelation of the hidden meaning of the tradition leads to a version of history that is not, of course, that which the tradition claims to report, but whose elements it nonetheless provides.

Alföldi is the best representative of this type of exegesis, defended throughout a substantial body of work and set out in a dense little book of impeccable erudition, *Early Rome and the Latins* (1965).[1] It is clear that on many points the analysis relies on Pais's work for support; the general conclusion of the book, that the tradition of the beginnings of Rome is nothing but a forgery, is also reminiscent of the thesis of *Storia di Roma*. But Alföldi avoids the abyss that opened at his predecessor's feet, by hypothesizing a deliberate falsification of Roman history. He is even presumptuous enough to identify the man responsible, in the person of Fabius Pictor, generally considered the most ancient Roman historian.

Thus, when Alföldi presented the tradition as false, he, unlike Pais, was not led to annihilate the very possibility of writing history. Rather, he proposed that to rediscover the true sequence of events one must simply read the tradition

---

[1] A. Alföldi, *Early Rome and the Latins* (Ann Arbor, 1965). The German translation of this work by F. Kolb in fact constitutes a revised edition. It appeared under the title *Das frühe Rom und die Latiner* (1977). The interpretation of Rome's origins presented by Alföldi owes a great deal to the work of A. Rosenberg, a scholar who did not produce a monograph on the question, but who published several fundamental articles during the interwar period.

backwards as it were. For example, when the tradition says that the Etruscan king Porsena did not succeed in capturing Rome despite a relentless siege, one should understand that in reality, Rome did fall to Porsena, as it had already fallen to other Etruscan chieftains whom the tradition also shows vanquished by Rome. As for the city of Rome, which sources show flourishing under the reign of the Tarquins, it was for a long time no more than a little town without great importance. The history of the following century proves it: after the fall of the Tarquins, the tradition shows Rome struggling with difficulty for its survival in a hostile environment.

The point of view adopted by Alföldi led him to examine the slightest contradictions, the slightest obscurities of the tradition, with an attention sustained by faultless learning. For a specialist in Rome's origins, few readings are so demystifying. But as the years pass, we have been forced to admit that the thesis has not survived either the mass of new data or the test of criticism. Indisputably, archeology has shown with increasing clarity Rome's prestige and power in the sixth century B.C.E., confirming the brilliant intuitions that the Italian philologist Giorgio Pasquali expressed in 1936, primarily on literary foundations and in total contradiction to Alföldi's thesis.[2] But through the keen debate it provoked, the work of the Hungarian scholar had the enormous merit of compelling historians more clearly to define and refine the problematic associated with the fideist reading of the tradition concerning Rome's origins. Moreover, on one essential point, the probable conquest of Rome by the Etruscan Porsena, recent research generally suggests Alföldi was right.

To escape the impasse in the exegesis of the most ancient legends of Rome to which the strict application of the principles of both hypercriticism and fideist analysis led, in other words, to avoid an "unmediated" reading of the tradition and succeed in writing the history of Rome's origins in a manner other than hypercritical negation and concession or fideist repetition, hermeneutic interpretation thus turned to a reflection on myth as a privileged avenue of research.

In the nineteenth century, Ludwig Preller had studied the corpus of the oldest legends of Rome in accordance with modalities defined by the comparative mythology of the time. On the foundations of the achievements of Indo-European linguistics, created by Franz Bopp in his *Vergleichende Grammatik* (Comparative grammar), first published in Berlin in 1833, the Orientalists Franz Adalbert Kuhn and F. Max Müller (the latter summarized Bopp's method in *Comparative Mythology: An Essay*) provided a first model for rediscovering the fable of Rome's origins. Nonhistorical in content, their work provided the analyst with very ancient Indo-European schemata. But in granting a decisive importance to language in the formation of myths—Müller's 1863 lectures on the science of language, translated into every European language, created quite a stir—this type of analysis rapidly transformed research into a

---

[2] G. Pasquali, "La grande Roma dei Tarquini," *Nuova Antologia*, 1936.

hunt for the generative word. In the end, it granted too great a place to the investigator's imagination for there to be any hope of solid results; nonetheless, the method continued to be used for some time. On the other hand, the particular nature of the Roman legends, in which the historical coloration was always very strongly marked, stood in the way of a simple transfer of the methods that had been used for the mythologies of ancient India. When Alföldi wanted to shed light on the Indo-European character of the most ancient Roman society, he focused more on discerning social and religious structures than on studying myths in detail.[3]

It was Georges Dumézil who finally bestowed legitimacy on the study of the details of myth. Many have seen his vast corpus, perpetually reworked over a period of more than half a century (as the author himself indicates, it is not uncommon to rediscover the same arguments from one book to the next) as the final solution to the problem of Rome's origins.

However astonishing or even scandalous it might seem, I do not share that view. In a survey on the earliest times of Rome recently published in Italy,[4] in which more than fifteen of the best specialists analyzed all the social and economic aspects of Roman society from the beginning of its existence, producing a total of nearly six hundred pages, the name of the inventor of trifunctional theory appears only incidently. I too might have practiced such discretion, especially since, in specialized research, the ideology of the three functions is no longer at the center of the debate on Rome's origins.[5] The increasing flow of archeological discoveries, with the procession of interpretations and controversies that follow them, has once more pushed the problem of the historicity of the tradition to the foreground. And that historicity seems increasingly certain to the majority of scholars. Nevertheless, at the risk of appearing presumptuous, I feel it would be more honest to make clear declarations and explanations of my fundamental disagreement with Dumézil rather than refrain from a critique by seeking refuge in objective descriptions.

This disagreement—is it really necessary to point this out?—is not in any way directed at Indo-European itself. The discovery of that language at the beginning of the nineteenth century and the wave of research that followed constituted a major achievement of linguistics (in fact, linguistics came into being as a science in the very course of that research), and one of the most dazzling accomplishments of the modern scientific mind. But it is a huge leap from linguistic research to the establishment of an Indo-European mythology or ideology.

---

[3] See A. Alföldi, *Die Struktur des voretruskischen Römerstaates* (Heidelberg, 1974).

[4] A. Momigliano and A. Schiavone, eds., *Storia di Roma*, vol. 1, *Roma in Italia* (Turin, 1988).

[5] On this point, Poucet speaks of "polite indifference" in his essay in *Actes du Colloque International "Georges Dumézil, Mircea Eliade,"* ed. C. M. Ternes (Luxembourg, 1988), 29.

Thus, to take only examples mentioned by Dumézil himself, it is clear that, despite their indisputable linguistic kinship, the Vedic god Dyau and the Greek god Zeus (or the Latin god Jupiter) are very different from one another.[6] Dumézil himself recalls that "despite the Indo-European structure of their language, the Hittites—one of the emigrant groups that 'arrived' the earliest and one of the first to keep archives—had a religion and honored gods who barely resemble those we find, for example, in India or Scandinavia."[7]

Nonetheless, according to Dumézil, on the banks of the Tiber in the eighth century B.C.E. and before, "the prehistoric Romans conceived of their society, and no doubt of the world, within the same tripartite functional framework as the Indo-Iranians, the Celts, and the Teutons."[8]

But what exactly was that famous ideology of the three functions? It was, to repeat the exact terms of its inventor, a conception according to which "life in all its forms—divine and human, social and cosmic, and no doubt physical and psychic—was governed by the harmonious and varied play of three and only three fundamental functions, which can be given the names 'Sovereignty,' 'Power,' and 'Fertility.' The first assured the control—both magical and legal— of things, the second provided for defense and attack, and the third was open to numerous specifications concerning the reproduction of beings as well as their health or healing and their food and wealth."[9] And the tradition concerning Rome's origins provides a transposition of just that functional tripartition, in the guise of a historical account. Thus, "regardless of the real event it covers, any particular legend . . . which presents itself as history, is the epic transposition or its equivalent of complex, significant myths that also appear in other Indo-European societies, either conserved in the form of myths or, as in Rome, related to heroes of the past."[10] That is why, according to Dumézil, the traces of history must not be sought in Roman legends, since "the structured, significant legends, in their elaboration of a schema that predated Rome, did not emerge from the facts and cannot reveal the facts."[11]

When was the tradition as we know it formed? Embracing the conclusions of nineteenth-century hypercriticism on this point, Dumézil dates that formation from the fourth and third centuries B.C.E.: "It was between the fourth century and the beginning of the third that Rome, having managed to become the great power of Italy, resolved to give itself an official past."[12]

[6] See G. Dumézil, *Mythe et épopée* (Paris, 1968), 1: ll; and his earlier work *L'héritage indo-européen à Rome* (Paris, 1949), 67.

[7] Dumézil, *L'héritage indo-européen*, 17. That said, we would now have to temper that judgment. See, for example, C. Watkins's essays in *Innsbrucker Beiträge zur Sprachwissenschaft*, 1974, 101–10; and 1979, 269–88.

[8] G. Dumézil, *Jupiter, Mars, Quirinus* (Paris, 1941), 188.

[9] Dumézil, *L'héritage indo-européen*, 65; cf. p. 178.

[10] G. Dumézil, *L'oubli de l'homme et l'honneur des dieux* (Paris, 1985), 313.

[11] Dumézil, *Mythe et épopée*, 1: 432.

[12] Ibid., 1: 269; id., *L'héritage indo-européen*, 175–76.

Numerous polemics, in the course of which Dumézil displayed an incomparable degree of irony and talent, were influential in establishing the authority of a doctrine whose success equaled the scandal it had at first caused. That scandal, as Dumézil himself showed very well, can be explained in two ways. In the first place, it seemed shocking to the proponents of a certain classical tradition that they were now being forced to turn to other areas of philology, in short, to other humanistic disciplines, to explain the world of Greco-Roman antiquity, which had survived for so long in the splendid isolation of an arrogant and dominating model. But that resentment at seeing a proud intellectual autarky end was combined with the disappointment of being forced to abandon any hope of finding history in the most ancient legends of Rome. That resentment and disappointment stood in stark contrast to the swaggering self-assurance of the high priest of "the new comparative mythology" (Dumézil did not invent the term, but he found it acceptable). In reality, these animated and often passionate controversies did not really situate the debate on its true foundation. For example, Dumézil had no difficulty in showing how pointless was the criticism of the Italian historian Momigliano,[13] who had sought out texts written by Dumézil before 1938, that is, before his discovery of the trifunctional system. The theory of the three functions no longer appears helpful in understanding the structures of the most ancient Rome, but not because it would be possible, as some have shown (though at the risk, perhaps, of a certain artificiality), to construct a trifunctional interpretation of the Bible.[14] Nor need we consider (though here we are getting closer to the heart of the matter) the strange idea that Dumézil consistently defended—namely, that even in the classical age, Virgil and Propertius were the "conscious"[15] [*sic*] users of an ideology elaborated during the Bronze Age. This is no doubt the expression of a certain humor and of his predilection for virtuosity in commentary, of which he gave more than one example, particularly in *Le moyne noir en gris dedans Varennes* (1984).

To avoid such false debates, let us begin with the actual events of Rome, as Dumézil himself did in a number of his studies, and particularly in his major work *La religion romaine archaïque.*[16] Let us first measure the validity of the theory by the yardstick of Roman data. Nothing is more logical, in fact, for a comparative method properly understood, as Dumézil himself clearly and

[13] Let us add that Momigliano, no doubt sensitive to Dumézil's criticisms of his own critique, returned to the question of functional tripartition in one of his last public lectures. The text of this lecture is published in *Saggi di storia della religione romana* (Brescia, 1988), 45–66.

[14] See J. Brough's essay in the *Bulletin of the School of Oriental and African Studies, London,* 1959, 69–85.

[15] There are numerous and recurrent declarations of this kind. See Dumézil, *L'oubli de l'homme,* 314: "I proposed . . . that Virgil, like Propertius, was conscious of these functional notes traditionally attached to the three ethnic components of nascent Rome and that, in the 'Trojan' plagiarism of 'Roman' origins, he retained, underscored, and exploited the play of functional characteristics with the resources of his art."

[16] G. Dumézil, *La religion romaine archaïque* (Paris, 1966; 2d ed., 1974).

adamantly emphasized in the opening pages of *Jupiter, Mars, Quirinus.*[17] For him, the Roman world was much more than an element to be compared with structures observed elsewhere; on many occasions and on many of the most important points, he himself provided all the initial raw material for elaborating schemata that were only then applied to the traditions of other civilizations. It follows that the reexamination of the Roman aspect of his theory ought to have significant repercussions for the status of the theory overall, though such concerns lie beyond the scope of this book.

Let us confine ourselves to Rome itself. Even taking into account the fact that, as of about 1950, Dumézil stopped believing that trifunctionality had ever had a social and historical reality,[18] we can only be struck by the dual and intrinsically contradictory postulate implied by the theory of the three functions. How are we to accept the idea that the memory of the most ancient schemata of Indo-European thought could have coexisted with the irremediable and almost total eradication (if we except proper names and a few concrete details) of the historical content of the most recent eras?[19] After all, in terms of the chronology of Indo-European eras, it is quite certain that the eighth century B.C.E. can be considered recent! And what about the following centuries, of which the tradition supposedly conserved nothing or almost nothing? According to Dumézil, the "facts" "revealed or highlighted by comparisons at various levels, despite the precision of the names of places and of persons, dissuade us from seeking real events under the accounts considered, and commit us to consigning them to pure literature, a literature that itself fed on traditional religion and on a conception of the world that was older than Rome."[20]

Such declarations clearly contrast with recent works claiming that "Dumézil's work does not concern, or concerns only indirectly . . . the solution to the fundamental problem raised for specialists in Rome, which, let us recall, is that of the historicity or nonhistoricity of the traditional account of the regal period."[21] In reality, these salvage operations have been carried out under the increasing pressure of recent discoveries, which illuminate the tradition as much as they are illuminated by it.

We can detect other contradictions of the same order in this interpretive system, even though Dumézil's astounding skill has often seemed able to resolve them without difficulty. Dumézil claimed he had to abandon the idea of finding the tripartite Indo-European ideology in lived experience; yet the definition of

---

[17] "Comparison and the comparative spirit must intervene *from the beginning*, with the collection and evaluation of the sources, and with a reading and classification of the documents" (Dumézil, *Jupiter, Mars, Quirinus,* 31).

[18] See Dumézil, *L'oubli de l'homme,* 301–2.

[19] And the conscious memory, in fact! But let us set that point aside once more, so as not to lead the discussion astray with problems that could be considered secondary.

[20] Dumézil, *Mythe et épopée,* 3: 12.

[21] Poucet, in *Actes du Colloque,* 38 and 40.

myth that follows from that partial retraction seems peculiarly impoverished in relation to an initial, and more classical, conception, later formulated in *Jupiter, Mars, Quirinus*, which claims that "myths cannot be separated from social life as a whole."[22] Whatever the point of view adopted, it is an established fact for all the analysts (and for Dumézil himself) that myth in Rome must usually be explained as a function of religious ritual with its grounding in the topographical, ceremonial, institutional, and, in short, social context in the broad sense. Under these conditions, the articulation between the eternal—that is, the Indo-European—and the temporal—the historical—that is manifested in myth, becomes at the very least tricky to grasp.

In addition to these basic difficulties, other obstacles, perhaps less visible at first glance, emerge when we examine the trifunctional analysis of the primordia. As can be expected, it is the most legendary part of the narrative of origins, that which concerns the four pre-Etruscan kings—Romulus, Numa, Tullus Hostilius, and Ancus Marcius—that has received the most attention from the new comparative mythology. It thus seems possible, though this remains more implicit than explicit, that for Dumézil himself the account of subsequent reigns is more substantially historical.[23] In fact, later developments in research have ratified that scholarly Yalta agreement. As the archeological discoveries have depicted the Etruscan reigns with more precision, these reigns have, so to speak, been abandoned to historicist exegesis, and little by little the conviction, accepted by all, has taken root that the first part of the narrative of origins illustrates Indo-European ideology, and the second part lends itself to historical interpretation after all.[24]

In reality, to confine ourselves exclusively to Dumézil's demonstration, that dividing line is utterly without foundation. There are only two choices. Either the tradition about the origins is of recent date, and in that case, why would that concerning the Etruscan kings, who clearly predated the time when the tradition is presumed to have been elaborated, be true? Or the tradition is much older, and in that case, why would the account of the older, pre-Etruscan kings be "false"? In reality, the new comparative mythology has no choice at all in the matter. It has an absolute epistemological need to suppose that the tradition of the origins was codified only at a recent date. Otherwise, if it admitted that the account of the primordia was fixed earlier, it would find it impossible to maintain, as it does, that no historical memory of the ancient periods was con-

[22] Dumézil, *Jupiter, Mars, Quirinus*, 15.
[23] See, for example, G. Dumézil, "Les rois romains de Cicéron," in his *Idées romaines* (Paris, 1969), 193–207.
[24] Note Poucet's characteristic stance. After declaring that "the views of G. Dumézil . . . constitute . . . the most complete and most coherent explanatory hypothesis currently on the market," he concludes his inquiry as follows: "In the present state of our knowledge, it is not until the reign of the Etruscan kings that one sees a few authentic pieces of historical data slip into the traditional account. For the origins and the first four kings, the tradition seems to develop exclusively in the realm of fable" (*Origines de Rome*, 173 and 300).

served.[25] This means, though in general this is rarely taken into account, that it is of central importance to the entire validity of the trifunctional system to determine the character (historical or nonhistorical) of the Etruscan reigns as the tradition recounts it.

If, as seems to be the case, we must move back the date of the elaboration of the tradition, or at the very least of its most ancient kernel, we are obliged to accept hypothetically that the periods that immediately preceded the Etruscan monarchy could also have left some *precise* traces in legend. After all, Dumézil's interpretation adopts the same procedure when, placing the formalization of the narrative of origins as we know it in the fourth and third centuries B.C.E., it also concedes that the Etruscan reigns, situated more than a century and a half before that, could have left some precise memories (see the initial pages of *La religion romaine archaïque*). But the more information archeology provides on the reality of the power of archaic Rome as the traditional narrative of origins depicts it, the more difficult it is to maintain that everything was transmitted within and by a trifunctional ideological framework emerging from the fount of ages and remaining unchanged in its substance. It is increasingly difficult to say, without immediately running up against the discoveries of historical research, which is annexing new territory daily, that "when the legend was constituted, the ideology of the three functions was still powerful enough to enclose and conceal it." These claims, formulated quite recently by Dumézil,[26] have already been transposed, mezza voce and in a minor key, by certain of his disciples, who attenuate their scope in a peculiar manner. Since the progress of archeology makes it increasingly difficult to consider the indications about the Etruscan reigns transmitted by the literary sources as the mere residue of a primarily mythological tradition, Jacques Poucet prefers to limit explicitly the validity of Dumézil's hypothesis to the pre-Etruscan period. This hypothesis, he claims, accounts for "numerous elements of the tradition on the first kings of Rome."[27] In many respects, in fact, this tempering of a theory that initially had very broad ambitions is the work of Dumézil himself. We can only admire the rigorous intellectual honesty that has often led him, even as he repeated his fundamental principles, to limit their field of application. One of the best-known and most important examples of this kind of correction is provided in his analysis of the three primitive tribes of Rome. He first saw them as the illustration and the proof of his trifunctional system but later abandoned the idea of explaining them from this point of view.

---

[25] Of course, the date proposed by Dumézil for the birth of the tradition remains valid if we confine ourselves to the final formulation of what has come down to us. But on that point, everyone is agreed, and the real question is whether we cannot detect more ancient strata in what we possess, or whether, with Dumézil, we have to push the elaboration of the narrative of origins forward to the fourth and third centuries B.C.E.

[26] Dumézil, *L'oubli de l'homme*, 302.

[27] Poucet, *Origines de Rome*, 173.

We can predict that, with the development and refinement of our knowledge of archaic Rome, the tide will continue to turn. Yet we can easily imagine that some critics will always find it possible to appeal to the schemata of Indo-European thought, as long as a few concessions are made. The debate, which at present is confined to the Etruscan centuries of Rome, will soon shift to the protohistorical periods, which are increasingly well known and documented archeologically as a result of progress in excavation techniques. And this shift in time will affect the core of trifunctional theory. After the lively polemics of the 1960s, recent research, pressured by the flood of new discoveries, has not returned to the basic questions that in my view deserve to be asked, despite the fact that the essential problems of chronology, still open in the 1960s, can now be considered resolved.

Whatever the future of trifunctional theory, it will always have to suppose, as it has in the past, that a very ancient Indo-European ideology persisted, despite the fact that the historical content of incomparably more recent times vanished. And since new discoveries and new analyses are shedding light on the substantial validity of the legend of origins, we can predict that, like hypercriticism when confronted with the great discoveries of the Forum, trifunctional analysis will also make use of *concession*, without abandoning altogether its defense on principle of the value of its schemata. But to all appearances, it will have to prune the tradition ruthlessly of all the branches most threatened by historicism, even at the risk of reducing it to a shapeless trunk. It will be left only with its original supposition, increasingly doomed by the troublesome variants it considers "secondary developments."

The history of philology already offers one famous example of this epistemological process: the passionate search, pursued by the whole of German scholarship in the nineteenth century, for the "real Homer," the most ancient and only authentic kernel (*Urkern*) in the epic cycle. It is not surprising to learn that the identification of these primordial vestiges, though carried out according to the same criteria and as a function of apparently identical objectives, led every scholar who attempted it to different conclusions. Thus, brought together, these conclusions led to an authentification of the Homeric corpus as a whole!

It would be unfair to say that the theory of Indo-European tripartition, elaborated by its author at a time when archeology had provided only rare, fragmentary, and uncertain data on the early centuries of Rome, was built on the presuppositions of hypercritical exegesis as I have described them. Dumézil began, first and foremost, with considerations of a linguistic nature.[28] But we can only note that, in the end, he repeated and integrated into the logic of his

---

[28] Although we sometimes find surprising anticipatory comparative analyses in Pais's work, as is the case, for example, for the myth of Horatius Cocles (*Storia di Roma*, 473). That said, according to Dumézil himself, the article that served as a starting point for his research was J. Vendryès, "Les correspondances de vocabulaire entre l'indo-iranien et l'italo-celtique," *Mémoires de la Société de Linguistique de Paris* (Paris, 1918).

vast enterprise conclusions that in the preceding century had been the domain of the hypercritical school. It is more surprising that the present-day successors of the hypercritical school have often enthusiastically adopted the vision of origins that Dumézil proposed. In my opinion, the profound reason for this allegiance must be sought in their desire to avoid the impasse to which hypercritical analysis, pursued to its logical end, would lead. Thanks to the Indo-European three functions, the discouraging abyss opened by destructive analysis can be filled in, and the darkness of a false tradition can be illuminated by a light coming from farther off.

How so? Through the persistence of "schemata of Indo-European thought," which the comparatist can identify in the form and content of the tradition as it has been transmitted.

It is therefore clear that the question of the transmission and formation of conceptions that are Indo-European in origin constitutes the crucial point of trifunctional theory as a whole. Such "schemata of thought predating Rome" may evoke Kant's a priori categories, and the terminology adopted by Dumézil lends itself to this facile association. But philosophy's garments do not fit history very well, and Kant, author of the *Critique of Pure Reason*, would have certainly found peculiar the idea of categories that originate in contingency and change. On the other hand, to make functional tripartition a mode of a priori mental perception preexisting the realities of space and time would entail suppressing its Indo-European origin and placing it definitively outside the field of historical analysis. That is why, to resolve that theoretical difficulty, Dumézil insisted, even in his last works and at the risk of embarrassing his proponents,[29] on the conscious character of that tripartite ideology. The result can only be a radical, almost ontological, dissociation between ideas and facts, between an ideology that remained the same throughout all its subsequent metamorphoses and a history condemned to oblivion and nonbeing as a result of that ideology's survival.[30] Reversing the commonly accepted relationship between ideology and history, Dumézil takes up the old metaphysical opposition between substance and accident, to the advantage of ideology. Never was history so completely reduced to "the mere froth of days," never was Rome more deserving of the name Eternal City!

In the field of the historical analysis of Roman reality, Momigliano formulated the major objection to the system of functional tripartition. In 1962, in a dense survey of early Rome published in the *Journal of Roman Studies*, he notes that "the fundamental fact of Roman society remains that warriors, producers, and priests were *not* separate elements of the citizenship, though priesthoods tended to be monopolized by members of the aristocracy."[31]

---

[29] See Poucet, *Origines de Rome*, 291.

[30] See the revealing line in Dumézil's *L'oubli de l'homme*: "ideology, which may be astonishingly conservative, and history, composed of unpredictable events" (p. 301).

[31] Momigliano, "Origins of Rome," 114. Dumézil's response was published under the ironic

Dumézil devoted one of his last *Esquisses* to a response to the objections of his persistent adversary. It is nonetheless very curious to see that, on this fundamental point, he confined himself to recalling that he had rapidly been led to dissociate "the idea of 'functions' from the notion of 'social classes.'" In other words, he abandoned the notion of finding traces of tripartition in social reality. But that brief response, or rather, that reminder of a distinction that was in fact quite necessary, again places the debate on the level of facts, if only negatively.

In fact, however, the real problem is that functional triparition not only has no concrete corollary—and for good reason—but also has no existence on the ideological level. It is not simply in the order of facts that "warriors, producers, and priests were not separate elements of the citizenship"—a claim the new comparative mythology had no trouble appropriating long ago—it is also true in the order of mentalities, of the social imaginary, or, to speak in Dumézil's terms, of ideology. If we really wish to isolate "the schemata of thought" of Roman society, we must note with John Scheid that "the priest was a citizen like any other, assigned duties which he performed only if he was formally vested with political authority. In sum, he was a 'magistrate' of a particular kind."[32] As a result, the idea of a functional tripartition that was Indo-European in origin and that survived solely as "system of representations" vanishes.

Dumézil's univocal reduction of the narrative of origins to a mythology that had been transformed into history, though it certainly corresponds to the truth to a great extent, does not take into account the reverse and complementary movement that has often been observed. To cite a single example, it is clear that the divine birth of Servius Tullius, sixth king of Rome, was not a schema artificially concocted centuries after the events by historical scholars but was contemporary to the history of the man himself. The same is true of the privileged relation that the tradition establishes between that king and Fortune, a relation that closely resembles the link between the sovereign and a protecting deity, which is clearly attested in Phoenician and Cypriot mythologies, that is, in civilizations that had long had close ties with early Rome. Thus, while it is true that the narrative of origins contains "a mythology that is lost as mythology and recuperated by history,"[33] it also contains, to paraphrase an expression in Dumézil's *Mythe et épopée*, "a history lost as history and recuperated by mythology." For the Roman citizen of archaic times, just as surely as history was grounded in myth, it was also myth's realization. This dual and doubly complementary correspondence cannot be reduced to a simple relation without grave

---

title "Une idylle de vingt ans" (A twenty-year idyll), in *L'oubli de l'homme*, 299–318 (see esp. pp. 300–302).

[32] J. Scheid, *Religion et piété à Rome* (Paris, 1985), 38. This book also includes an exposition of Dumézil's system, with which the author declares himself in agreement.

[33] Dumézil, *Mythe et épopée*, 3: 9.

error. One must seek both the reality of history in myth and the truth of myth in history.

In the end, in confining itself to the first of these operations, the new comparative mythology reduces history to a play of shadows, eliminating from it everything involving change, movement, *otherness*, to the advantage of continuity, stability, *sameness*. It sets in place an exegesis through which the historical part of history is reduced to the bare minimum. Indo-European functional tripartition thus constructs a history that in the end escapes disturbing turbulence and the gravity of change, taking refuge in the essential identity of being, which lies behind a curtain of appearances that can quickly be torn away. There is a great deal of nostalgia in such an enterprise. It is Jacques Bossuet's providentialism transfigured—and with an impressive scientific and scholarly apparatus!—by the trappings of absolute determinism, which the entire nineteenth century dreamed of attaining, but without success. So the origins of Rome truly did have a meaning!

In what way is this determinism? Even though the matter was not formulated explicitly, it is difficult to avoid the idea that, beginning from Dumézil's theory, functional tripartition is not only a mental framework that informs or deforms the tradition of Rome's origins, but may also have been, in Rome first and then in other places and other times, a true motor of history.

Recall, for example, the functional interpretations of the three orders of ancien régime society,[34] which, though not proposed by Dumézil himself, were given his endorsement.

Of course, in spite of all that, we cannot deny the presence in the most ancient Roman society of elements that are Indo-European in origin. Rituals such as the October Horse, the goddess Aurora, Mater Matuta, and, above all, the undeniable analogies between the Roman *flamen* and the Indian *brahman* (illuminated by Dumézil in a memorable 1938 article)[35] attest to the reality of that legacy. But it is another matter to move from observing these dispersed and residual elements to reconstituting an entire mythology, and yet another step to explain *the whole* of the narrative of origins in terms of such a "world system."

Nonetheless, it is this totalizing ambition that explains the considerable success encountered by a body of work[36] in which discoveries of details and audacious syntheses abound. On a historical question that had too often been viewed as mysterious and secret, trifunctional theory suddenly seemed to reveal the key to the enigma of Rome's origins. And that key fit all the locks, even those that had resisted the efforts of several centuries of exegesis (the Mater

---

[34] I am thinking in particular of G. Duby, *Les trois ordres ou l'imaginaire du féodalisme* (Paris, 1978).

[35] Reprinted in Dumézil, *Idées romaines*, 155–66.

[36] Which itself constitutes only part of Dumézil's oeuvre. He was also the author of numerous linguistic monographs, which remain fundamental.

Matuta and the October Horse are exemplary in this respect). That key seemed to open all the doors.

Within this vast corpus, Dumézil's readers wandered the world and human time, from ancient India and Iran to Scandinavia, from the darkest eras of history to medieval civilization, and rediscovered the classic legends of their childhood. But those legends had been revitalized, illuminated, reinvigorated, by an analysis that, like psychoanalysis, claimed to read in the texts what was expressed but silenced, hidden but visible, essential but subterranean.

For their part, the specialists found, no doubt for the first time,[37] Roman religion treated as a unitary and organic whole, where the deities, their functions, rituals, and sacerdotal collegia, their theology and liturgy, were given a definition both structural and differential. Far from being considered an aggregate of rudimentary practices and beliefs, Roman religion from its archaic period was elevated to the dignity of "a system where representations and actions are not only juxtaposed but mutually adapt to and support one another."[38] This enterprise was all the more necessary in that, at the same time, a primitivist vision was gaining the ascendant, a vision that rediscovered in every Roman deity and myth the trace of an original and vague feeling for the divine, baptized mana by analogy to the Melanesian world. Dumézil's enterprise was crowned with full success: under the cutting remarks of his demonstrations and refutations, the notion of mana, which had been diffused in a number of monographs and manuals, soon ended up in the cemetery to which obsolete theories are consigned.

Out of concern for the long term, a concern inherent in his theory, Dumézil was led to shed light on the value and authenticity of the information transmitted through the channels of religious rites and formulas, which had for too long been scorned by rationalizing scholarship, heir to the Enlightenment. And much still remains to be done in the field he pioneered.

Seeking the explanation for Roman events outside Rome itself, Dumézil put an end to the myth of Italic cultural autochthony, which was so robust at the time. After Dumézil, there was less hesitation in accounting for some Latin or Roman particularity by turning to data borrowed from other civilizations, notably those of the Near or Middle East, with which, as is too often forgotten,[39] archaic Rome was in contact very early on.

No doubt the universalist ambitions of trifunctional theory, the aspects we might find excessive, were the very condition for its scholarly productiveness. Once fashioned, the instrument could detect facts that had escaped the most alert eyes. Whatever the judgment we might make of trifunctional theory today,

---

[37] Confining ourselves to French works, let us make a particular place for J. Bayet's remarkable *Histoire politique et psychologique de la religion romaine* (Paris, 1957).

[38] Dumézil, *L'héritage indo-européen*, 36.

[39] On this matter, let us mention the pioneering role played by J. Bachofen, *Die Sage von Tanaquil* (1870).

it possessed a dual value: first, though it may have seemed to intersect the hyper-critical reading of the narrative of origins at certain points, it in fact showed the substantial value of the tradition and illuminated the need for apprehending that tradition over the long term; second, in contradistinction to a directly historicist fideist reading, it showed the impossibility of deciphering the sources without preliminary mediation and interpretation.

This means that, despite the illusions that have risen up here and there, we can no longer turn back on this well-traveled road; but, after the failure of the great interpretive systems of the past, we can also no longer avoid asking, in ever more explicit terms, how we are to gain access to a tradition whose complexity continues to resist efforts at simplification.

What paths, then, must we take to arrive at the Rome of origins without losing our way?

CHAPTER 4

THE HISTORIOLOGICAL
DIMENSION

A FTER THE POLEMICAL turmoil of the 1960s, current research
has chosen the path of meticulous, fastidious, and technical investigations, leaving suspended the great debates of the past on the historicity
of the narrative of origins. There is of course much modesty and efficacy in such
a suspension of judgment, much optimism, but also much naïveté. The implicit
conviction is that the patient accumulation of "objective data" will replace to
advantage long discourses, that the "facts" laid end to end will substitute for the
proliferation of brilliant ideas, unverifiable hypotheses, and risky deductions, and
that the anonymous, discrete, and ineluctable advance of research will assure,
without much ado, the progress (or rather, the Progress) of knowledge, without
false debates and the useless expenditure of energy.

But such a view forgets that the facts and events are not—especially in the
history of ancient eras—"data" that simply offer themselves for analysis. They
are rather constituted as such only at the end of a long critical process that one
ignores at one's peril.

As we come to the end of our historiographical itinerary, the nature of that
peril becomes clear. The failure of an exclusively philological reading of the narrative of origins is matched in the contemporary era by the failure of an
interpretation claiming to be founded on archeology alone. Philology followed
the path that, from Niebuhr to Pais, led to hypercriticism; but the archeological
approach, with the Swedish historian Gjerstad at its head, led only to "plausible
history," which Paul Veyne aptly describes as the genre

> to which archeologists turn to reconstruct after a fashion the history of dark
> centuries. That genre is the flip side of utopianism and shares its overly logi-
> cal insipidity. The rule of the game is to make the fewest suppositions possible
> (the historian must be prudent) to account in the most economical manner
> for the few traces that mere chance has selected and allowed to reach us.[1]

To expect examinations of these traces alone to provide "economic and
social insights of supreme value," to think they communicate "precious informa-

[1] P. Veyne, *Comment on écrit l'histoire* (Paris, 1971), 29.

49

tion on religion, sacrifices, votive repositories, offerings, and sanctuaries," or to believe that the "prodigious harvest of material data" (however accurate the expression may be) allows for an "archeological reconstruction of the origins and early centuries of Rome"[2] is to fall back, though on the basis of different material, into the kind of illusion that inspired Niebuhr's reconstructions in the past. Despite appearances, we can only fear that the edifice will be neither less fragile nor less precarious than such reconstructions,[3] even though the objectivity attributed to the material facts confers a semblance of solidity. If it remains faithful to its own principles, such a synthesis will be nothing more than a collation of all the traces and vestiges, classified by typology and chronology. But economics is not simply the accumulation of numbers and indexes, and only Jacques Prévert can make an inventory into a form of literature! The catalog of all the stones existing in all the sanctuaries from ancient Rome and Latium (however descriptive it might be, and even supposing that such an identification is possible based solely on archeological considerations) would depict a religion without gods (unless they could be identified by an inscription, which is rare), without rites, and without myths. This is not even a depiction, but simply an empty framework.[4] Despite the disappointment that such a statement will no doubt cause, I must repeat that the history of Rome's origins cannot be reduced to the developments of archeological investigation, which historians would do no more than faithfully and patiently record. That is a technicalist dream, typical of an era that likes to imagine its computers are "intelligent machines" that can function and decide on their own. It is the ultimate incarnation of a positivism that is pained by the fact that all knowledge is also interpretation.

Anxious to avoid the ambiguities of an uncertain literary tradition, hypercriticism has thus entrusted archeology with the task of telling the truth about origins. Because it distrusts the texts it knows so well, it seeks a cure for its uncertainties in archeology. Or rather, it finds in archeology a way to ground that uncertainty in a principle, at the risk of falling prey to other mirages. Archeology, only a servant yesterday, is today the master. And because it is confident in the certainty of its discoveries, which it believes it owes only to itself, archeology is tempted to resolve to its own advantage the old border skirmish with philology, by establishing a definitive law of separation with the help of hypercriticism.

But the constraints and risks of that methodological asceticism are too obvious, and the pressure of new discoveries too strong, not to favor a form of interpretation that in its principles corresponds to ancient habits. This type of

---

2 I borrow these expressions from Poucet, *Origines de Rome*, 304.

3 This is not, of course, to misconstrue the enormous importance of *Römische Geschichte*.

4 Take the example (among hundreds of others) of the great sanctuary of Vulci (described by G. Colonna in his essay in *Santuari d'Etruria*, 79), which is known only through excavations. No one even knows for what deity it was built. In fact, in the absence of explicit texts, all of Etruria (present-day Tuscany) manifests this phenomenon of a mute religion.

interpretation is all the more widespread in that it seems self-evident. In fact, aware of the impasse to which the solipsistic use of archeology leads, and unwilling to give up on an exceptionally rich literary tradition, present-day research increasingly tends to take what may seem to be a middle, and thus a reasonable, road. The age-old conflict between archeology and philology is resolved in a policy of alliances whose balance is dictated by the expediency of the historical circumstances. At first glance, that policy seems capable of laying claim to the prestigious support of "interdisciplinarity." Depending on the case, there is a bit more archeology, when the texts have little to say (the recent example of Satricum), or a bit more literary tradition, when the texts are abundant and the remains scarce (as in the case of the Romulean pomerium). In this joint reading of stones and texts, this simultaneous and reciprocal translation of one by the other, the different series of data are mutually "confirmed" (a word often used these days).

I do not deny, of course, that with the many discoveries made in recent decades, the literary tradition concerning the origins has benefited from an overall reevaluation that holds out the possibility of a historicist reading. But the risk now exists that on the basis of "confirmations" established with increasing ease, we will end up with what I have termed a modulated repetition of the tradition, a reading that ignores its characteristics and complexity. In reality, despite what seem to be profound differences, the hypercritical and the fideist (or traditional) view intersect in a shared lack of understanding of the literary tradition, a lack that in each case results from too rigid and too unitary a vision.

Hypercriticism insists on the multiplicity and diversity of the tradition, to the point of undervaluing the overall effect the tradition produces. Historicism has a tendency to overestimate the substantial unity and validity of the tradition, at the expense of countless and often important variants, which appear as soon as one moves to the details of the analysis. But fundamentally, hypercriticism and historicism have much in common. In other words, they are less two approaches to the tradition that are radically different from each other than two ways of responding to a single question, namely, the truth value of the tradition.

Is the legend of origins true or false? That is the question that both hypercriticism and historicism ask, in a noisy and never-ending quarrel. And, like old adversaries who have finally come to know and respect each other, they need each other and use each other by turns to assert their own worth. But that Manichean dualism, that false debate illusorily maintained, is not designed to resolve the matter one way or the other, but rather to feed on the new material endlessly proffered by contemporary archeology. Whatever the response given to a question that turns out to be always the same, the final interpretation is lackluster, reductive, and repetitive. Either it is impossible to know (the hypercritical view)[5] or it was all known beforehand (the fideist perspective). And the

---

[5] Pais's version of hypercriticism claimed that nothing is known. Thus the current formulation

approach that has recently been adopted, an uncertain and ill-defined amalgam of tradition and archeology, does not allow for any escape from that impasse.

The legend of origins, endlessly evaluated in terms of the choice between true and false, far from revealing its own truth, has simply reflected that of every particular age. It adorned itself in the sparkling colors of the supernatural during the Middle Ages, then submitted to the rational fervor of the Renaissance, the skepticism of the Enlightenment, the enthusiasm of the Revolution, the scientism of the nineteenth century, and, finally, the archeological technicism of our own time. The pendulum of criticism has continued to swing rhythmically back and forth between hypercritical condemnation and fideist exaltation.

But beneath an apparently identical problematic and the formal recurrences, an almost imperceptible slippage in the terrain has occurred. These silent shifts often bring into being new objects of knowledge, new utterances, new concepts, and new themes, despite the use of the same words. This diversity has continued beneath a surface unity of what, since the advent of humanism, has gradually constituted itself as a "discursive practice"[6] properly speaking, clearly delimited and autonomous within the larger field of the history of antiquity. Under these conditions, to say that the monks of the Middle Ages, the libertines in the age of Louis XIV, and the scholars of Bismarck's Germany directed their efforts toward the same goal, and all sought truth to an equal degree when they examined the account of Rome's origins, is to cover over the variety of points of view, the multiplicity of categorizations and of conceptual definitions, the methodological developments, shifting notions, and changing stakes, with the artificial veil of a unitary description (which is not false, but insignificant). In situating the historians of the past within their own time, historiography does not in any way claim that history is always only the history of the present, or that "the historical object does not exist independent of the viewer of history," a conclusion that is as imprecise as it is banal.[7] In the first place, under the surface declarations of intentions and explicit choices flow less visible currents that over the long term shape the geography of disciplines and of commentaries. Beyond Niebuhr's or de Sanctis's individual corpus lies a history of the notions of "primary source" and "oral tradition." And for that history, to repeat a famous formulation, "time is not the factor of evolution, but only the framework."[8]

---

is slightly different, somewhat toned down in relation to the first.

6 Michel Foucault has identified the parameters of this discursive practice in his study of "discursive formations" (such as medicine, grammar, and political economy). See M. Foucault, *L'archéologie du savoir* (Paris, 1969), 44–54. In his 1970 course at the Collège de France, Foucault gave this definition: "Discursive practices are characterized by the cutting up of a field of objects, the defining of a legitimate perspective for the subject of knowledge, and the fixing of norms for the elaboration of concepts and theories" (*Résumé des cours, 1970–1982* [Paris, 1989], 9).

7 See J. Le Goff, "Storia," in *Histoire et mémoire* (Paris, 1988), 179–352. As Le Goff points out, this idea goes back to B. Croce, *La storia come pensiero e come azione* (Bari, 1952), 5. See also Veyne's apt critique in *Comment on écrit l'histoire*, 103–5.

8 E. Benveniste, *Problèmes de linguistique générale* (Paris, 1966), 1: 5.

In the second place, when we define the "situation" of the historian in a context that is itself historical, we account less for the content of the discourse than for its boundaries, less for what is said than for what is not said, less for what is chosen than for what is set aside. That is why the writing of history escapes any simplistic definition, any unifying causality; it is the site of a convergence between age-old problematics and momentary interests, forgotten moments and suddenly recurring memories, the old and the new, in ever-changing proportions. But this does not mean that the historian's choices can be justified solely by the sheer play of chance. Historiography does not restore the ultimate and transcendental Truth of History as eternity created it, but rather produces the new cogito of the historian: I think *from whence* I am.

Thanks to critical historiography, history no longer escapes the purview of history; it acquires a reflexive lucidity that has long been the privilege of philosophy alone. Thus historiography should not be relegated, as it too often is, to a merely ornamental and rhetorical role, nor should it remain on the universal plane. To be truly effective, historiography must become an essential and permanent component of the historical approach. And in the study of the earliest times of Rome, where nothing is certain, but every new piece of knowledge represents an achievement, historiography will allow us, throughout the progression of research, to show how (if not why) what was said was said in precisely that way. In drawing borderlines and establishing genealogies, it will locate the errors, the impasses, the illusions of the past, providing the means to avoid errors, impasses, and illusions in the future. No bibliography, however exhaustive, can be sufficient, unless it is accompanied by an exact understanding of the choices and conceptual configurations that allowed for discoveries and may have caused errors in the past. Contrary to popular opinion, these choices and configurations are no less present in "pure" scholarship than they are in "great" narrative histories.[9] That is why historiography, to realize its heuristic productiveness, cannot be left outside historical demonstrations but must be placed inside, using a method magnificently implemented,[10] in the field of Rome's origins (and in many other fields as well), by the great Italian historian Momigliano. Practiced in that manner, historiography allows us to move beyond outdated divisions and their surviving relics, providing, parallel to the research, an incomparable range of prospective tools.

Can we further expect historiography to shed light on the constants, the laws, the universal typologies of historical discourse, which, beyond the detailed analyses and the variety of subjects discussed, constitute history's secret framework? No. That would simply be displacing the aspirations and errors of earlier forms of determinism and historicism from the level of facts to that of dis-

---

[9] *Pace* Veyne, they are merely more difficult to detect in pure scholarship. See Veyne, *Comment on écrit l'histoire*, 273–76.

[10] In the avenues opened by Croce, *La storia come pensiero*.

course.[11] In the end, the search for such a "metahistory,"[12] whose aim is to show that historical reality is conceivable only through the filter of a rationality that is always identical to itself, is nothing but a variation on the themes of the old Hegelian idealism, transposing the transcendental dimension from the level of the philosophy of history to that of a philosophy of knowledge.

The history of historiography as it has developed is familiar with this sort of temptation.[13] In the end, there is nothing surprising about that, since the proclamation of such objectives is the best legitimation that a discipline still unsure of itself can find. But, taken to the extreme, the current tendencies on this point would once more lead to a pointless discourse on method (pointless inasmuch as it is universal), which would erase the singularity and irreducibility of the historical object. That is why, unlike the traditional history of historiography, the reflexive approach (which I term historiology)[14] is not limited to the study of the slow, sure development of scientificity taken only for itself. To dissipate the mirage of false universalities, of supposed continuities, and of apparent unities, I appeal to the analytic principles defined by Michel Foucault as an "archeology of knowledge."[15] In place of the illusory and fluid notions of "mentality," "discovery," "oeuvre," "evolution," and "change," the archeology of knowledge shows the exact rules that scientific utterances (or those claiming to be scientific) of a particular period obey, the transformations these utterances undergo, and the networks of positivity that, through dissension and discontinuity, shape the shifting geography. The archeology of knowledge abolishes the universal and immutable categories of historical discourse in itself and of eternal and (progressively) revealed truth. It posits a historical discourse studied in the detail of its emergence and of its insertion into a discursive practice, studies its modalities of expression and the delimitation of its field of application. In short, historical discourse itself becomes fully historicized.

Applied to the discourse on Rome's origins, these criteria of analysis point to different thresholds. In Foucault's terminology,[16] these are a threshold of positivity (Pouilly and Beaufort); a threshold of epistemologization (Niebuhr and his

---

[11] On historicism, see M. Mandelbaum, *History, Man, and Reason: A Study of Nineteenth-Century Thought* (Baltimore, 1971).

[12] I borrow this term from H. White, *Metahistory: The Historical Imagination in Nineteenth-Century Europe* (Baltimore, 1973) but use it in a different sense.

[13] As witnessed, for example, by the hope formulated by K. Pomian (in his remarkable article published in *Annales, E.S.C.*, 1975) of "a history of knowledge and of the different uses made of it" (p. 952). In any case, for the moment we can agree on the need for preliminary and discipline-specific investigations, since critical historiology is possible only once the scientific aspects of knowledge, through which historiology studies history, have been mastered.

[14] I use the term "historiology" to distinguish it from historiography, which normally designates the historical literature on a given subject. I elaborate the analysis outlined here in "L'avenir du passé: De l'histoire de l'historiographie à l'historiologie," *Diogène* 151 (1990): 56–78.

[15] See Foucault, *L'archéologie du savoir*.

[16] Ibid., 243–47.

successor A. Schwegler);[17] a threshold of scientificity (Mommsen, Pais, and de Sanctis—for, as opposed as the exegeses of Pais and de Sanctis are, they belong to the same conceptual configuration in my opinion); and a threshold of formalization (which current debates transcend). Congruently, we may study the history of Rome's origins at the very beginning of the nineteenth century from the same perspective. Simple intuition suggests the importance of this period: at stake in Niebuhr's and Micali's work during the years 1810–1830 or thereabouts is the very possibility of history presenting itself as a science. It is no accident that the nineteenth century, the great century of history, began, historiographically speaking, with a debate on a field whose most notable characteristic is the lack of primary sources (at the time, the contributions of archeology were nonexistent). It is not *despite* that absence but rather *owing to* it that the account of Rome's origins became the site where a new field of knowledge (we take this word in a broad and not exclusively "scientific" sense) fashioned its first weapons and asserted its specificity, detaching itself from its old masters—rhetoric, aesthetics, and philosophy. It is within that context that A. W. Schlegel's attacks on Niebuhr take on their full meaning.

But what is the importance of all that for the research being done today on Rome's origins? To avoid finding ourselves once more at the theoretical and practical impasse to which the false debate relentlessly pursued by hypercriticism and historicism leads, current research must find the means for reading its historiographical traditions in a manner that is not directly positivist. In that sense, the "archeological" techniques just mentioned acquire all their usefulness. In contrast to traditional historiography, which studies the explicit and continuous unfolding of scientificity as an autonomous whole closed upon itself, these techniques reveal the risks of a history that is neither implicit nor latent within this scientificity but is quite simply different. Thus, for example, in the exegesis of the account of Rome's origins as it was formulated in the sixteenth century, we were able to locate one of the sites where the possibility for a critical analysis of Scripture was played out.

But although historiology appropriates, at least in part, the type of analyses practiced by "the archeology of knowledge," it does not set aside the cognitive aims of traditional history. Here again, the exact evaluation of what could be called the cognitive material—material elaborated on a particular question by several centuries of exegesis—is the preliminary and indispensable condition for its adequate use by contemporary research. And that evaluation cannot result from the reassuring contemplation of theories considered by the tradi-

---

[17] See A. Schwegler's *Römische Geschichte* (Tübingen, 1893), which displays an incomparable knowledge of the literary sources and is still used by specialists. Schwegler was Niebuhr's successor in that he conceived of his work as the final word on the great scholarly movement initiated by the work of his illustrious predecessor. In relation to the implicit confrontation with the debate on the historicity of Scripture, it is interesting to note that, according to Schwegler's biographer, reading D. F. Strauss's *Das Leben Jesu* played a major role in the historian's intellectual formation.

tional history of historiography in the diachronic totality of their evolution. On the contrary, beyond the apparent obviousness of nominal and formal continuities, and beyond the unmediated confrontation (spontaneously practiced by every researcher) of some past hypothesis with the current state of the discipline, historiology requires a diachronic interpretation of the methods and systems that made theories, hypotheses, and results possible in the first place. Hence the notion of oral tradition, often mentioned in reference to the famous *carmina convivalia* described by Cato, had an entirely different function in Perizonius, a sixteenth-century scholar, than it had in Niebuhr. Significantly, Niebuhr was long unaware that he had a predecessor in this matter.[18] Thus to attempt to use the theses formulated by these two scholars as if they occupied the same plane, as if they marked successive stages in the discovery of a Truth always identical to itself and finally accessible to modern research, would be to risk making a serious mistake.

Conversely, in other cases, a certain discursive coherence takes shape behind obvious discontinuities. We have seen, for example, the complementarity that exists between hypercriticism and the new comparative mythology. Such a critical historiography, far from being merely an agreeable pastime for specialists who wish to leave the austerity of their usual work for a moment, points out the path that historians of Roman antiquity (to speak only of them) ought to take, and more particularly, the path that the historians of Rome's origins ought to follow if they wish to avoid the possibility that new archeological discoveries will lead them back into the deep ruts dug by historicist fideism and hypercriticism.

Of course, I have no wish to announce the birth of a new discipline or propose a new theory in a field that has already seen so many. Nor do I wish to set out a new system that would claim to resolve in a single stroke all the difficulties that present themselves. More modestly, and more precisely as well, I wish to give the historiological dimension all its theoretical legitimacy, to take the full measure of its effectiveness and of its necessity. It is less a discipline to be pursued for its own sake, autonomous in its approach and in its objectives, whose rules delimit a scholarly field that was totally unknown in the past, than a landscape full of already familiar objects. But in that landscape, a new source of light uncovers things in the background that were unsuspected before; and through the effect of the reflexivity proper to historiology, the landscape takes on an added dimension.

Thus the transcendental aura that surrounded the notion of historical truth dissipates. Under the apparent uniformity of an identical formulation ("Does the tradition tell the truth about the origins of Rome?") the historiological gaze discovers different issues, provisional meanings, precarious systems. How are we then to believe that we can continue to ask the narrative of origins in an

---

[18] See A. Momigliano, "Perizonius, Niebuhr, and the Character of Early Roman Tradition," in *Roma arcaica*, 449–65.

unmediated manner the question of its historical veracity, while at the same time avoiding the mirages, hopes, and errantry that question expresses? We cannot say that the notion of historical truth is false, since that would again be situating ourselves on the transcendental plane; it is simply that the notion of truth, itself part of a determined historiographical context, is today inoperative because inadequate. There is no longer any absolute referent that can serve, even implicitly, to support a historical discourse that would set itself the task of recapturing a lost totality. This historiological reshaping of the notion of historical truth also allows us to explain the contradiction that the Truth revealed by the work of history is at once absolute, progressively discovered, and always provisionally articulated.

But if the question of truth is itself a historiographically dated and circumscribed question, does it follow that history must renounce all cognitive aims? After so many accomplishments and metamorphoses, has the time come for history to finally return to the origin, and, since it cannot be a science, concern itself with being literature, as Cicero recommended so long ago? In other words, if the exegesis of the narrative of Rome's origins must now leave the field where hypercriticism and historicism so long stood in opposition to each other, can it do anything else but rewrite Livy once more? And if so, isn't it now exposed, through the effacement of its transcendental legitimation, to the mere chance of the talents, subjectivities, choices, and biases of each historian? That might appear to be the case, and a tendency in that direction, exacerbated by the recurrent pretensions of a certain kind of neopositivism, has been articulated several times. Because the knowledge of the past cannot be a science, some claim, it must renounce the idea of seeking scientific legitimation for itself. And since it does not belong to the domain of universality and generality, it must be satisfied with being what it is, the singular description of a singularity.[19]

In such renunciations, which are as absolute as were the ambitions of the past, we can detect a feeling resembling the bitterness of love lost. The historiological view shows not that we must abdicate any cognitive aim for the history of Rome's beginnings, but simply that the questions raised in the past in relation to the narrative of origins, far from allowing an immediate relationship to historical truth, are themselves the product of unconscious mediations and deformations. The ancient tradition of the *primordia Romana* has long been the object of an inquiry that hopes to find a direct response to what, according to the famous definition of the German historian Leopold Ranke, is the very question of history: "Wie es eigentlich gewesen?" (So what really happened?)[20]

---

[19] "The barrier between history and science is not history's attachment to individuality, or its relation to values, or the fact that John Lackland will never pass this way again: it is the fact that the *doxa*, lived experience, and the sublunary are one thing, science is another, and history is on the side of *doxa*" (Veyne, *Comment on écrit l'histoire*, 206).

[20] In examining it closely, we find that Dumézilian hermeneutics has its source in such a disappointed hope. As late as 1985, Dumézil declared: "I shall never know, nor shall others with me, the events and actors that were at the origins of Rome" (*L'oubli de l'homme*, 302).

But gradually, and more quickly in this field than elsewhere, the notions of "facts," "events," and "documents" have crumbled away, and the edifices built from such fragile materials have become cracked. Thus, throughout the nineteenth century, philologists and historians wondered if Rome had been conquered by the Etruscans. Although useful for writing the history of the Europe of nations, this type of question turned out to be quite inadequate for archaic Rome, since the entire difficulty was to define first what was meant by the terms "conquest" and "Etruscans." Similarly, the monarchy of Servius Tullius was very often analyzed in the light of the implicit notion of "constitutional sovereignty"—a notion that was more appropriate for describing political regimes in nineteenth-century England and France than in archaic Rome.

Or again, we are surprised to find that historians of urbanism analyze Fustel de Coulanges's famous *Cité antique* as an important manifestation of what they call the culturalist movement, on the same level, for example, as the work of John Ruskin.[21] Yet Coulanges's book, which appeared in 1864, has for several years been the object of a very clear renewal of interest among historians of antiquity: It is sometimes considered by them to be a classic, particularly pertinent for the study of archaic Rome, and is thus used as a means of direct access to the truth of those obscure times. What can this mean, except that questions that seem to directly engage the notion of historical truth are themselves mediated and presuppose preliminary choices—in short, that they are already partial responses?

It is thus not enough to say that historians no longer confine themselves to the study of events, and now allow objects into their field of observation that had previously been excluded from it. After all, a neopositivist conception of historical truth can very well accommodate such an extension of historians' territory; in fact, it would celebrate it.

In reality, something very different is at issue. The viewing eye cannot see itself. But the historiological approach at least allows historians to know that such a blind spot exists in their vision of the past, and allows them to detect implicit presuppositions in the work of their predecessors. Thus historians can see that the criterion of simple historicity (which corresponds to Ranke's question) is not only dated for the study of the Rome of origins but is obsolete and inadequate, whether the historian in question is studying the short term, the medium term, or the long term. Such a criterion supposes that history has only to clear the field of its investigation of the dirt and refuse that covers it, in order to find, buried but still intact, the Truth, like those archeologists of the past who, with a stroke of their picks, exhumed a Venus de Milo or an Apollo Belvedere, come to reveal the eternal truth of the Beautiful, or so they thought.

[21] See, for example, F. Choay, *L'urbanisme, utopie et réalités* (Paris, 1965), 21. But see Momigliano's clear reservations about a direct use of *La cité antique* in *Roma arcaica*, 494–98.

No, there is no historical truth that is already there, sub specie aeternitatis. There is only a series of questions, which do not emerge ready-made from an abstract absolute but must be formulated, calibrated, adjusted each time as a function of the view chosen, the sources available, and the existing historiographical work. In other words, historical "truth" is not an ontological given. It is constructed from the analysis of a network of mediations and is the product of a relation between different elements. To be more precise, historical truth lies in the very definition of that relation.

Thus, to know the truth of the legend of Alba Longa,[22] the mysterious metropolis where, according to legend, Romulus and Remus originated, it is pointless to wonder whether the tradition's account is true or false. That would involve returning to the arena where hypercriticism and historicism vainly seek an outcome to their endless quarrel. All the philologist's and historian's work must focus on elaborating finely honed questions to ask of the tradition, on thoroughly analyzing that tradition to determine its different strata, and on evaluating the archeological sources free of the inadequate postulates inherited from historiography.

Because both the historicist and the hypercritical readings (and "reading" ought to be understood in literal terms) of the narrative of origins situate themselves in a relation of immediacy to a tradition, which they cross-examine even while restricting themselves to what the tradition explicitly said, they make the tradition a place without depth, without perspective, and, finally, without great interest.

The great historian Moses Finley, taking the side of the skeptics, recently observed that "the confirmation that is now being claimed proves to be extremely restricted. Not surprisingly, therefore, the best modern accounts shift quickly from the question of Roman origins to the no less interesting, but wholly different, area of the intellectual and ideological history of the Roman Republic."[23]

At the risk of seeing this book definitively classified by its readers as one of the "worst modern accounts," I shall not abandon the problem of the origins of Rome, which in my view must on the contrary be apprehended in all its complexity and richness! It is true that the legend of Romulus is an excellent source for the study of republican times and of the Principate.[24] But that should not lead us, as is too easily done, to abandon all heuristic aims for the earliest times of Rome, only to dress up that decision in the noble costume of a new scholarly Pyrrhonism. The ideological use of Romulean legends by the

---

[22] To avoid any secondhand impressions, I have deliberately chosen as example the theme of a personal research project. The legend is detailed in chap. 9 below.

[23] M. I. Finley, *Ancient History: Evidence and Models* (New York, 1986), 22.

[24] The scholarly debate surrounding what is called the constitution of Romulus focuses on this problem. See E. Gabba's essay in *Athenaeum*, 1960; and J. Poucet's essay in *Sodalitas: Scritti in onore di Antonio Guarino* (Naples, 1984–85).

Romans of the Republic and the Empire does not preclude their constitutive role as the indispensable foundation for our knowledge of archaic times. Such a use accounts for the survival of these legends, not for their existence or for the whole of their content.

What we must abandon, in contrast, is the long-maintained hope of reducing the problem of Rome's origins to a single hermeneutic system embracing all facets of the question, a unitary explanation that would suddenly illuminate the narrative of origins as a whole.

To perform the exegesis of the tradition of the *primordia Romana* and to write the history of Rome's beginnings, we must, with the historian of religions, be attentive both to the historicization of the myth realized by the narrative of origins and to the theological and ritual continuities implied by a liturgical practice that continued for centuries. With the archeologist, we must not neglect any of the data available from excavations and must focus closely on typologies and chronologies before making any interpretation. With the jurist, we must learn to recognize the process by which the tradition shaped narratives from the schemata and precedents borrowed from the world of law. And, last but not least, with the philologist, we must learn to detect the contradictions, silences, variants, repetitions, anticipations, rationalizations, and biases, which, in the narrative of origins, are so many marks of its diversity and of its long existence. Let us note in passing that the hypercritical perspective, though erroneous, gave its proponents an incomparable advantage in this respect.

But none of these elements is significant in isolation, since the complex composite of the problem of Rome's origins results precisely from their dynamic interaction. And an analysis is possible only if we practice the critical and reflexive historiography I have identified by the name historiology. That analysis is not limited to cognitive aspects, nor is it the sole valid means for avoiding the deformations due to the double prism of particularly dense ancient and modern traditions. Thus, on the threshold of this veritable house of mirrors, facing these illusory plays of transparent or silver-backed glass, this maze with its countless detours, facing this spectacle of images, sometimes enlarged, sometimes in miniature, these unstable sights, and these multiple reflections, we can understand why some have decided with Finley to "turn elsewhere."[25]

This is especially tempting since the Ariadne's thread that determinism once offered the historian has disappeared. For a long time, in fact, historians sought the first fruits and causes of the later development of Rome in the era of the origins. Marc Bloch once remarked that "in popular usage, origins are a beginning that explains. Or worse, a beginning that is adequate for explaining."[26] This

---

[25] "Two decades of intensive inquiry into early Rome have culminated in the cul-de-sac of Satricum, suggesting that the ancient historian interested in evaluating his sources had better turn elsewhere" (Finley, *Ancient History*, 22–23).

[26] M. Bloch, *Apologie pour l'histoire*, rev. ed. (Paris, 1974), 38.

laconic comment can apply just as well to a large part of earlier scholarly writings on the *primordia Romana*. Like mirages that lead the confused traveler ever deeper into the desert, the search for origins, seen as the first cause, has often led archeologists and historians to detect the signs of the emergence of the city of Rome in the darkness of the most remote prehistory. Hence they speak of a "preurban" settlement to describe the few huts that, toward the tenth century B.C.E., occupied the hills on the banks of the Tiber, the site of the future Rome. This means that, with the progress of linguistics and archeology, the determinist view, which used to interpret the beginnings of Rome as the necessary starting point for any history of the peninsula, now sees it as the ineluctable end of a long prehistory. In both cases, however, we rediscover, applied to different temporal dimensions, the characteristic conviction of all forms of determinism, that what was could not not have been. As transition periods, the beginnings of Rome and the end of the Roman Empire are both sites where history, understood as the search for determining causes, tested its inquiries and its methods. In that respect, it is certainly no accident that a number of eminent historians of the primordia have directed their efforts toward what is today called, precisely to avoid any determinist connotations, not the Lower Empire, but late antiquity. Let us merely cite the names André Piganiol, Jérôme Carcopino, Alföldi, and Santo Mazzarino.

In Latin, the same verb (*condere*) means both "to hide" and "to found": hence the origin, always hidden, always absent, always present, founded the discourse on the history of Rome, particularly its religious history, even as it concealed it. But gradually, the search for first causes, like that for last ends, ceased to be the objective of modern-day historians. In other words, the possibility of a unifying causality that could place the narrative of origins under a single light dissolved in the multiplication of discoveries and the proliferation of hypotheses and divergent interpretations.

Does that mean, to cite Veyne's expression, that "the problem of causality in history is a relic of the paleo-epistemological era"?[27] Yes, if we remain at the level of a causality that would be immediately accessible and directly decipherable in the mere succession of events. In reality, the problem of causality remains a heuristic principle for the historian, but that causality is no longer absolute, general, universal, univocal, fixed, finite, and definitive, but rather relative, partial, multiple, plural, shifting, infinite, and provisional. It is no longer static and closed upon itself, but dynamic and in a state of permanent expansion. In these processes, the reflexivity historiology makes possible plays a major role, since, even as it traces the limits of a given problematic, it also delineates the conditions for scholarly productiveness.

In the skies of history, nothing can be seen without optical instruments. Once the instrument has been selected, the objects within the field of observa-

---

27 Veyne, *Comment on écrit l'histoire*, 115.

tion will appear, but not those outside its purview. That is why the historiological approach cannot be considered merely a provisional scaffolding that would allow historians to construct the edifice of historical Truth definitively. It is in fact a constituent part of a "truth" that cannot exist without it. But this does not mean that there will now be as many causalities as there are historians: once defined and set in place, the elements historians work with lead to conclusions that are not so much arbitrary and personal as logical and necessary. Disintegrated and dissolved in the light of historiology, the false continuities and false unities of neopositivism and determinism cede their place to a form of history that reflects as much on the questions it asks as on the responses it seeks.

What, then, are the consequences for the history of Rome's origins, given that simultaneous effacement of both the transcendental and the determinist legitimations of history? Historians have not adequately taken into account the fact that this effacement leads to a complete overhaul of the status of the discursive practice constituted by the study of the *primordia Romana*. The search for origins gives way to the search for discontinuity, that is, to a question that is finally the very question of history.

Break or transformation, threshold or fracture, passageway or fault? How are we to conceive of this discontinuity manifested so intensely by the foundation of Rome, a foundation that no longer stands as the mere starting point for a long historical evolution, but is increasingly revealed as one of the major sites where history attempts to find the key to its own enigma.

Niebuhr once defined philology as "mediating eternity."[28] I do not share in that illusion of identity with the classical tradition, which is betrayed by that expression. A single system or a single theory, however definitive it may, cannot reveal in a single stroke the truth of Rome's foundation. That does not mean, of course, that we must give up conceptual interpretation. It is still true that the writing of history can result only from the asymptotic tension between the irreducible singularity of the "fact" and the need for classifactory universals.

Roma condita. For a long time, that lapidary expression sounded obvious, but a question can now be discerned in it, a question that every new discovery revives, for Rome is no longer, has not always been, and might have not been . . .

---

[28] Niebuhr, *History of Rome*, 1: 18 [translation modified].

PART 2

DAWN

CHAPTER 5

SURVEYING LATIUM

TO THOSE WHO SOUGHT the explanation for what was at the time called the Greek miracle in the quality of light in Hellas, Hegel responded irritably: "Don't tell me about Greece's sky, since the Turks now live where the Greeks used to be. Leave me be and don't bring up the matter again."[1]

This famous anecdote suffices to put us on our guard, if not against historical geography itself, then at least against an immoderate use of it, which would lead to a form of determinism as facile as it is pointless and inexact.

Must historians for that reason turn away from the landscapes and sites where the events constituting their object of study occurred, where, as a very significant expression would have it, they "took place"?

No, of course not, for that would deprive historians of a good deal of the pertinence and accuracy of their analyses. But they must abandon a geography whose ambition is to explain history directly and definitively and must confine themselves to detecting the elements, lines of force, and characteristics of the lie of the land, the climate, and the composition of the soil, which are valuable as so many conditions (and not causes) that allow the unfolding of human history.

In addition, it would be a grave mistake to make geography and history into two separate, autonomous entities opposed to each other in the way motion can be opposed to stability or change to permanence. More than any other region of Europe, perhaps, Latium illustrates how fragile these rather academic distinctions are. Although most of the time geographical facts obviously preexist historical facts, the reverse can also be true. We must therefore seek the origin of certain sometimes major geographical evolutions in history itself.

"No birds, no plowmen, no rural life, no lowing of cattle, no villages," wrote Chateaubriand of a Roman countryside that was flourishing in antiquity, but to which the upheavals of history had brought profound geographical changes.[2]

On the other hand, although geography is ordinarily measured within a time frame that is not that of human evolution, it also has its own history, which

[1] See J. Brunhes and C. Vallaux, *La géographie de l'histoire* (Paris, 1921), 2.
[2] F.-A.-R. Chateaubriand, lettre sur la Campagne Romaine, 10 January 1804, reproduced in *Correspondance*, ed. L. Thomas (Paris, 1912), 155.

sometimes interferes with human history. Modern science has established that the lava spewed by the volcanoes of Latium—now peaceful, verdant mountains—was seen by human eyes.[3] We can only conjecture the exact consequences, which were certainly decisive, that such phenomena had on the survival and environment of the human communities existing at the time.

But there are other closer examples, where we are fortunately better able to evaluate such correlations. "The Tiber itself has its ruins," observed Charles de Bonstetten, a traveler contemporary with Chateaubriand, in *Voyage sur la scène des six derniers livres de l'Enéide* (Journey to the site of the last six books of the *Aeneid*), published in Geneva in 1804.[4] In fact, following a particularly violent storm and flood, the waters of the Tiber abandoned their former bed in Ostia (still quite visible under the name "Fiume morto") to follow a new course. This happened in 1557, which is to say, very recently in geological terms. We also know that, since antiquity, the shoreline at the mouth of the Tiber has receded by several kilometers, making way for the continuing mass of alluvia brought by the yellow waters of the river. As a result, the ruins of Ostia, which was once a Roman port, rise up in the middle of grassland.

Attesting once more to the indissociable link between geography and history, the Tiber also empties a great part of its waters into the sea through a canal first dug by Trajan and gradually transformed into a "natural" bed called the Fiumicino.

To appreciate rightly the influence of natural surroundings over the course of history, we would need to set aside the Latium that now appears after centuries of abandonment, followed by the intense development of farm lands in the modern era, lands that are today being devoured by urbanization. We would need instead to describe the Latium of the early Romans and the ancient Latins. That Latium hardly exists any longer and disappears a bit more every day. In reading what Jérôme Carcopino wrote about the origins of Ostia, we can measure the scope of the changes that, in less than a hundred years, have affected, often irremediably, many of the landscapes and sites of the ancient territory. It has been a long time since Carcopino on horseback, Arnold Toynbee on bicycle, and Thomas Ashby on foot could hope to find the landscapes that Livy and Virgil had seen and described nearly two thousand years before them! That is why, quite often, the researcher who wishes to resolve questions of topography, confronted with a reality that has often become deceptive and unrecognizable, turns to the descriptions of travelers or scholars of the past, to find the terms of comparison and the precisions that are indispensable for reflection. Not only

---

[3] The first manifestations of volcanic activity in Latium can be dated by eruptive strata at more than 700,000 years B.C.E. And *below* them, traces of human presence have been found in a few places (especially near Anagni). The collective work of A. P. Anzidei, A. M. Bietti-Sestieri, and A. de Santis, *Roma ed il Lazio dall'età della pietra alla formazione della città* (Rome, 1985), provides an excellent overview of the data concerning the prehistory of Latium.

[4] C. de Bonstetten, *Voyage sur la scène des six derniers livres de l'Enéide* (Geneva, 1804), 78.

time passes, but space as well, though we believed it motionless and untouchable. Of course, past efforts and enthusiasms were rife with illusion. After all, didn't Virgil himself demonstrate he was aware of the historical character of every natural landscape, when he had Aeneas, under Evander's guidance, visit the future site of Rome, still covered by woods and prairies? In a general way, the ancients were sensitive, if only for reasons of literary aesthetics, to the effect of human activity on nature.

And of course, not everything has disappeared, and it is still possible in certain cases to rediscover at least part of the geographical and ecological realities of primitive Italy.

But we are increasingly aware that this type of restitution, along with the analyses to which it leads, cannot result from a direct view of things. That is why the old historical geography is changing into what is now called the archeology of the landscape, a discipline to which the English school has made a major contribution, with, in the case of Italy, studies dealing primarily with southern Etruria and Veii, the territory of the ancient rival of Rome. Researchers no longer simply describe the landscape as it appeared in a particular era, but attempt to understand how the natural conditions could have oriented (or not) lifestyles, forms of farming, and kinds of settlements, while not neglecting any aspect of the extremely complex relations established between a population and the environment in which it developed. There again, they focus less on defining fixed categories with the aim of linking a history to a landscape, based on the too simple model of cause and effect, than on studying the dynamic of a network of complex and shifting interdependencies.

Several new disciplines or scholarly approaches have contributed to the quest for answers to what is, finally, a very old question, that of the relation between nature and culture. Used for the last several decades, aerial photography of all of central Italy is still rich in possibilities. More recently, satellite photographs have also been used. Aided, for example, by periods of drought, differential growth of cultures, and extensive tilling, superficial and precarious traces have appeared, revealing ancient structures of human occupation that used to be invisible.

Natural science also plays an increasingly important role in helping us understand the relations between human beings and their environment over the course of history. In the particular case of Latium, which used to be a region rich in lakes, the work of specialists in dendrochronology (the observation of concentric rings of tree trunks to fix precise dates), sedimentology (the analysis of lacustrine sedimentation to establish variations in water levels), and palynology (the examination of preserved pollen grains to retrace the composition and evolution of vegetation) will probably prove to be extremely valuable. These specialists not only accumulate the data, however precise they may be, but also restore the entire agricultural chain of production for a given chronological stage, in order to describe as completely as possible the way a population used the earth's resources, and the resulting changes in the environment. From this perspective, the paleoethnobotanical approach, "which rests on the analysis of the vestiges of ligneous oils and seeds conserved in the deposits,"[5] gives precious information on "the composition and structure of forest populations" and on the nature of the soil cultivated. More generally, such an approach can hope to arrive at a significantly increased knowledge of the techniques implemented both in farming and in raising livestock, in short, a knowledge of everything concerning the life of a human community within a "natural" environment. It is for that reason as well that this archeology of the landscape is increasingly combined with the problematic of ethnology (thus one speaks of ethnoarcheology), elaborated through an observation of traditional societies still surviving today. In a certain way, specialists on primitive Latium do the same thing when they refer to data collected by historians of the medieval periods of the region, or even by economists who, beginning in the early nineteenth century, founded their projects of reform on surveys of the sites, which are precious because they are so precise.[6] All these methods, often stemming from recent developments in the field of prehistory, require prospecting the surface, that is, systematically and quite rapidly identifying the directly visible traces as a whole throughout an entire zone. In contrast to an excavation limited to one site, this is the only procedure that allows scientists to raise the difficult but essential question of how settlements were distributed in relation to the types of farming and to demographic trends.

In many ways, contemporary research is only at the beginning of an approach that will soon lead to a thorough, new apprehension of the role natural conditions in Latium and central Italy played in developing the human collectivities that succeeded one another in these territories.[7]

In taking into account the most recent studies (without neglecting older accounts), we can already provide a rough sketch.

In the first place, the western coast of Italy offered infinitely greater possibilities for human activity than the eastern coast:[8] much more spacious coastal plains; more numerous natural ports; navigable rivers and not just devastating torrents; soil that was fertile because volcanic in origin; less violent terrain, relieved by valleys that were so many natural paths of communication; a more moderate climate that spared Latium and Etruria from the formidable periods of

---

[5] See H. Richard, "Sciences de la nature et archéologie," in *Le courrier du CNRS, Dossiers scientifiques* (Paris, 1989), 24.

[6] One of the first to our knowledge to have practiced this type of comparison was Bonstetten, who ended his *Voyage sur la scène* with "a few observations on modern Latium," obviously designed to demonstrate a contrario the prosperity of the region in antiquity. One of the best-known and most useful surveys reconstituting the appearance of Latium before the upheavals that began in the 1880s is P. de Tournon, *Études statistiques sur Rome et la partie occidentale des états romains*. On this subject, see C. Ampolo's remarkable essay in *Dialoghi di Archeologia*, 1980.

[7] A general survey by G. Barker appears in the journal *Archeologia Medievale*, 1986.

[8] See T. Cornell and J. Matthews, *Atlas of the Roman World* (New York, 1982), 12–14.

drought that were the usual lot of Apulia (between Bari and Taranto); and a system of lakes facilitating the establishment of human communities. Beginning with the great migrations of prehistory, all these advantages assured the indisputable superiority of the west over the east. It was from the west that the Greeks, the Phoenicians, and no doubt other peoples before them arrived in Italy, and it is in the west that a people, giving their name to the Tyrrhenian Sea, made it their goal to extend their domination to the whole of the peninsula, first to the Etruscans and then to the Romans. In the archaic age, Hesiod's *Theogony* thus speaks of the Tyrrhenians in Latium,[9] leaving the modern historian the task of determining whether they were Etruscans or Latins (at that date, the hypothesis that they were Romans is unlikely).

With the exception of Strabo and Pliny,[10] who give only an enumeration of peoples, legends, cities, roads, and wines in Latium, no author of antiquity provides a real analysis of the natural framework within which Rome constructed the instruments for its future greatness. This absence is no doubt explained in part by a profound sense of the altogether singular nature of Rome's destiny, a destiny irreducible to any natural causality, and by the character of geographical descriptions among the ancients. But such an absence also illustrates the geographical diversity of a region that escapes any unitary definition.

This is, in the first place, a geological diversity.[11] The most ancient rock formations, which appeared more than 130 million years ago, during the Secondary (Mesozoic) era, persist in the form of a few chalky reliefs on Monte Circeo; in the center and south of the region, and in Sabine; to the southeast of the Alban Hills, beyond present-day Velletri, between Segni and Priverno; to the northwest, behind Palestrina and Anagni; and, finally, in Sabine, near Palombara Sabina. At an altitude often exceeding a thousand meters, they constitute the hard core of massifs, which are lower in elevation and more "recent." The peaks that surround Palestrina, like those running the length of the Aniene River, belong to the Tertiary era and are rich in clay and sand marls.

The region also owes a good part of its present appearance to the volcanoes of the Quaternary era, which are distributed in the northwest around Monti Sabatini and Monti Cimini, and in the southeast around the Alban Hills. Lake Bracciano (a former flood basin), on the one hand, and Lake Albano (a crater lake), on the other, mark the center of these two geological systems, of which the present-day Tiber constitutes the approximate line of separation. The eruptions of volcanoes in Latium, which began about 900,000 years ago and ended in about 280,000 B.C.E., played a major role in the formation of the soil. In a large part of Campagna di Roma (especially in the south), volcanoes were responsible

---

[9] Hes. *Theog.* 1011ff.

[10] Strabo 5; Pliny *HN* 3.56–70.

[11] For what follows, see the numerous indications in Anzidei, Bietti-Sestieri, and de Santis, *Roma ed il Lazio*.

for the local variant of tufa called cappellaccio, which is also found in a number of the buildings of archaic Rome, especially in walls. Often situated just below the humus, the cappellaccio stratum remains impermeable to water. To drain stagnant waters, obtain cultivable land, and assure its irrigation, early settlers often undertook large-scale projects, leading to the proliferation nearly everywhere of canals, called *cuniculi,* which long puzzled specialists. They now agree to date the great majority of these canals to the fifth or fourth century B.C.E., though the first of them were probably begun during the archaic era.

When a troubled history prevented the inhabitants from maintaining the canals, the spread of marshlands and malaria transformed these regions into unhealthy isolated areas, feared by all travelers until the beginning of this century.

Higher up, and particularly on the sides of the Alban Hills, the soil is more friable, more fragile, but also more fertile. Vineyards already famous in antiquity still prosper there today.

Elsewhere, the first chalk formations, decomposing as a result of erosion, often produced red granular soil, which did not easily lend itself to early exploitation. Although good land was not rare, therefore, it was not found everywhere in Latium and required attentive and persistent care. There were numerous lands, especially along the coast and south of the Tiber, that were more suitable for grazing than for farming.

Nonetheless, "it would be a grave mistake," in Carcopino's words, "to imagine the Rome of the early centuries, the city that unified Latium and then conquered Italy, as similar to that fixed in our minds by the Lower Empire and the Middle Ages, rising up as a victorious army in the middle of a desertlike, unhealthy steppe." Sixty-four years after admiring the view from the property of the princes Torlonia in Porto near Ostia, Carcopino still remembered the "blooming farm lands on hundreds and hundreds of acres, stretching to the horizon," and described in luminous terms the "already high wheat, compact and turning green," which "undulated to the point of infinity."[12]

Hence the geomorphological diversity of the region was at the origin of a great variety of landscapes. The etymology lent credence by the ancients, who derive the name Latium from the adjective *latus,* "broad," is tempting but incorrect. In any case, the region is not simply the plain that, just beyond Soracte (the mountain so dear to Horace), suddenly reveals its entire expanse to the eyes of the motorist coming from the north. In fact, the origin of the Latins can be sought in the Alban Hills, renowned for the mildness and relative coolness of their climate, which have made them a particularly appreciated vacation spot in our own times, as in the times of Cicero's Rome. If we had to define the natural geography of Latium in a word, it would be more accurate to speak not of a plain but of a continuous "tangle" of plain and mountain. Thus the great geographer Paul Vidal de La Blanche described "the mountains, snowy in winter

[12] J. Carcopino, *Souvenirs romains* (Paris, 1968), 109 and 110.

but offering cool pasture land in summer; the plain, hospitable in winter, after the renewal following the autumn rains, but subject to summer droughts that can interrupt vegetation for a full two months." And he adds: "Sheep, the characteristic form of wealth (*pecunia*) in the Mediterranean region, move about easily and find what they need on the plain and in the mountains by turns. A pastoral form of administration was the result of that interdependence."[13]

Although we need to nuance the retrospective determinism of an assessment that was fully valid only for the beginnings of primitive Rome, it is certain that, on the whole, geomorphological duality constituted one of the major characteristics of the territory of Latium. Moreover, the plain itself was rarely just an expanse without reliefs and without variety. Much of the modern visitor's impression of uniformity is the result of erosion and, even more, of human activity. Many trenches and lakes were filled in, and many hillsides leveled; many forests disappeared to give way to farm lands or to an inexorably progressing urbanization. To those who traveled over it in archaic times, the plain of Latium offered a rich and unforeseeable alternation of fields and forests, waterways, shaded valleys, and sometimes steep hills, as we still see in Lavinium and Ardea.

Lacking the mining resources found in Etruria (on the island of Elba), Calabria, or Sardinia, Latium was renowned for the beauty and quality of its forests. Certain of the legends of origins, belonging to the old Latin fount, retained the memory of the shadowy grandeur of the primitive silva. Thus one tradition, probably very ancient, gave the mythical kings of Alba the name *silvii*, which is directly related to the Latin word for forest. In the lines Theophrastus devoted to that forest at the end of the fourth century B.C.E. (thus inspiring Jean de La Bruyère), we also discover that this wealth of forests was one of the principal things that attracted seafaring peoples, whether Etruscan, Greek, or even perhaps Phoenician, to Latium. These navigators, who found Circeo "thickly wooded," were anxious to find material to build their boats. "The country of the Latins is well watered," writes Theophrastus— a very important characteristic to seafaring peoples, who need to lay in regular provisions in calm waters. In addition, "the lowland part contains bay, myrtle, and wonderful beech. . . . They cut timbers of it of such a size that they will run the whole length of the keel of a Tyrrhenian vessel. The hill country produces fir and silver-fir."[14]

All in all, framed by the mountains of Tolfa (on the Civitavecchia side) to the west, the mountains of Sabine and Palestrina to the east, and by the Lepini and Ausoni Mountains and the promontory of Monte Circeo to the southeast, Latium could be defined as an amphitheater with Rome at its center. And in this wall formed by mountains, which are always visible somewhere along the

---

[13] P. Vidal de La Blanche, *Principes de géographie humaine* (1921), 82.
[14] Theophrastus, *Enquiry into Plants*, trans. A. Hort (Cambridge, 1961), 5.8.3 (p. 465).

horizon, there are numerous natural breaches. In many ways, the history of primitive Latium is only a series of battles, which the communities living on the plains, whether Latin or Roman, had to wage against invaders coming down from the mountains: the Sabines, the Samnites, and the Volscians.

In addition to this axis of communication lying (north)east to (south)west and formed by the general incline of these reliefs from the interior to the sea, there is another lying in the north(western)-south(eastern) direction, particularly marked by the valleys of the Sacco and Liri Rivers. With no gaps between them, these valleys established ties between Rome and the rich and cosmopolitan Campagna, ties that were to find their administrative corollary when Augustus formed the first of fourteen regions in Italy by regrouping Latium and Campagna. The wide corridor called the *via Latina,* carved into the massive mountain, was dotted with Latin (that is, Roman) colonies, to which it owed its name. It was also regularly defended by these colonies and constituted the principal instrument for the first expansion of republican Rome. Even in modern times, it was the path the highway—and before it, the railroad—took, putting Naples two hours from Rome. Along the same line, but less visible on the terrain, another itinerary can be reconstituted. It runs a short ten kilometers behind the riverbank line, and the centers of Ficana, Lavinium, and Ardea—and before them, the Etruscan cities of Tarquinia and Caere (Cerveteri)—could be found along it in archaic times. The desire to prepare against surprise attacks coming from the sea, but especially the inhospitality of an often marshy coast, explain the choice of these settlements. Having known an indisputable prosperity in archaic times, to which the size of the archeological finds made on the site and their role in the legend of origins attest, they later found themselves supplanted by Rome.

Thus the more we try to define the geographical unity of Latium, the more it escapes analysis. Sometimes, to conform to the suggestions of the landscape, we would have to extend the limits of the region far beyond what its history suggests; at other times, to best follow the reality of the terrain, we would have to reduce or eliminate territories that are known for their "Latinness." If there is any unity, it lies in what makes Latium, before anything else, a borderland, a sphere of contacts (albeit violent), a space for encounters. That is why there is no strictly geographical definition that is adequate in itself, and the old question of Latium's boundaries, the torment of so many specialists of ancient topography,[15] calls for a response that is in the first place historical.

If, for all these reasons, the ancients did not seek to describe the region of Latium as a whole from the point of view of natural geography, the same is

---

[15] Like the analagous question of the respective borders of the territory in every Latin city. In that regard, Beloch's analyses in *Römische Geschichte* illustrate the impossibility of a purely geographical point of view.

not true for the site of Rome, whose description was a theme dear to classical historiography.

Rome could be only . . . at Rome. Such was the profound conviction of the ancients when they reflected on the long history of their city, even though, on at least one occasion (after the taking of Veii), the Romans themselves imagined leaving their city, which had been devastated by the Gauls, to settle on the site of their ancient Etruscan rival. But Camillus prevailed over those who wanted to move, and Rome remained faithful to itself. Whether or not the speech Livy attributes to Camillus was ever uttered matters little here. It is clear in any case that the reasons set out by the conqueror of the Gauls to convince his fellow citizens to remain were for the most part religious in nature.[16] Of course, Camillus did not neglect to speak of the natural advantages of the Roman site: "salubrious hills," "a river at hand," "a fairly close sea," and "a unique situation in the heart of Italy." But the essential point of his argument had to do with the impiety involved in abandoning places that had, so to speak, been consecrated or sanctified by religious practices.

On the same subject, the reflections Cicero attributes to Scipio, at the beginning of the second book of *De republica*, leave a much greater place for strictly geographical factors. But the rest of Latium is hardly present in these considerations, which are situated at a very general level.

For the modern historian who raises the question of geography in reference to the city of Romulus, Rome is not, as it was for the ancients, a monad that found its principles of development within itself and offers for analysis something like a mirror of the universe. The modern historian knows that, in the Middle Ages, the ancient capital declined to the size of a large town. And before that, it was abandoned by the imperial powers, which left to establish their palaces and pomp elsewhere, on the banks of the Bosphorus. Thus the old proverb takes on the allure of a question: Do all roads really lead to Rome? Or more exactly, why did they lead there, even to the point of making the gathering of a few huts "the site and center of the greatest of empires"?[17]

---

[16] Livy *Ab urbe condita* 5.51ff. The passages cited appear in chap. 54.
[17] Cic. *Rep.* 2.5.

CHAPTER 6

THE SITE OF ROME

"THE POSITION OF that world capital," observed Johann von Goethe in his *Italian Journey,* "immediately takes us back to its foundation."[1] Even today, with a little imagination, it is possible to discern the specificity and exceptional character of the site of Rome, despite all the metamorphoses brought about by centuries of urban development. And without succumbing to the naive astonishment of Jacques-Henri Bernardin de Saint-Pierre, who was amazed to see every great city traversed by a great river, we cannot avoid noting the major role played by the Tiber in the emergence and development of Rome.

Curiously, outside a few felicitous exceptions, and despite the obvious topography, modern historical research has denied or minimized the importance of the river in the origins of the city. Thus, in a book of indisputable and lasting value, Léon Homo wrote in 1925: "The rôle of the Tiber in the economic life of Central Italy, vital during the classical period, could not be invoked in the same way to explain progress at the time of Rome's remote origins without a flagrant anachronism."[2] Nonetheless, ancient texts do attest to the importance of the river beginning with the dawn of the city; and, in addition to the texts, the reality of the place speaks for itself.

Yet for a long time, history and philology, under the effect of a systematic prejudice that always presented itself as the conclusion of a demonstration, declared that the texts were wrong. After all, to make the prosperity of the Eternal City depend on the flow of a river seemed a bit too simple, and frankly, a bit trivial. It was no doubt more elegant to declare that "Rome's greatness . . . was . . . chiefly—based on intelligence and will."[3] In addition, didn't the relatively late creation of Ostia during the republican era show a contrario that the Tiber had played only a very secondary role in the early history of Rome? To be fair, let us add that the almost total absence of material evidence from the most ancient times in Ostia, apart from a few indexes brought to light by Carcopino, led scholars not to lend credence to the tradition, which placed the first Roman

---

[1] J. von Goethe, *Italienische Reise* (Leipzig, 1912), 196.
[2] L. Homo, *Primitive Italy and the Beginnings of Roman Imperialism* (New York, 1968), 79.
[3] Ibid.

colony in Ostia, dating it from the time of the kings. Nor did such an absence turn their attention to the muddy waters of a river that seemed to lead nowhere. In addition, beginning in 1870, the river was progressively enclosed and walled up in a veritable corridor of stone, on the model already realized for the Seine in Paris. Thus it became very difficult to imagine the part the Tiber had played in the history of the city born on its banks and so often invaded in the past by impetuous floods.

Fortunately, the most recent research has corrected that forgetfulness,[4] and everyone is now agreed in recognizing the importance of the river in Rome's development, beginning at the age of origins. In recent years, archeological finds, the result of methodically conducted investigations, have become more numerous. In Ostia, for example, and in surrounding areas, such as Castel Fusano, the remains of archaic settlements have come to light. Rediscovered near the present mouth of the Tiber, an anchor of the Aegean type, buried for more than three thousand years, has provided an archeological counterpoint to the legendary account of the arrival in Ostia of the sailing ships of the Trojan Aeneas.[5] That is not to say, of course, that one thing proves the other! But the existence at an early date of navigation on the waters of the Tiber indicates that this type of legend is not just the completely artificial and belated product of an erudition that was Greek in origin, but is rather nothing less than the embellishment and transposition to the mythical plane of very real activity. We must not forget, in fact, that before the harnessing of the river in the modern age, which has tamed it and reduced its flow, the vastness of the river offered ample opportunities for navigation. We must therefore not judge the possibilities by anachronistic criteria. Nearly everywhere, particularly in the mountains of Sabine, archeologists are rediscovering scale models of barks in tombs from Latium's protohistory, an obvious reference to the boating practices of the deceased.

Nonetheless, to account for the primordial importance of the Tiber in the birth of Rome, it is not enough to recognize the early existence of river navigation. The river and its valley certainly constitute a magnificent natural path of communication between the mountains in the interior of the peninsula and the sea. But the river alone does not explain the human traffic now attested from the first periods of Latial civilization. It only allows for such traffic, which is a different matter. There must have been something else to attract to these rather desolate banks people who were not yet seeking beaches to sun themselves on.

[4] In 1986, an important colloquium was organized by the very active Comitato per l'Archeologia Laziale on the theme "Il Tevere et le altre vie d'acqua del Lazio antico" (The Tiber and other waterways of ancient Latium). Moreover, an exhibit held in Rome at the same time produced a catalog containing a rich panorama of the entire history of the city. See *Tevere, un'antica via per il mediterraneo* (Rome, 1986). J. Le Gall's *Le Tibre, fleuve de Rome dans l'antiquité* (Paris, 1952) led the way.

[5] L. Quilici, "*Terrarum alumna,*" *Archeologia Classica* 23 (1971): 1–11.

And, unless we are to fall into pure and simple tautology, we must also explain why, on one site of the bank rather than another, human activity developed to the point of giving birth to a city that would one day be able to proclaim itself eternal. In short, if people were traveling on the Tiber or along the Tiber, what was the reason for it? And why did they stop at the site of the future Rome rather than somewhere else?

To respond to the first of these questions (and in fact, to raise it in the first place), we have at our disposal a remarkable study by the Swiss historian Adalberto Giovannini, which reveals the role of salt in "Rome's fortunes."[6] Giovannini gathers together all available indexes and judiciously compares them to those of the medieval world. The formation of the word *salarium*, in which the Latin term for salt (*sal*) is easily recognizable, and which gave us the word "salary," already suggests the importance of this food product. Salt is as essential to animals as to human beings (in antiquity the annual consumption of salt per capita can be fixed at a minimum of twenty kilograms) and is also indispensable for food preservation in any society that does not possess refrigerators. Through literary and epigraphical sources, it is possible to identify the presence of salt fields, beginning in antiquity, at the point near Ostia where the Tiber empties into the sea (the Latin word *ostia* in fact means "mouth"). These salt fields allowed for the extraction of salt from seawater through evaporation.[7] Since it is clear that the displacements linked to the transhumance of livestock cannot fully explain the increasingly numerous archeological finds, we must add to that generally mentioned reason the presence of salt fields that attracted, there and not elsewhere, herders and their herds. Salt is rare in Italy: Apart from the deposits of rock salt, which are almost nonexistent on the peninsula, the only place besides Ostia that possesses salt fields is on the other side of Italy, on the Adriatic coast (near ancient Canusium, north of Apulia). For a civilization that long remained predominantly pastoral, the deposits of this veritable white gold (which is actually grayish in color when not purified by chemical processes) became, by that very fact, frequented and coveted sites. It is thus very tempting to explain the incessant wars Rome waged against Veii, which were elevated to the dimension of legend in the narrative of origins, as at least in part a struggle for the control of the Ostian salt fields, which were for the most part located on the right bank of the river, that is, on the Etrurian side.

Granted, then, the Tiber was the great artery along which this salt trade occurred. The second question raised is not solved for all that. Why, after all, did

---

[6] A. Giovannini, "Le sel et la fortune de Rome," *Athenaeum*, 1985. The role of salt in earliest Rome was sensed by Clerici, *Economia e finanza dei Romani* (1943); P. de Francisci, in his posthumous *Variazioni su temi di protostoria romana* (Rome, 1974), 89; and Carcopino, *Virgile et les origines d'Ostie*, 418–19. The importance of salt also appears in religion. Salt was used by the Vestals to make the *mola salsa* (sacred cakes) and *muries* (sacred brine) used in sacrifices.

[7] In the classical age these were known by the name Campus Salinarum Romanarum. As the archeologist R. Lanciani showed in 1888 (in an article in the *Bulletin de la Commission Archéologique de Rome*), they were located on the right bank of the river.

these herders coming down from the mountains stop on their long journey at the future site of Rome, in the midst of these "woods and marshes,"[8] in preference to some other site? Must we return to the old thesis that the city and its river were two chance companions, with the city benefiting from the river for its development (the level of river traffic during the imperial age makes that concession necessary), but only long after its birth? In this view, far from the city coming into its own as a result of the river, we would have to imagine the reverse scenario. In other words, perhaps Bernardin de Saint-Pierre was right to have been amazed by such a fascinating coincidence.

As a matter of fact, we now possess elements that allow us to go beyond mere plausibility and to establish that there was a primordial and essential relationship between the (future) city and the river. The names of ancient roads along the Tiber, from the Sabine mountains to the estuary, can be deciphered as latent signs of the major role played by the Roman site in the traffic of salt.[9] It was only at a relatively late period that the classical custom of giving the builder's name to new roads became established, following the example of the censor Appius Claudius in 312 B.C.E., famed for the Appian Way. Before that, roads were given the name of the city to which they led.[10] In an even earlier time, when there were no cities in Latium, roads took their names from the region (and not the city) where they ended. Roads in that category obviously belong to the most ancient phase of history, preceding the formation of the urban centers and, so to speak, preceding history itself.

That is the case, for example, of the *via Latina*. Every year, the entire population of Rome, escorting its highest magistrates in procession, took that road to the summit of Mons Albanus to witness the solemn sacrifice of a white bull in honor of the Latin god Jupiter. It is also the case, precisely, for the *via Campana*, which, leaving Rome, ended at the coastline. Since, obviously, no trace of a city by that name exists, it follows that the road was so designated because it led to the salt fields, the "*Campus* Salinarum," bordering the coast and located on the right bank of the Tiber. The name *via Salaria* can in no case be applied to that road, as has sometimes been done without any real evidence. The road by that name has been verified only as far as Rome. It is clear that the designation *via Salaria* is explained by the transport of salt along its route; this has in fact been recognized since antiquity. Hence the *via Salaria* ended in Rome, and the *via Campana* began in Rome. In addition, the former road ran along the left bank of the Tiber, the latter followed the right bank, and the river crossing occurred

[8] The expression comes from Livy, who attributes it to Camillus in his famous speech to the Romans ("in his locis nihil praeter silvas paludesque," *Ab urbe condita* 5.53.9).

[9] According to F. Coarelli's argument in a forthcoming book on Ostia. For the moment, see his *Il foro boario* (Rome, 1988), 113, and "I santuari, il fiume, gli empori," in *Storia di Roma*, vol. 1, ed. Momigliano and Schiavone.

[10] See G. Radke, "Viae Publicae Romanae," in Pauly-Wissowa, *RE* Suppl. 13 (Stuttgart, 1973), 1479.

at Rome. Thus two changes, in the name of the road and in the riverbank it followed, clearly designated Rome as a major and "unavoidable" stop on the journey of the mountain people headed toward the sea and salt. Although the classic problem of the relation between a city and the road that passes through it very often bears an annoying resemblance to the eternal and grave question of which came first, the chicken or the egg, the elements we have just set forth provide the means for reconstructing the emergence and development of Rome on more certain foundations than in the past. Drawing its name from the product it made accessible and not from the center to which it led, the *via Salaria* is by its very existence evidence of the preeminence of the road over the city, a city that in part owed its birth and early expansion to the salt trade. If the traffic in salt along the *via Salaria* had been created and developed only once Rome was founded, would not the *via Salaria* have been called the *via Romana*?

The same reasoning applies to the *via Campana,* which, unlike the road the Romans built when they founded the new colony of Ostia in the fifth (and not the fourth) century B.C.E., was not called the *via Ostiensis.*[11] In my opinion, the Romans probably did not have control of the salt fields on the coastline at the beginning of their history, as they had control of the route that seekers of salt coming down toward the sea were obliged to take. The oversight, maintenance, and control of the sites where the precious product so necessary to all could be collected was too important to the communities of central Italy as a whole for them to agree on their own to entrust it exclusively to one entity. Simple plausibility suggests that this control was first shared and "international." That could explain the traces of a federal organization, preserved at the level of religious ritual in particular, of which tradition has kept a vague memory for the Ostian territory. Carcopino attracted attention to this tradition at the beginning of the century in speaking of a "pre-Ostian Ostia." The fact that this center did not have an urban form, that it therefore predated the formation of cities in Latium, is once again demonstrated by the absence of any reference to a city in the name of the *via Campana.* We must imagine a federal sanctuary, the traces of which might well have persisted in the cult of the god Volcanus, still present in the Ostia of classical times. In short, we must return to the hypothesis formulated by Carcopino in 1919, which, in the light of recent finds, seems of particular contemporary import.

Must we then refuse all credence to the legend of Ancus Marcius, the elements of which have been dispersed over time into a fine dust of evidence but without a total modification in their profound unity? No, on the contrary. The tradition that makes Ancus Marcius, fourth king of Rome, the founder of Ostia can be considered credible.[12] Contrary to what was believed in the nine-

[11] In fact, the construction of the fortified town of Ostia seems to have been linked to the destruction of Fidenae, a rival city located beside a ford of the Tiber. See Coarelli, "I santuari," 138.

[12] See Coarelli, *Il foro boario;* id., "I santuari."

teenth century, it was not the adulterated product of the incommensurate vanity of the Marcii, a family living at the time of the Republic. It retains the memory of an episode, essential in its assertion of early Roman power, that saw the sons of Romulus seize for themselves the most sought-out natural resource of the entire region.

In other words, it was precisely because Ostia did not exist that it had to be founded, in such a way as to guarantee the city on the banks of the Tiber control over the course of the river to its mouth. This was accomplished by establishing a colony, in accordance with a method consistently practiced by Rome in the following years, which constituted one of the surest bases for its expansion. No doubt the Romans of the time were not confirmed sailors, but it does not follow that access to the sea was of no interest to them. In creating a colony at Ostia (we must not imagine, however, that the colony had the same form that Roman colonization would later assume), archaic Rome looked less to the high seas (which it seems to have frequented more than was long believed, however) than to a source for supplies and riches. Obviously, in all that, history was simply obeying the necessities of geography, since from the moment an autonomous entity, having grown through contact with the river, asserted itself on the site of Rome, it could only aim for mastery of the wealth the river provided. But although, at the beginning of its existence, the expansion of Rome into Ostia was programmed as it were, the city still had to wait to be powerful enough to organize for its own benefit the harvest and diffusion of a product necessary for all. That is why, even as we grant the tradition an attention that was long refused it, we must nonetheless avoid taking literally the evidence it provides. The classical sources speak most often of a foundation of the salt fields by Ancus Marcius, parallel to the foundation of Ostia. To say that these sources are now "confirmed" by the existence of increasingly numerous archaic remains[13] on the Ostian shore would be to travel the same path, but this time in the opposite direction, that directly links past hypercriticism to present-day fideism. As it happens, many other traces predating those from the seventh and sixth centuries B.C.E. attest to human activity dating to protohistory.

In fact, the tradition assigns the creation of the Ostian salt fields to Ancus Marcius, in the same way it assigns the creation of the Feriae Latinae to the Tarquins. In both cases, a very ancient reality, which was Latin and federal, was reorganized at some point and placed under Rome's control, following an identical process that was called a foundation in each case. Thus even when the tradition tells the truth, it does so in the language of lies, but lies that are also *its* truth. That is why the revalorization of the classical sources concerning Rome's origins, as necessary as it is inevitable, can be made only on the basis of a com-

---

[13] See the indications and bibliography assembled in Poucet, *Origines de Rome*, 151–55; and V. Santa Maria Scrinari's essay in *Archeologia Laziale* 6 (1984): 358–63.

plex interpretation remote from the too simple judgments of hypercriticism ("everything is false") or fideism ("everything is true").

Up until this point, we have spoken of the Tiber as a path of communication, but we should not limit ourselves, as is often done, to river navigation properly speaking. Of course, the Tiber was also valuable, perhaps especially in the most ancient periods, for the facility of transport offered by its valley and its numerous roads.

Although salt was a determining factor in the attraction exerted by the valley of the Tiber, it was not the only one, and the texts at least suggest the important role played by the forests that amply covered Latium in those remote times. Wood, as both building material and fuel, was desired by everyone and constituted a natural resource of the first order. It established Latium's renown far and wide—among the Etruscans, the Greeks, and no doubt the Phoenicians as well.

Were the foundation of archaic Ostia—described by the texts and suggested by archeological indexes—to be definitively proven, give or take the nuances mentioned, it would be a further sign of the importance of the Tiber in the emergence and development of Rome. In this regard, traditional historiography has demonstrated its internal logic by rejecting the importance of both sites, a rejection grounded in the last analysis on the conviction, abundantly belied by modern archeology, that Rome could not have been a powerful city as early as the sixth century B.C.E.

But in all fairness, indexes have never constituted proof, and, all things considered, such proof seems to be lacking. Archeologists, who for nearly a century now have turned over the soil throughout Ostia, a city whose pink ruins dotted with cypress trees decorate the Roman periphery, have not identified, among the thousands of houses and the hundreds of streets uncovered more than a very few vestiges that might be attributed to the times of the foundation by Ancus Marcius. And, above all, the archeological exploration of the fortified camp, or *castrum*, around which Ostia developed in republican and imperial times, has revealed nothing that could lend credence to the tradition of a royal colony. This silence in itself has long seemed decisive proof of the fabricated and fallacious character of the tradition.[14] Are we faced with a mere legend, which, as such, would have nothing to do with historical reality?

I do not believe so. Since Rome was on the left bank of the Tiber, as was Ostia during the Empire and the fortified city that preceded it under the

---

[14] Only a fragment of architectonic terra-cotta dating from the fifth century has troubled somewhat the careful order of a reconstruction resting on a void, in both its presuppositions (that there was no royal Ostia) and conclusions (that the *castrum* dates from the fourth century). But, like the absence of archaic remains (which is neither total nor decisive on the left bank), the dating of the *castrum* from the end of the fourth century B.C.E. does not rest on solid foundations, and even the single fragment from the fifth century might suggest other hypotheses to those seeking them. Here is another good example of the ambiguity and fragility of archeological "data." For those holding the view that there could not have been any Roman colonization before the end of the fourth century, the Ostian fragment moves from the status of document to that of mere refuse.

Republic, it seemed logical in the past to seek the eventual traces of the settlement attributed by a consistent and unanimous tradition to King Ancus Marcius on the left bank as well. But rarely has the contrast been so great between the prolixity of the literary sources and the silence of the archeological data, with the result that this silence appears to invalidate the data definitively. This was not so troublesome at the time of triumphant hypercriticism but has become more so within the new context of the rehabilitation of the tradition. Nonetheless, with reference to a pre-Etruscan king who even today is believed to be completely mythical, there was in the end nothing very surprising about the situation. And after all, was not the right bank of the Tiber Etruscan land and, as such, forbidden to Roman enterprises?

But, as Beloch briefly but vigorously emphasizes,[15] Roman influence also extended to the right bank, beginning in the archaic era. Tradition places the mysterious *septem pagi*, or "seven cantons," there, the object of endless battles between Rome and Veii. It is thus altogether legitimate, as Filippo Coarelli points out, to look for regal Ostia on the right bank rather than the left, where it has always been sought but never found—and for good reason! Let us note, moreover, that it is precisely this type of contested territory—vital by reason of the attested presence of salt fields (Campus Salinarum)—that made necessary the establishment of an outpost "near the mouth of the river,"[16] to cite the words of the Latin erudite Festus, writing in Augustus's time, whose information is always of remarkably high quality. Dionysius of Halicarnassus, a Greek writer living in Rome, left an indication of the place where we might perhaps seek the traces of an archaic site: "In the angle formed by the river and the sea," he wrote, "the king founded a city, which he named Ostia, given its situation."[17] If we take into account the shift in the Tiber's bed alluded to earlier, the bend the classical historian mentions occurs in front of the walls of the medieval castle built by the future Pope Julius II. Once we set aside the prejudice excluding the right bank, we can surmise that the city founded by Ancus Marcius may have been situated *within* the almost complete ring formed by the river. Ostia would then have been protected on three sides by the waters of the Tiber, which, in this case, would have served as a natural defense.[18] How can we then not see, in the very name the tradition conserved for the creator of that

[15] Beloch, *Römische Geschichte*, 146.

[16] "Ad exitum fluminis" (Sextus Pompeius Festus [who condensed the Augustan erudite Verrius Flaccus], *De verborum significatu*, ed. W. M. Lindsay [Leipzig, 1913], 214). As Carcopino has noted, the Latin term *ad* indicates that Ancus Marcius's creation was not located on the bank itself but merely in its vicinity, set back from the coast.

[17] Dion. Hal. *Ant. rom.* 3.45. See Coarelli's commentary in *Storia di Roma*, ed. Momigliano and Schiavone, 1: 140.

[18] Compare, mutatis mutandis of course, the situation of the medieval city of Cahors, France, which is encircled and protected on three sides by the Lot River. That said, significant protohistorical traces have recently been found on the site of the medieval town. See *Archeologica Laziale*, 6: 358–63.

first Ostia, namely, *Ancus* Marcius, a vivid memory of its placement on the terrain, in the hollow, the *angle,* formed by the sinuous course of the Tiber? In other words, that name, no doubt a nickname at first, would be explained not by the physical deformity of an unfortunate king unable to straighten his arm—a desperate hypothesis invented by ancient scholars, who, like their modern successors, had already ruled out the idea of seeking archaic Ostia on the right bank—but rather in the curve of the river where the first Roman colony had first been established. And all the literal obviousness of the link between the name of a king believed to be entirely legendary and the word designating a curve was required to convince Carcopino, almost in spite of himself,[19] of that interpretation, which I borrow from him.

Once more, contemporary archeological discoveries, supported by a rereading of the sources unencumbered by the postulates of hypercriticism, end up enlarging somewhat the territory of history, which, until very recently, has been occupied by the shadowy kingdom of legends beyond our grasp. In other words, the analysis of episodes linked to the reign of Ancus Marcius leads us to reconsider totally the commonly accepted dividing line between the pre-Etruscan regal period, which would belong to the mythical and legendary domain, and the Etruscan period, which would mark the entry, albeit partial, of Rome into history.[20] This insurmountable wall, which delimited the field of Dumézilian hermeneutics even in its last version, collapses under the pressure of recent discoveries. Does that mean that legend gives way to history? Asking the question in those terms amounts to maintaining a theoretical Manicheanism, which has less and less reason for existing. Rather, the legend of origins appears increasingly in all its complexity. That complexity resists classifications, which are so many misleading simplifications. The legend can now be analyzed, if we still wish to attach a definition to it, as the mode by which a society such as that of archaic Rome conceived of its own development over time.

The legend of the foundation of Ostia thus deserves to be taken completely seriously, despite the fragmentary and dispersed character of the elements that compose it. As is often the case, such a dispersion is in reality the very sign of the fundamental authenticity of the traditions attached to the reign of Ancus Marcius. The coherence and significance of those traditions appear only from a global point of view, which brings together all the materials, sparse and insignificant in themselves, transmitted by the numerous sources.[21] Once rehabilitated,

---

[19] See Carcopino, *Virgile et les origines d'Ostie*. Carcopino speaks of "the entirely literary aspect of the pseudo-founder Ancus Marcius" and yet recognizes that "in the composition of this fictive character, the site of the pre-Ostian settlement enters in as an element of truth" (p. 459).

[20] On this delimitation, see chap. 3 above, esp. pp. 41–42.

[21] That is why, unlike Poucet, we cannot consider them "antedated transpositions" and "indisputable anachronisms," on the pretext that they "have not succeeded in penetrating into the great annalistic tradition[, and this fact] may betray their recent character" (Poucet, *Origines de Rome,* 223). If that were the case, they would constitute a coherent set that was significant and immediately

the tradition of Ostia founded by regal Rome unequivocally bears witness to the importance of the Tiber in Rome's development.

That statement is valid only as a starting point and not as a conclusion. We are not seeking to discover, by a different path than that of the natural environment and the economy, a facile kind of determinism—and, in history, any kind of determinism is facile—the traces of which we followed at the beginning of this book. Although the existence of an archaic center near the Ostian coast is evidence enough of the role played by the Tiber in the history of Rome in the most remote ages, there is another site that shows in an obvious manner (though this has not been taken into account) the limits that the search for a simplistic causality very quickly encounters in the explanation of the birth of Rome.

That site is Ficana: such was its name in antiquity, and such is the name restored to the city by recent research. It displays similarities with Rome that allow for a kind of counterproof, which makes the originality of Rome appear all the more obvious.[22]

Like Rome, the site of Ficana, identified in the hills of Monte Cugno near Acilia, lay on the bank of the Tiber. Like Rome, it benefited from a position that assured it indisputable defensive advantages. And like Rome, it was located on natural lines of communication that put it easily in contact both with the Etruscans of Caere and Veii and with the Latins of the hinterland. For a long time, in fact, Ficana seems to have had a development that, period by period, corresponded almost exactly to the phases observed on the Roman site. Even setting aside its prehistory, attested to by vestiges more than forty thousand years old, we find, beginning in the tenth century B.C.E., traces of a human settlement that shows evidence of at least periodic and perhaps already sedentary human occupation. In any case, by the eighth century B.C.E., all doubt is gone. In recent years, archeologists have discovered traces of a fortification (*agger*) surrounded by a trench. This fortification protected the valley separating the principal peak of Monte Cugno on the west side from the adjacent hill of San Paolo. How can we not think of the "Romulean" trench that Italian archeologists discovered in Rome, located between the peaks of the Palatine and the Velia (as close to each other as the hills of Ficana), which also dates from the eighth

---

recognizable. Yet we are dealing not with a recently constructed edifice but with ruins, outcrops of an ancient tradition that was eliminated, precisely, by the system set in place by the annalists. Added to these sparse data, the traditional attribution (Livy *Ab urbe condita* 1.33) of the construction of the Pons Sublicius, the oldest bridge in Rome, to Ancus Marcius, assumes all its significance. One very revealing fact is that, in the habitually infallible *Realencyclopädie*, there is no complete entry devoted to Ancus Marcius, who appears only in the lines concerning his supposed descendants (14: 1543).

[22] On Ficana, in addition to the brief description in C. Pavolini's *Ostia* (Bari, 1983), 11–13, I have consulted the catalog of the successive exhibitions organized in Rome from 1975 to 1980: *Ficana: Une pietra miliare sulla strada per Roma*. There are also very useful entries in the catalogs of two other exhibitions: *Enea nel Lazio* (Rome, 1981), 102; and *Case e palazzi d'Etruria* (Florence, 1985), 164–77.

century? Here and there, on the principal hill, excavators have found imprints made in the soil by huts, the oldest of which also go back to the eighth century B.C.E. These huts do not form a dense and continuous settlement but are sparse and at some distance from one another. It is obviously possible to suppose that the open spaces can be explained by the disappearance of the vestiges once found there, but the total abandonment of the site to agricultural activities in the second century B.C.E., without any new urban settlement thereafter, makes that hypothesis unlikely. The dispersion probably attests to a scattered settlement, and this proves to be a precious indication for the Palatine. Indeed, throughout its history, the Palatine was subject to municipal projects that, overturning and destroying earlier remains, made any hypothesis on its most ancient phases of occupation very fragile. In Ficana as well, beginning in the middle of the seventh century B.C.E., and concurrent with the earlier huts, we find the appearance of permanent constructions with tufa walls and tile roofs. That period seems to mark Ficana's apogee. Nonetheless, recent excavations have shown, in direct contradiction to the letter of the tradition, which speaks of the city's destruction by Ancus Marcius, that life continued thereafter. But, in this case as well, we must avoid concluding too quickly, as hypercritical philology once did, in the radical falseness of the tradition, and must understand the supposed destruction of Ficana as the sign of its integration, by force no doubt, into the Roman sphere of influence. That integration, as archeology demonstrates, did not result in immediate disappearance, but rather in a slow and irremediable decay, which eventually reduced Ficana to the mere shadow of its past splendor, gradually erasing all trace of it on the terrain. Surviving only in the form of a name devoid of all reality, Ficana figures among the disappeared cities of Latium that Pliny the Elder listed during the Empire, in the laconic form of a funerary inscription.[23]

Yet Ficana could have been Rome, and Rome could have been in Ficana! If we attribute a determining role in the birth of Rome to the Tiber and to salt, Ancus Marcius's conquest had the benefit of an equally favorable topographical and strategic situation. Moreover, Ficana had an advantage over its rival, its greater proximity to the mouth of the Tiber and to the precious salt fields. Why, then, did it not know the fate of its more fortunate neighbor? Is chance alone responsible for the extraordinary fortune of a city that in many ways resembled the city conquered by Ancus Marcius?

Chance is, after all, one cause among others in history, and although we are not satisfied with that type of explanation in this case, it is not out of an aversion on principle. It is rather because, in this instance, an examination of the particular details of the site of the future Rome allows us to discern, apart from any determinist prejudice, certain obvious "natural" advantages.

[23] Pliny *HN* 3.5.68.

Let us therefore return to Rome and proceed down the Tiber, which guided mountain shepherds to the fields and to salt.[24] After a first bend that leaves behind a plain, alluvial in origin (the future Campus Martius), on its left, another loop toward the east bumps up against the hills, which once more push the course of the river toward the west. In the curve of the second loop, Tiber Island, slightly closer to the left bank than to the right, facilitates movement from one side of the river to the other. Immediately downstream, a ford allows for the crossing of the barrier formed everywhere else by the course of the river. Above all, on the left, concave bank, against which the current beats and shifts, this ford opens onto a vast expanse of land. And there, across from the river, three hills, with pathways between them, frame and dominate that natural landing site, somewhat like the block of spectator seats in an ancient theater frame and dominate the orchestra and stage. These hills are of course the Aventine, the Palatine, and the Capitol, and it is precisely in the theater formed by their architecture that the first act of a great history was to be played out, a history whose dimensions would one day extend to the far reaches of the world known at that time and would last for nearly two millennia.

But why, in the remote ages in which we have placed ourselves, should we pass on the right bank? First, because all along the coastline, the largest salt fields were on the right bank, whereas the mountains of Sabine were located on the left. More generally, it was on the right bank that the rich Villanovan civilization flourished; during the so-called Orientalizing period in the eighth century, as a result of complex processes, said culture would give birth to what we know as Etruscan civilization. Why, then, did Rome prosper on the left bank and not the right?

A first response, appealing solely to geographical determinism, would focus on the need for the Sabine mountain people to have available a pathway to the right bank. And obviously, if a ford by definition assures the link between two banks, one of them benefited in this case from indisputable possibilities for defense, owing to the hills that bordered it. But it is also true that, on the right bank, the hills of the Janiculum offered possibilities on that order. That is why a second response is needed to introduce the historical importance of the Latin element in Rome's formation. It is precisely because, in about the tenth century B.C.E. or even before, a "geopolitical" center of gravity existed on the side of the Alban Hills and in the southeastern part of the Tiber basin, that a center developed on the left bank of the river. On the same bank during the archaic age,

---

[24] The description of the site of Rome is obviously a commonplace for all of ancient and contemporary historiography, and I have no pretensions here except to recall what is already well known. As Bonstetten declared in 1804, "It is the misfortune of those who write on Italy to repeat themselves in their accounts, which they do without copying from one another, but simply because they all follow the same route. I shall attempt to leave it and not say what everyone knows" (*Voyage sur la scène*, 32).

many other cities also emerged on the edges of the Tiber, such as Antemnae, Fidenae, Crustumerium, and of course Ficana, all cities that Rome was to conquer and subjugate to secure itself sole control of the entire valley.

Hence Tiber Island, as it has often been claimed, did play a determining role in the foundation of Rome. Like Lutetia for Paris and Kölln for Berlin, it had an importance that should not be underestimated. But it would be a grave error to explain the formation of the city of Rome solely by the presence of the island, which was a necessary cause perhaps, but not a sufficient one. The abandon in which it seems to have been left in the first phases of the occupation of the Roman site are proof enough of that. Unlike Lutetia,[25] Tiber Island does not seem to have been inhabited originally, to judge from the absence of any archeological documentation (which, it is true, cannot be valid proof). According to the most recent discoveries, the first inhabitants settled on the Capitol, whose promontory dominates, protects, and controls the island and the area known by the tradition as the Forum Boarium, "cattle market." However incongruous it might seem at first glance, that name should not be at all surprising, since it is part of the logic of the exchanges that developed with the salt trade:

> Since salt is above all necessary for feeding cattle and for preserving the products of livestock and fish, an important supply source of salt brings its fortunate owners an abundance of these products. . . . A city where salt is bought and sold becomes by force of circumstance a place for exchanging and processing products of livestock and fish.[26]

The Forum Boarium obviously did not acquire its name during the age of the Republic, when the elegant little building known by the (inaccurate) name Temple of Vesta was constructed. As often happens, the toponym retained a memory of the most ancient history and must be traced to the dawn of Rome. In a general way, the name change from *via Salaria* to *via Campana*, which occurs from one bank to the other, allows us to identify the site of Rome as the place of a transhipment of cargo in the salt trade. The very name Forum Boarium, moreover, allows us to presume that this shift was made in conjunction with Tiber Island. And a further index designates, in an even more precise manner, the place that served as a veritable hub for these exchanges. At the foot of the Aventine, the classical tradition conserves the memory of a placename, Salinae, which, quite obviously, does not refer to the salt fields, since

---

[25] For the situation of Lutetia Island and its role in the origins of Paris, see P. M. Duval, "De Lutèce à Paris: Les origines de Paris," *Travaux sur la Gaule* 2 (1989): 901–11: "The presence of an island during those insecure times had an inestimable value, because the island was well placed to facilitate crossing a great river and, with an area of ten hectares or so, could welcome an urban center from the outset" (p. 902). To continue the analogy, let us add that the Tiber at Rome receives waters from the Aniene, just as the Seine at Paris receives waters from the Marne.

[26] Giovannini, "Le sel et la fortune," 380 and 381.

the coastline is located nearly thirty kilometers away, but rather to a site for unloading, stocking, and supplying the precious product.[27]

If these views are correct, shouldn't the Forum Boarium have been called the Forum Salarium? Apart from the fact that there is an undeniable and inevitable complementarity between cattle raising and salt, the name Forum Boarium attests to the role played by the pastoral populations of the interior peninsula in the development of the Roman site. Let us now suppose for a moment that the narrative of origins, so dense and rich in its account of Rome, had been entirely lost and buried in the silence of oblivion. Let us wonder, at the same time, how the memory of these populations of mountain people, involved from the beginning in the vicissitudes of the Roman site, might have been conserved from the dawn of history. How could we imagine anything but a legend that represented such peoples and their leaders grappling with the mythical creators of the Roman city, and particularly with Romulus? How could we imagine anything but a succession of confrontations and reconciliations, in accordance with the narrative logic proper to any mythographical account that presents two peoples coming face to face with each other?

And we in fact have that legend, attested to by a rich textual tradition. It is of course the legend of the Sabines of Titus Tatius, deprived of their women by Romulus and his companions, then finally reconciled with their earlier adversaries. In other words, the Sabine legend, whose importance in the narrative of Rome's origins is well known, corresponds, despite everything that may have been said, to the profound logic of the sites, the history, and the toponomy, and also to the logic of the elaboration of a mythographical tradition that, given the basic elements it had to transmit, could hardly have followed a different "diegetic" schema.

Once more, we do not claim that these characteristics of the Roman site as we have described them are sufficient to explain the birth of Rome. After all, many sites offering favorable natural conditions for exchange and passage experienced no development comparable to that of Rome, or became simply "international" sanctuaries, of which archaic Italy offers numerous examples. Thus Rome might have been only another Lucus Feroniae, to take the case of a gathering place in a neighboring geographical context, at the foot of Soracte, which was frequented by Sabines, Etruscans, and Latins alike, but which never became a major center.

As for Rome, it asserted itself as Latium's center of gravity only at the end of a long and complex process, and a mere geographical description could not adequately account for it, especially if it confined itself to selecting one of the numerous characteristics of the site and conferring the weight of a determining factor on it. The great originality of the sites that saw the birth of Rome has to do with the diversity of the elements, the natural assets found there. Taken sepa-

[27] Sources and commentary in Coarelli, *Il foro boario*, 111.

rately, each of these elements can hardly be distinguished from what can be found elsewhere, in the entire central part of the peninsula. However important the valley of the Tiber, there are other sites that could have laid claim to an advantageous position in relation to the river. The very presence of an island facilitating passage from one bank to the other certainly appears to be a note-worthy particularity of the Roman site, but there were other places, in Fidenae, for example, where the Tiber could easily be crossed, and also other islands, like that found near present-day Nazzano, not far from Lucus Feroniae. In fact, in looking closely, we find that, in these troubled times when history was taking shape, ease of passage also constituted a serious inconvenience, since it offered a temptation to eventual invaders coming from territories that would later be those of the Etruscans. This has led Léon Homo to say that "Rome was created to mount guard, like a vigilant sentinel, over the frontier of the Latin world."[28] But in that view, many other places could have offered their occupants an easily defensible refuge against attacks from the outside, including attacks from the river, as the example of Ficana shows. In fact, in the first periods of Latium's civi-lization, between what specialists call the Middle Bronze Age and the Late Bronze Age, most of the sites where archeology has identified the traces of human settlement possess, by their natural situation, significant defense facili-ties.[29] Thus Rome, on this point as on many others, merely fits into a very general framework. As for the possibility of easy communication with the inte-rior of the Latin region, and particularly with the Alban Hills, that also existed at other sites, or at least in Ficana. We might even say that, regarding the link between the two great zones of civilization that enclosed Latium on both sides, that is, between Etruria and Campagna, Rome was not truly better placed a priori than other centers. What is more, Rome had to struggle against these cen-ters subsequently. To go from Palestrina to Volsinii, for example, or from Ardea and Lavinium to Caere and Tarquinia, passage through Rome was, geographi-cally speaking, neither necessary nor unavoidable.

To detect in one of these characteristics of the site of Rome the single cause for the city's future greatness, historians must immediately attribute to that factor a determining role, at the expense of other particularities, ignored or rele-gated to the rank of mere secondary causes, situated later in time.

Thus those who emphasize the importance of the Tiber and the salt trade, whose significance is indisputable, do so by declaring that Rome "was badly placed both for maritime commerce and for overland commerce between Etruria and Latium."[30] It is useless to point out that exactly the reverse view-point can also be found.

---

[28] Homo, *Primitive Italy*, 79.

[29] As R. Peroni has shown in several studies, especially his essay in *Storia di Roma*, vol. 1, ed. Momigliano and Schiavone.

[30] Giovannini, "Le sel et la fortune," 381.

In contrast, those who respond to what seems to be the essential lesson of the tradition and identify the seat of early Rome as the Palatine[31] (a hypothesis now contradicted by the most recent discoveries of archeology, by the way),[32] have to ignore the river, or nearly so, whose waters flow beneath the Romulean Hill. They are obliged to attribute a decisive and definitive preeminence to the Palatine Hill over the other peaks of the site, where, however, as we now know, human presence was sometimes of earlier date.

Thus, according to the point of view adopted, the Roman site as a whole is the object of very different evaluations. Some insist on the conveniences it offered human activity, and some, in contrast, on the difficulties and inconveniences of those places, cluttered with swamps and poorly linked to one another. This divergence, in reality, goes back to antiquity itself: Livy, in Camillus's voice, claimed that "it is not without reason that the gods and men have chosen this place to found Rome"; yet, according to the geographer Strabo, "the site of its foundation" was "dictated by necessity rather than freely chosen."[33]

The disagreement is no less significant among moderns, though most of them tend to adopt Livy's geographical determinism. Tiber Island, for example, is unanimously recognized as being of decisive importance in the foundation of Rome, but some see it as a point of passage that slowly and almost imperceptibly led to the aggregation of a human community around it, while others view it as a strategic stronghold, placed from the beginning under the control of a kind of permanent garrison. This implies that the exchanges between the center (Etruria) and the south (Campagna) of Italy were, according to the first group, significant and regular, but, according to the second, limited and rare. In both cases, in any event, the Tiber is considered only an obstacle that Tiber Island made it possible to surmount, and not a possible path of communication.

Even those who reduce the role of the Tiber to almost nothing do not agree on the principal "land" actors in Rome's development in its first phases. Thus, for some, the early Romans were transhumant herders from the mountains of Sabine, who settled, temporarily at first, on what were at the time nameless hills. For others, they were Latins coming from the nearby forests of the Alban massif, who were stopped in their explorations by the barrier of the river.

What should we think of these analyses, all different from one another, all similarly dependent on the obviousness of the sites and the evidence of the texts? None seems inaccurate, but neither does any appear adequate. As long as analysts argue in terms of priority, seeking a causality that excludes the other possibilities, they will always come up with incomplete explanations that cannot account for this singular process by which a center of activity and settlement emerged there and not elsewhere, to become a city that would one day be *the* city.

---

[31] That was Homo's thesis, for example, in *Primitive Italy*, 77ff. See also *Cambridge Ancient History*, 1st ed. (Cambridge, 1928), 7: 353–54 (H. Last).

[32] Since the most ancient vestiges have now been found on the Capitol side. See below, chap. 9.

[33] Livy *Ab urbe condita* 5.54.4; Strabo 5.3.7.

However pertinent they may be, the hypotheses just mentioned delineate in each case facts that, as such, are a matter for description, discussion, evaluation, and comparison. But in reality, it is a *process,* that is, a set of facts, or more exactly, a set of elements, whose interaction and interdependence constitute this phenomenon called the birth of Rome. And in that emergence, in that expansion that fed on itself, there are "natural" geographical causes and causes that are not natural; there is the part played by chance, but also that played by human beings; there are contributions from the outside, but also forces that are born despite opposition from this external world, or rather as a result of that opposition.

That is why, in seeking here or there, if not the sole then at least the principal cause for the foundation of Rome, the historian is like a physicist who would attempt to establish whether, in the structure of the evolution of the atom, the foremost role should be given to the electron, the proton, or the neutron. And just as the physicist in such a case would be unable to grasp what constitutes the essential character and complexity of the atom, the unity of which results precisely from a perpetually shifting diversity, the historian could not give a satisfactory explanation for the appearance of the Roman nebula.

For what made Rome was not only its river or the salt that river conveyed or the island its waters encircled. It was not even the hills, however "fated." It was not the proximity to the sea, since Ficana was even closer. The river washes over other banks, there are other islands, and other hills rise up elsewhere along its shores. Not one of these topographical and geographical particularities is decisive in itself. But these factors, relatively commonplace in the landscape of the peninsula when considered one by one, confer on the place that brings them all together a truly exceptional aspect and dynamism.

We must therefore stop seeking in one or another of its aspects the first and ultimate cause of the development of the Roman site. What made Rome Rome, or rather what made possible the conditions that allowed it to be Rome there and not elsewhere, is the extraordinary conjunction in the same place of a ford (or, at least, ease of passage), of a landing site (the natural port of the Forum Boarium), and of fortifications (the hills), along a route vital for all of central Italy, not far from the sea, but still close enough to the mountains of the interior. The concentration of so many different and complementary advantages in a single space thus made Rome the point of intersection for roads linking the north and south of the peninsula, and for others joining the hilly interior to the coastal plains. Hence came about what we could call, using an expression borrowed from the vocabulary of astrophysics, a center of gravitational attraction, which pulled in scattered dynamic forces, and then, having reached a sufficient threshold of density, began to expand, into Latium first, then into Italy as a whole, and finally into the whole of the Mediterranean world.

But make no mistake: To a very great degree, it was only when its existence was assured and its development already begun that the Roman community could take advantage of the possibilities that, though they existed in latent form in the configuration of the site, still remained unexploited. If Rome, to speak in Spinozan terms, became what it was, it was to its history, as much as to its geography, that this was due, a history that the most recent discoveries of archeology allow us to see in a new light.

CHAPTER 7

THE DISCOVERY OF LATIUM:
FROM TREASURE HUNT TO MODERN
ARCHEOLOGY

S INCE THE BEGINNING of the century, archeology has contributed decisively to progress in our knowledge of Rome's beginnings,
even though we may judge after the fact that such progress was a long
time coming. We have seen the importance of the excavations directed by
Boni, in the very heart of classical Rome, in the Forum and on the Palatine.[1]
In every respect, and not only for specialists of the most ancient Roman history, the discovery of the Lapis Niger and those that accompanied it marked a
major step. In the history of archeology, it was the first time a technique was
applied that today constitutes the very basis of any investigation of the terrain.
That technique, called stratigraphy, consists of excavating the soil by distin-
guishing and separating the layers of successive deposits, whose relative
chronology is thus determined. The farther down an archeologist digs in the
soil, the farther back in time one moves, with the remains situated at the deepest level being the most ancient.

But before Boni (and even, alas, somewhat after him!), archeology was practiced in a completely different manner and pursued with completely different
objectives. We must never forget the concrete conditions under which old discoveries were made if we are to know how best to evaluate them in documentary
and historical terms.

For a long time, archeologists went in search of the art object, precious for
its material or its execution. Archeology began as a treasure hunt and had difficulty working itself free from its origins and becoming what it is today, a
science through and through. Thus, during the period when the discovery of
Herculaneum and then Pompeii (in 1748) gave a new dimension and new
meaning to the already old habits of "antiquarians" (in other words, specialists in
antiquity), the nascent discipline did not differ very much from what we now
call art history. For Johann Winckelmann,[2] who is considered its founder, archeology was only the means for acceding to a knowledge of Eternal Beauty. Under

---

[1] See above, chap. 2.

[2] Significantly, J. Winckelmann titled his major work *Geschichte der Kunst des Altertums*
(History of the art of antiquity) (Vienna, 1764). See also his famous "Réflexions sur le sentiment
du beau dans les ouvrages de l'art et sur les moyens de l'acquérir."

such conditions, what truly mattered was to uncover works of art, destined to figure subsequently in the collections that rich amateurs assembled from one end of Europe to the other. These amateurs considered themselves "enlightened," but, using completely different criteria, we often judge them to have been wreckers. No one had any idea at the time that archeology could serve to give a concrete and precise knowledge of every aspect of life in ancient societies. That conviction, which has led archeologists to consider not the artistic value of the objects exhumed but their documentary interest, and hence to grant equal attention to all finds, even the most modest, occurred only slowly, and in particular in the light of the excavations of Pompeii, which for the first time offered the possibility of exploring with relative ease an ancient city in its totality. But for a long time yet, archeology was conceived only as art history applied to antiquity.[3]

Thus Chateaubriand, ambassador to Rome for the second time in 1829, undertook excavations in the environs of the *via Cassia*. He was happy to keep Madame Récamier, who had remained in Paris, apprised of his findings, in letters reproduced in his *Mémoires d'outre-tombe*: "I hope to find something that will reimburse me for the money lost in this lottery of the dead. I already have a block of Greek marble large enough to make the bust of Poussin."[4] "What does one pay the owner of the site where treasures are buried?" he inquired in another letter, immediately replying: "The value of the grass destroyed by the excavation. Perhaps I shall return my own clay to the earth in exchange for the statue it gives me: I shall merely be exchanging the image of man for the image of man."[5]

Now compare this excerpt from the record of an excavation carried out in 1982 in the Forum:

> The ascent into *opus incertum* is attested, if only in a partial manner, along the entire length, from item 1 to item 9. Supported by the arches of a series of shops opened to the west (items 3–6), it rises through alternating staircases and stories, which corresponds well to the indications of the *Forma Urbis*. An inclined plane, covered with shards, is visible at the bottom of item 2, and the next story is conserved as an impression in item 5 (number 17.20). A second staircase probably surmounted item 5, which was originally divided in two; a third began at the height of item 7. There, at a level clearly higher than the clay floor that seems to constitute the pavement for item 4 (respectively, num-

[3] To take only one example among many others, the classic manual by G. Perrot and C. Chipiez, published in several large volumes, was still titled *Histoire de l'art dans l'antiquité* (History of art in antiquity) (Paris, 1884–1914). Archeological science has thus developed by progressively liberating itself from traditional art history.

[4] F.-A.-R. de Chateaubriand, *Mémoires d'outre-tombe*, ed. M. Levaillant and C. Moulinier (Paris, 1982), 3: 478. Since the painter Nicolas Poussin had died in Rome, Chateaubriand took it upon himself to have a cenotaph erected in his honor.

[5] Chateaubriand, *Mémoires*, 548.

bers 13.27 and 15.17), is a pavement made of white clay studded with chips of colored stone.[6]

Between these two voices lies not only the obvious chronological gap of 150 years that separates them, but a difference in nature. In reality, they belong to different worlds, and the second has little in common with the first.

This is all well known, but the phenomenon is easier to point out than to explain. Indisputably, the idea that every vestige, as insignificant as it might appear, could, at the exact place and depth where it was found by the excavator, have a documentary value equal to the most prestigious find, was not accepted all at once. The eras that worshipped Greco-Roman antiquity were also those that perpetrated irreparable destruction. That is the case, in particular, for Renaissance Rome, where ancient ruins, often still numerous and imposing at the time, disappeared one after the other under the picks of the demolition crews. Yet "with the renewal of interest in classical literary works, one might have hoped for increased respect for the material memories left by these same men, who on paper were considered demigods."[7] As we know, exactly the reverse occurred. The marble slabs of the Coliseum went to cover the steps of Saint Peter's, and the Pantheon was stripped of its tiles and bronze capitals to make, not the baldachin of Saint Peter's, as some have said, but cannons to defend the Castel Sant'Angelo.[8] The age that rediscovered Tacitus and Livy was paradoxically the same age that annihilated the still imposing remains of the Capitoline temple of Jupiter and the notorious Septizodium of Emperor Septimius Severus.

But the paradox, it seems to me, is only apparent. In a certain way, the demolition workers were also builders, and, in addition to the destruction just mentioned (two examples among many others), there were numerous new constructions that emerged almost everywhere. In a relation of both continuity and rivalry, the new Rome was built from the ruins and materials of the old, through a gigantic act of transmutation. Why should they conserve when they were going to improve? Thus, to build the new Saint Peter's Church, the old church built by Emperor Constantine was torn down, its mosaics covered in gold crushed into dust and oblivion. In other words, the Renaissance destroyed the remains of the past because, in a certain way, the past was not experienced as such. That is, it was not considered irreducible to the present. It would take the Industrial Revolution, with its awareness of a radical newness and otherness in relation to earlier ages, for a concern to emerge—very slowly and with great resistance—for conserving

---

[6] *Roma: Archeologia nel centro* (Rome, 1985).

[7] Grimal, *Italie retrouvée*, 51.

[8] This episode was clarified by the famous archeologist R. Lanciani in *Ruins and Excavations of Ancient Rome* (New York, 1979).

monuments now considered "historical." We know, for example, the role Prosper Mérimée played in this respect in France in the 1830s.

Before that time, from one end of Europe to the other, and as had been done during antiquity itself, workers continually destroyed in order to build, without any concern for safeguarding on principle the traces of a past, a simple bygone present not yet valued by a historical consciousness. We should not believe that the Romans of antiquity who took care to restore or reconstruct a damaged temple after a fire did so for "archeological" reasons. Not at all. Their conservationism can be explained solely on religious grounds. It was important that the worship of the deity not be interrupted. And although they conserved the orientation and placement of the building, they did not deprive themselves of the pleasure of redoing it to the taste of the day, and often of reconstructing it completely. The deity and the city could only celebrate such embellishments! Thus, without any interruption in rites and ceremonies, the new edifice emerged progressively from the debris of the old, just as, in medieval France, Gothic cathedrals rose up on the very ruins of the Romanesque buildings that preceded them.[9]

All that may begin to explain the immeasurable destruction in a city that was eternal because perpetually destroyed and reconstructed. That destruction, of course, greatly encumbered the knowledge we might have had of the ancient ages of Rome. In particular, on sites where human occupation was constant and where, in antiquity, great building projects were carried out on several occasions, it may explain the situation of the almost total archeological silence we encounter for the primitive periods, on the Palatine, for example, or on Tiber Island. In cases of this sort, it would obviously be risky to attempt to draw historical conclusions from this void.

For the period of Rome's origins, an additional factor has contributed to limiting the archeological documentation we now possess. The most visible and most archeologically perceptible traces that the most ancient civilizations of central Italy and Latium left of themselves are piles of more or less crudely formed terra-cotta vases. Exhibited in European museums beside precious Greek vases, they make the beauty of line and the delicacy of decoration of the latter stand out. It is understandable that, for an archeology that was long only a treasure hunt, the humble pottery of Latium's civilization suffered from marked disfavor and lack of interest. How many "funerary urns" from the primitive necropolises of Latium were broken to see if they concealed gold pieces? How many others were quite simply transformed without further ado into flower pots?[10] As for those that escaped such a sad fate, like many finds made until fairly recently, they entered the often obscure circuits of traffic in antiquities. There, merchants

---

[9] See A. Erlande-Brandeburg, *La cathédrale* (Paris, 1990).

[10] This has been reported by Gierow in his excellent *Iron Age Culture of Latium*, 2: 39 n. 2 and 354.

often found it more prudent to remain silent about the exact provenance of the object they sought to sell to the passing amateur, or more profitable to claim it came from some site that was fashionable at the time, even if the assertion was untrue. Outside a few privileged work sites, which came under the vigilance of the authorities fairly early, these practices reigned for a long time, especially in Campagna di Roma. It is not difficult to imagine the damage and deformations that resulted in our knowledge of Rome's origins.

Under such conditions, what can the modern archeologist and historian do in the face of these thousands of items exhumed at the end of the last century from the Esquiline Hill, the site of the great necropolis of archaic Rome, items that all bear, with tedious uniformity, the simple and identical stamp "Rome"?[11] We know today that the important thing for establishing an exact chronology and an overall interpretation at each site is to possess the most complete information possible on the layout and stratigraphy of each element of the "material" (the sanctioned term) discovered. For the most ancient periods of Latium and Rome, and for the tombs that constitute the essential, if not unique, documentary material, different chronological phases are characterized less by objects that are totally different in nature from one another, since there is a great deal of continuity in this case (the style of vases, jewels, and weapons changes only very slowly), than by variations in the way one class of object is associated with another. Thus it was by establishing collection tables detailing the types of associations encountered in the necropolises, and not by considering the evolution of a single type of objects, that, beginning in the 1950s, the German archeologist Heinrich Müller-Karpe succeeded in establishing a chronology for the most ancient phases of the archeology of Latium. With modifications and additions (notably those of archeologists Renato Peroni and Giovanni Colonna), that archeology has today become the basis for any archeological analysis of the *primordia Romana*.[12]

But what are we to make of these "collections" (the word itself reveals a great deal) put together in the last century or at the beginning of the present one, in which thousands of objects, forever separated from their exact context and location, which alone would allow us to date and interpret them precisely, stand in close rows for the specialist's discouraged meditation?

That is why the latest efforts to master the documentary evidence lead researchers in new directions; in addition to considering new excavations, they

[11] See the exhibit catalog *L'archeologia in Roma Capitale tra sterro e scavo* (1983), 140–55. The same phenomenon can be verified elsewhere, for example in Capua.

[12] H. Müller-Karpe, *Vom Anfang Roms* (Heidelberg, 1959); and id., *Zur Stadtwerdung Roms* (Heidelberg, 1962); R. Peroni, "Per una nuova cronologia del sepolcreto arcaico del Foro: Sequenza culturale e significato storico," in *Civiltà del Ferro* (Bologna, 1960), 461–99; and id., article in the *Bullettino della Commissione Archeologica Communale in Roma* 77 (1959–60): 15ff.; G. Colonna, "Aspetti culturali della Roma primitiva: Il periodo orientalizzante recente," *Archeologia Classica* 16 (1964).

employ what could be called an archeology of archeology. In exploring the store-houses of museums, in reading the notebooks kept by excavators who did not have the time or the interest to publish the circumstances of their discoveries, in searching administrative archives where precious information about provenance may lie hidden, they find that it is sometimes possible to save from dark obliv-ion some object lying at the bottom of a museum's dark cellar and believed to be lost. Or they may identify more precisely some other item, exhibited and known to everyone, but whose origin remained unknown; or may recompose the mate-rial of an entire site, which had been randomly dispersed through sales and gifts.

Thus, in the collections of the Boston Museum, researchers found an inscription of primordial importance (the so-called Poggio Sommavilla inscrip-tion), since it was one of the only written pieces of evidence of Sabine civilization. It had been completely lost from view[13] since its publication in 1896.

In the same way, an Etruscan vase dating from the seventh century B.C.E. and inscribed with the name Mezentius, the same Mezentius said for so long to have been invented out of whole cloth by Virgil, has emerged from the depths of the Louvre, in whose storerooms it had dwelt since the middle of the last cen-tury. In that case, its location was well known, but the inscription it bore had been misinterpreted in the last century and was thus believed to be merely a bit of graffiti without historical interest.[14]

And there are other examples of that archeology of archeology. A monu-ment of major importance for the knowledge of archaic Rome, for instance, was recomposed for the occasion of a recent exhibition in the Vatican museums.[15] This monument is none other than the famous François tomb (named after its discoverer), which, at the moment of its discovery, contained hundreds of objects, since dispersed to the four corners of the world. Through patient and meticulous work, the tomb was reconstituted nearly as it had appeared one day in 1857, when its discoverer first admired it. That Etruscan tomb was decorated with frescoes depicting figures in combat, one of whom was a certain Tarquinius of Rome ("Tarchunies Rumach"). The interest in restoring these well-known frescoes to their original context is clear. This type of investigation, destined to increase greatly, clarifies and enriches dossiers that had remained incomplete or uncertain. But sometimes, and contrary to all expectation, it also leads researchers to call into question knowledge that was considered quite secure.

In 1980, a bomb went off in the scholarly world: the Palestrina fibula was a fake! Since the author of that assertion was Margherita Guarducci, a world-

---

[13] Reported in a survey devoted to non-Roman languages and writings in Italy. See D. Briquel and M. Lejeune's essay in the collective volume *Italia omnium terrarum parens: La civiltà degli Enotri, Choni, Ausoni, Sanniti, Lucani, Brettii, Sicani, Siculi, Elimi* (Milan, 1989), 435–74.

[14] See F. Gaultier and D. Briquel, "Rééxamen d'une inscription des collections du Musée du Louvre: Un Mézence à Caeré au VIIe siècle av. J.-C.," *Comptes Rendus de l'Académie des Inscriptions*, January–March 1989.

[15] "La tomba François di Vulci," exhibition organized at the Vatican in 1987 by F. Buranelli.

renowned specialist,[16] this was not simply one of the countless wet firecrackers that the press at the time had the habit of setting off, especially in the field of Etruscology. The arguments advanced were impressive both in their number and in their precision. They supported and amplified doubts formulated about the notorious fibula immediately after its indisputably mysterious appearance in 1887. To understand the emotion and passion elicited by the 1887 discovery and by the charges brought against it by Guarducci in 1980, we must remember that the inscription engraved on the gold jewel found in Palestrina had until that time enjoyed the eminent status of being the most ancient inscription in Latin.[17] As such, it occupied a place of choice in all manuals of Latin language and epigraphy, not to mention the major role that had fallen to it in all reflections on the origins of Rome. Yet, from one day to the next, all that lay in ruins as a result of an investigation of ruthless erudition.

We must not, however, judge the practices of nineteenth-century archeology (the Bernardini tomb containing the fibula was discovered in 1876) by our own criteria. For an archeology seeking art objects, if not treasure, above all else, it is hardly astonishing that there was so little and such poor information about the exact circumstances under which the fibula appeared. True, the Bernardini tomb was excavated in 1876, whereas the fibula was not mentioned until 1887, and then only through the intermediary of the German archeologist W. Helbig. But that delay, though suspect, can also be explained by the conditions of archeological operations at that time. The Bernardini tomb revealed many other precious objects, among them, engraved silver goblets, one of which also bore a fine Phoenician inscription. No one has ever doubted that inscription; and yet, in discovering and publishing a previously unknown letter from Joseph-Ernest Renan on the subject,[18] I had the opportunity to note the share of imprecision,[19] and, as we would say today, of negligence that accompanied any archeological discovery of the time. Thus, to stay with the example of the Bernardini tomb, despite a 1918 attempt at discovery, its characteristics, its typology, and even its location are still unknown.

No doubt the involvement of an archeologist, and moreover, one vested with an official function as Helbig was, in more or less clandestine trafficking seems to us inconceivable and inadmissible today. At the time, however, whenever an archeological site opened somewhere, museums sought to procure for themselves only the most beautiful pieces and, most of the time, spurned the

---

[16] M. Guarducci, "La cosidetta fibula prenestina: Antiquari, eruditi e falsari nella Roma dell'ottocento," in *Atti della Accademia Nazionale dei Lincei* 7 (1980): 24. See also the companion essay published in volume 28 of the same collection.

[17] The inscription reads: "Manios med vhevhaked Numasioi" (Manios made me for Numasios). The object itself is supposed to be speaking, a fairly common practice in the archaic era.

[18] A. Grandazzi, "Une lettre inédite de Renan à propos de la tombe Bernardini de Préneste," in *Bulletin de l'Association Guillaume Budé*, October 1989.

[19] This lack of precision bothered Renan as he was preparing to publish the inscription in the *Corpus Inscriptionum Semiticarum*, for which he served as director.

others. In addition, excavations were the result of private initiative, and the administration did no more than authorize it, with only minimal supervision, in the form of periodic visits by inspectors of antiquities. One telling fact is that the report on the Bernardini tomb, published in the 1876 issue of the very official review *Notizie degli Scavi di Antichità,* was not signed by the archeologist responsible for the site, as it would be today in a similar case. In fact, there was no one there to play that role. At the time, the operation remained to a great degree in the private domain, and it was the general director of Antiquities and Fine Arts of the Kingdom of Italy, Senator Fiorelli, who, because of the importance of the discovery, briefly presented the principal results. A bit farther on in the same publication, which, by the way, had just been created by the newly formed Italian state to serve in making public all excavations carried out on the soil of the peninsula (a great innovation and great progress toward more scientific information), there appears a second contribution on the Bernardini tomb. The administration had charged a commission with negotiating the purchase of the art objects that had been exhumed. This second description was the appraiser's report. On one side, then, was an informational note from the highest administrator, and on the other, the report of a purchasing commission. Between them lies a gap, a space, which is today occupied by the professional archeologist.

In forcing the paradox a bit, we might say that in that affair, archeology in the strict sense was never at issue. That of course would be going too far, but it is nonetheless true that the use of the same word, "archeology," must not hide the changes that profoundly affected not only archeological practices from one century to the next (that would be saying too little), but, fundamentally, the very conception of the past these practices manifest. In the last third of the nineteenth century, archeology in the sense we understand it today did not yet exist, or, more exactly, its modern methods and requirements were only in the process of being formed. The real question, not only on this occasion but more generally, is to understand why the new "archeological positivity" (in other words, what we now call archeology) was formed only at that moment (or even later, if we follow the process to its end), well after the emergence of historical science. Attempting to respond to that question would lead us beyond the scope of this book, but it seems difficult to ignore the role played by state authorities in that area.[20]

To return to the Bernardini tomb, we can therefore explain why, even independent of the particular character of its protagonists, the Palestrina fibula affair was surrounded by so much obscurity. That type of uncertainty affected nearly all archeological operations carried out during this gestation period for the new

[20] From this perspective, certain historical coincidences speak for themselves. In 1870, the Italian capital was established in Rome; in 1876, the *Notizie degli Scavi di Antichità* was published for the first time (though we cannot forget the precursory role played by the International Institute of Archeological Correspondence, beginning in 1829).

science. And what is more tempting, or easier, than to pinch a gold jewel? As precious as they are portable, such objects are predisposed as it were for great adventures! If it were to turn out that the inscription was actually engraved by Helbig himself (Guarducci's hypothesis), we might still suppose he had copied an authentic text that was present on a less noble and less prestigious support.[21] In any case, from now on, the authenticity or inauthenticity of the fibula can be defended only by plausible arguments (unless we imagine the discovery of signed confessions!).[22] As a result, it is no longer possible to use the fibula and its famous inscription as it was once used, as an Archimedean lever for important questions, such as the origin of the Latin language or the diffusion of writing in earlier periods. But this is now much less important than it once was, because numerous other inscriptions, beginning with the famous Lapis Niger, have since 1887 augmented a dossier that was almost empty at that time.

We might think that just a bit more care and exactitude on the part of the various scholars who played a role in the exploration of the Bernardini tomb and in the fibula affair could have spared specialists of today the soap opera that continues to produce new episodes every year (the bibliography on the affair is already considerable).

But there again, we would be allowing ourselves to be taken in by the deceptive uniformity of words and expressions. In reality, between the archeology practiced by Fiorelli's and Helbig's contemporaries and our own, the entire status of evidence has changed. In analyzing the epistemological process that led archeologists and historians in the nineteenth century to judge an object as authentic or unauthentic, we can only be struck by the decisive weight given to the search for witnesses. As in a criminal case, archeologists and administrators exerted enormous efforts, as soon as discoveries were signaled here or there, toward finding witnesses who, because they had been there, could guarantee the authenticity of the discoveries exhumed. The analogy, visible in the reports published by the *Notizie degli Scavi di Antichità,* is even more so in the mission orders from the director of Antiquities and Fine Arts at the time, and in the relevant documents that accompany them. These are conserved in the archives of the Italian administration.

But is not such a search for witnesses natural for institutional officials who had to secure the authenticity of the archeological discoveries brought to their attention? Yes, but that is precisely the point. Preliminary authorization (in principle at least!), oversight—partial and periodic—of the excavation, and the judgment of authenticity for essentially museographical ends (the state's collections had to be increased) determined the main aspects of an activity that was

---

[21] As G. Colonna proposed in an article in *Miscellanea archeologica Tobias Dohrn* (Rome, 1982), 39 n. 28. Note that Helbig's defenders are generally authors of Germanic culture, from V. Wilamowitz to F. Wieacker, and including K. Radke and H. Lehmann.

[22] See the copious rehabilitation dossier in H. Lehmann's article in the *Mitteilungen des deutschen Archeologischen Instituts, Römische Abteilung* 96 (1989): 7–86.

more supervision after the fact than creative initiative. On the site, an "inspector" from Antiquities (and it is not accidental that here again we find a word and function stemming from the legal profession) recorded . . . not the crime, but the reality of the archeological excavation, and looked for witnesses for the purpose of coming to what would be a *judgment* of authenticity in the strong sense of the term. Of course, in all fairness, there must be at least two witnesses. In the vicissitudes that ordinarily accompany ancient discoveries, the scientific criteria of modern archeology could come into being only through excavations undertaken on the initiative of specific and autonomous administrations, and realized, supervised, and made public by them. It is more important to note such a concomitance than to wonder, no doubt to little avail, whether the excavations preceded the administrations, favoring their development and the expansion of their prerogatives, or whether, on the contrary, the excavations became possible only once the administrations were well in place.

Law and legal practices appeared as the standard for that archeology that was coming into being as a science. Such practices provided the parameters and the language for the activity of recording finds, the material "witnesses" to the past, an activity that would long remain only a "discipline auxiliary to history."

These conditions explain in large part the proliferation of scandals involving fakes that monopolized the chronicle of the nineteenth century.[23] For archeologists anxious to discover works of art,[24] and only occasionally present on the excavation sites (usually left to unskilled laborers), for the countless amateurs (themselves most often trained in law schools) on the prowl for a beautiful item, the "discoverer's" word, provided of course it was corroborated by another witness, was sufficient to guarantee the authenticity of the excavation.

In sum, that hunt for witnesses was only the corollary of what was at the time the exclusive orientation of archeological practice: the search for art objects. That orientation gave way to other criteria of evaluation only as archeology itself extended its interest to the whole of the material vestiges brought to light with each new excavation—in short, when it ceased to look toward the fine arts and became the science it is today. For a long time, however, archeologists went to excavation sites in search of the Beautiful, in the same way that historians in their writings went in search of the True.

How distant those times now seem! Needless to say, the path that led to modern archeology was long and difficult. In many ways, however, the modern historian and archeologist work from documentation gathered during those

---

[23] Numerous cases are mentioned in the catalog *Vrai ou faux? Copier, imiter, falsifier* (Paris, 1991) of the exhibition held on this theme at the Bibliothèque Nationale in 1988. Just as what was held to be true in the past can be revealed false, the reverse sometimes happens as well. The Duenos vase stands as the mirror image of the Palestrina fibula. In the nineteenth century its exportation into Germany was authorized because it was considered counterfeit, whereas today we know it to be an authentic piece.

[24] See V. Bracco, *L'archeologia classica nella cultura occidentale* (Rome, 1979).

bygone ages and built on their foundations. Many classifications and many theories, not all of which have been submitted to a fundamental reevaluation, were originally elaborated from data collected through the filter of what are now outdated conceptions and systems. We may know on principle that some notion no longer corresponds to much of anything, that the available documentation on some subject resulted from investigations founded on obsolete postulates, but it is no use; we forget all about it when new problematics and new concepts seem to resolve all the difficulties and to open new horizons suddenly. In that way, without paying it any mind, we build recent edifices on foundations as old as they are fragile. That is why archeologists must reshape the documentation coming from excavations before using it, just as surely as historians must perpetually call into question the notions with which they work.

Until a relatively recent date, numerous examples have made that necessity obvious. Such is the case in particular for what Pierre Grimal calls the "terramara fairy tale." Terramarae are protohistorical villages built on piles and present in the Po Valley. It was believed they were characterized by an always identical plan, a regular parallelogram, whose layout anticipated that of Roman cities, with their sacred fence (*pomerium*) and the characteristic intersection of the two axes, the *decumanus* and the *cardo*. It was thought, therefore, that these were the first manifestations of the "Roman" people's existence before their arrival on the site of the Eternal City.[25] Did not the Palatine Hill, where tradition situates the city of Romulus, the mysterious Roma Quadrata (Square Rome), conserve in that very name the memory of a primitive settlement, built on "the ideal of a mountain spur that the Prisco-Latini demanded for their *oppida*"?[26] Such a claim forgets that the present appearance of the Palatine is the result of long centuries of human intervention, which have at several points cut into the natural slope, originally much less steep. Above all, it is grounded in pseudo-observations. All in all, the most peculiar thing is not that the theory of terramarae was formulated—the history of science is rich in other episodes that are at least as quaint—but that it took so long for historians to realize that it was founded on almost nothing, since terramarae, confined, moreover, to the Po Valley, are characterized by a wide variety of plans. We have known for half a century that "we must abandon the old equation: 'terramarae = Protolatin,' from which so many supposed 'truths' have been derived."[27] In toto, however, that scientific fairy tale, begun in about 1880, lasted until the eve of World War II.[28] Such durability cannot be explained apart from the indisputable talent of its principal

---

[25] The archeologist L. Pigorini's name is attached to these theses, set out in successive issues of the *Bullettino Paletnologico Italiano* (1883–1908).

[26] Homo, *Primitive Italy*, 79.

[27] Grimal, *Italie retrouvée*, 324.

[28] Although the very official *Cambridge Ancient History* clearly and quickly condemned the theory in 1927, it was not until 1939, with the work of G. Säflund, published in the *Acta Instituti Romani Regni Sueciae*, that a systematic and complete refutation was available.

defender, the archeologist Luigi Pigorini, and by the force of the hopes to which the system responded. That system, once more, seemed to suddenly dissipate "the mystery of Rome's origins." Let us refrain, nonetheless, from smiling at such outmoded theories. Let there be no doubt, contemporary archeology also has its terramarae. It is simply that, by force of circumstance, it is difficult, even impossible, for us to detect their existence. Some time from now, however, they will be obvious to the eyes of future historians and archeologists.

It is rare, in fact, that the prejudices that oriented and, so to speak, fashioned earlier archeological documentation or the theories we have habitually formulated from it (often forgetting they are only theories and gradually taking them for facts) appear so clearly. Most of the time, we know the broad scientific tendencies that characterized a particular period of historiography, but we do not see, or if we do see we immediately forget, their influence on some particular problem of scholarship. Added one upon another, they produce a falsified overall view, which often depends on a dated and outmoded historiographical context whose influence remains unperceived.

Among many possible examples, let us take the case of the legendary city of Alba Longa,[29] a mythical Latin metropolis from which Romulus and Remus, the founders of Rome, supposedly originated. We might say, then, that the city was at the origin of the origin.

How many scholars, "antiquarians," topographers, philologists, archeologists, and historians wandered the banks of Lake Albano in search of the fabled city? After nearly five centuries of scholarly investigation, there is not an acre of land along the circumference of this peaceful lake that cannot claim, in the mind of one or another of its countless visitors, the preeminent dignity of being the site of the mythical city founded by Ascanius.[30]

Nevertheless, as we now know, there were no cities in Latium (or in all of central Italy) until a period clearly later than the apogee of the civilization that appeared in the Alban Hills, and in particular, on the periphery of the lake dominated by the majestic silhouette of Monte Cavo, the Mons Albanus of classical texts. That is why the hut-urns exhumed here and there by wine growers going about their agricultural work throughout the last century, beginning with the famous discoveries of the archeologist Ennio Visconti in 1816, cannot in my opinion be linked to a single site, that of the legendary Latin metropolis. They are rather the traces of a dispersed settlement, prior to the formation of cities in Latium, and typical of the federations of which the narrative of origins has conserved the deformed memory, in accordance with a process the phases of which it is possible to detect. But there again, researchers took the classical literary tradition *literally* and sought in these remains the "confirmation" of the legend of a

[29] I summarize here an essay of my own from *Mélanges de l'Ecole Française de Rome*, 1986, 47–90.

[30] In fact, the ancient literary tradition made the son of Aeneas the founder of Alba.

city of Alba, a legend to which they tried to apply a directly historicist, positivist, and realist reading. From a strictly archeological point of view, they had to imagine—in the most restricted meaning of the term—the settlement based on the necropolises, and the famous hut-urns constituted the most visible remains of those cemeteries. As researchers have not failed to underscore since then, archeological investigation as it was practiced in the nineteenth century was incapable of identifying the traces of protohistorical settlements—fragile, discrete, ambiguous traces that only the refined techniques of modern archeology have been able to situate. And, to confine ourselves to provenances that are more or less known, we note that in reality the archeological vestiges allow us to identify not one but at least three necropolises. That is the minimal number established and accepted by the advocates of the historicity of a city of Alba. And we cannot expect most of the archeological items ordinarily taken into consideration in this debate to have a certificate of origin in good order! There was almost no regular scientific excavation in the modern sense of the term in the Alban Hills. Normally, peasants found these "funerary vases" (as the hut-urns were called at the time) in their fields and sought to sell them to distinguished amateurs (Chateaubriand's contemporary, the duke of Blacas, put together a remarkable collection of them). For the peasant, and for the antiquarian who sought to resell the vases, it was certainly more convenient, more prudent, more prestigious, and as a result, more profitable, to merely say they came from "Alba."

A mere historical fairy tale? It is, in fact, nothing other than an exact appraisal of the precise "human, all too human" conditions, in their concrete and historical dimension, under which discoveries, too often used subsequently as neutral, clear, and objective data, were originally made. In other words, in linking a set of remains scattered over a wide surface to the artificial unity of a place supposed to be that of the mythical Latin metropolis, archeologists of the past shaped their observations to accord with the explanation that seemed to impose itself on them. Once more, we find that the act of collecting information is inseparable from the theory that organizes its framework, modalities, and principles. There is not documentation on one side, located in its entirety in the realm of the object, and interpretation on the other, subject to the chance events of historical circumstances and subjective biases. Although it is true that the archeologist's task (and in any case, the word "archeologist" is inappropriate for the discoverers—unknown for the most part—of the Alban hut-urns) is to collect a maximum of "objective data," it is no less the case that archeologists can do so only by means of, or rather through, classifications and techniques that translate so many theoretical choices, favoring certain options over others.

Aware of this double pitfall, contemporary archeologists, with the help of computer techniques, have undertaken to construct the most detailed and most neutral typologies possible, including a very high number of parameters within them. But a nonchoice is still in a certain manner a choice, and archeology runs the risk of transforming itself into a mere technology. Such a technology, as anxious about its formal elaboration as it is far from any possibility of historical utility, finds its own end in itself.

All these obstacles (in the sense Gaston Bachelard understood that term) are all the more difficult to discern and avoid in that, in contrast to a well-established practice in the field of history, archeology does not present itself as a hermeneutics. It claims to be an activity of collection and classification above all else, more and more encyclopedic in its methods and objects. As a result, the problematic at the foundation of both history and archeology remains implicit and only rarely disturbs the surface of words and designations. This is especially true (and this goes without saying) because the process of selection is not in any way voluntary or conscious (in which case archeologists would quite simply resort to dishonesty and the falsification of facts) but is revealed only by a historiographical and epistemological analysis.

In this case as well, the example of Alba allows us to detect signs that manifest and reveal what I should like to call the subterranean choices that guide scholarly research. In going over the old writings on the question, we can only be struck by a phrase that recurs insistently between 1816 and the 1880s. Between those two dates, Alba Longa was very often designated by periphrasis as "the prehistoric Pompeii." And, in that name, which may appear purely ornamental, we can read the expression of a preliminary interpretation that oriented, determined, and delimited from the beginning the field of observation and the elements gathered. What is Pompeii? A city buried by a volcanic eruption. What, then, is Alba, the "prehistoric Pompeii" (the modifier is important)? Nothing other, quite obviously, than a city that was also buried by a volcano! But there is no volcano among the placid hills whose verdant slopes still provide Romans with a destination for their Sunday excursions. On the contrary. In the nineteenth century, geological science, so proud of its recent progress, established that the Alban Hills—especially the highest of them, Monte Cavo, where the ancient Latins had placed the sanctuary of their god Jupiter—were volcanic in origin (a finding that has since been confirmed). Hence, through a mode of interference that is not without precedent, the progress of one science came to block the development of another. A fortuitous material circumstance also favored the assimilation of the mythical metropolis to the famous city in Campania. Very often, the hut-urns unearthed by the peasants of Castelli Romani while digging deep trenches for their vines were covered by a layer of crushed earth so hard that it suggested the layer of lava that had buried Herculaneum. Same effect, same cause, it was thought. Archeologists imagined that, just as Pompeii and Herculaneum had disappeared after the eruption of 79, Alba Longa, which for lack of an exact chronological reference point was situated, without more precision, in the obscurity of remote times, had one day been erased from the map by the incandescent flow of nearby Monte Cavo. In that reconstitution, archeologists believed they were making a serious critique. They surmised that the Roman tradition spoke of a destruction of Alba by Tullus Hostilius because that tradition had transposed onto the human plane of commonplace historical causality, and for the greater glory of Rome, a natural catastrophe whose scope and suddenness had remained without example. Did that not show once more the artificial and fabricated nature of Roman annals? And did not these ingenious restitutions bring to light the now highly scientific character of philology and history? The scholars who formulated this theory in the nineteenth century, when, throughout the industrial world, urban civilization was expanding as never before, may have also been influenced by the example of the great modern metropolises (London, for example), which they saw developing before their eyes. Quite simply, what nineteenth-century philologists and historians did not see was that, in conceiving of Alba as a city, they were at the same time concealing the specificity of Rome, the innovation represented by the emergence of a city on the banks of the Tiber, and were thus condemning themselves to perceive the time of the "origins" as the slow unfolding of a nearly motionless and obscure process. In other words, that interpretation made it impossible to perceive the discontinuity introduced precisely by the sudden emergence of the "city" of Rome, and researchers then had to relegate the whole of the tradition of the primordia to the insubstantial shadows of legend, which they defined in negative terms as the absence of history.

The growth of archeological documentation, especially over the last three decades (at least for regions of Latium other than the Castelli Romani, which has remained a bit apart from modern research), and the elaboration of an increasingly refined chronology that was its most direct consequence allow for an approach to the tradition concerning Rome's origins that is more differentiated and more sensitive than in the past to the play between breaks and continuities. The study of the data, literary as well as archeological, now lends itself to an analysis of that kind. But very often, as the example of Alba demonstrates, the problematics and presuppositions of the past continue to invisibly guide and fashion present-day research.

That is why it is not enough to be aware of the factual lacunae that exist in the documentation. Because of the incessant upheavals to which the substratum of the city of Rome was subjected, these lacunae are glaringly obvious. After all, the city was inhabited continually for more than two and a half millennia. We must, in addition, constantly seek to measure what is historical, precisely, in the orientations of modern historiography. There is a great distance between the treasure hunt practiced by Winckelmann's contemporaries and the methodically planned discoveries of modern archeology in Lavinium, Osteria dell'Osa (Gabii), Castel di Decima, and Rome.[31] In 1738, when excavations

---

[31] I borrow the indications provided by G. Colonna in his remarkable survey "I Latini et gli altri popoli del Lazio," in the collective volume *Italia, omnium terrarum alumna* (Milan, 1988), 411–528.

began in Pompeii, the same year that Beaufort published his famous *Dissertation*, Ficorini discovered in Palestrina the cist (a receptacle of engraved bronze) to which his name is attached. Then, in 1784, a find of terra-cotta in Velletri revived interest in early Latium. Several years later (in 1790), Cardinal Despuig found a bronze head in Ariccia, where tradition had conserved the memory of a famous sanctuary of the Latin people. The publication of Bonstetten's pioneering book in 1804 was followed in 1816 by the influential publication of Visconti's memorable dissertation on the "Alban" hut-urns. In the same period, the Frenchman L. C. F. Petit-Radel's research on the Pelasgians (from 1810 to 1830) attempted to clarify the most ancient and inaccessible eras of the history of primitive Italy. We have already noted the long interval of time, apparently inexplicable, that separated Visconti's book and the first studies that sought to draw conclusions from it regarding the problem of Rome's origins. This can be explained by the fact that the discussion was seized upon and diverted toward purely paleontological ends (thus important studies on the archeology of Latium appeared in the first issues of the *Bulletin de Paléontologies Italiennes,* also in 1870–1879). It would be more than half a century before Schliemann, the discoverer of Troy, came to seek the traces of the mythical metropolis of the Latins in the vicinity of Lake Albano. He did not find them—and for good reason—but he demonstrated that the layer of earth under which the hut-urns were situated was not volcanic in origin, thus restoring to history what he took away from paleontology.[32] A technical error in interpretation was thus the cause of historians' lack of interest and silence regarding the first unidentified vestiges from the most ancient periods of Latium. In fact, it is more probable that that case was itself an effect of the little consideration that historians had for legendary times. During that period, history was anxious to be recognized as a full and legitimate science as soon as possible, and it eliminated from the narrative of origins everything that was only fable and legend.

Nonetheless, the progress of Etruscology, whose research on the origins of Rome long constituted only an auxiliary development, and the extraordinary revelations brought by the discovery of the royal tombs of Palestrina beginning in 1855 (and until 1878), gradually led to a reevaluation of the most ancient history of Latium and Rome. More exactly, although historians continued to deny all historicity to the literary tradition of the primordia,[33] they now considered with growing interest the material vestiges of the archaic periods of Latium. Nonetheless, they had a tendency to decree, when the objects exhumed were of an exceptional quality, that they were Etruscan, Greek, or Phoenician imports.

---

[32] Schliemann, however, did not succeed in convincing everyone, and for several more years, his adversary de Rossi defended the traditonal thesis that the hut-urns predated volcanic activity in Latium.

[33] See chap. 1 above.

Above all, the unification of the kingdom of Italy, accomplished in 1870, meant that the very young state, unlike the old pontifical administration, looked with fresh eyes on the most ancient past of the peninsula, and particularly that of its new capital. It was at that time, between 1870 and 1890, that a shift occurred from private collections, due to the pioneering activities of amateurs (for example, Augusto Castellani, Michele Stefano de Rossi, and Luigi Ceselli),[34] to museums created to receive the products of the new excavations. It is in such museums that the essential part of the archeological evidence of primitive Latial civilizations is conserved.

In studying the historical and philological perspectives on the origins, we saw that, after Boni's excavations in the center of Rome, the renewed interest in the primordia withered somewhat and was often transformed into a purely rhetorical exaltation of origins. (That aspect was already largely present in Boni but was redeemed in his case by his extraordinary capacities as an archeologist.) In terms of the archeological discovery of primitive Latium, Giovanni Pinza's *Monumenti primitivi di Roma e del Lazio antico* (1905) marked an exceptional achievement. Exhaustive in its time, it is still fundamental today.[35] As evidence that great currents of research transcend individuals, we might also note that, after World War I, Pinza himself attempted an overview that is not exempt from the faults we mentioned a moment ago and is far from having the value of his earlier work.[36]

The role of chance, uncertainty, ignorance, error, and preconceived systems is thus no less great in archeological documentation than in historical reconstruction. It would be illusory to believe that the documentation simply imposed itself, already there, ready for interpretation. On the contrary, it is a set of data that, in itself, in the detail of its organization and constitution, is the product and expression of the particular geography of a discipline, or rather, of an intersection of disciplines. And, when we speak of the limits of past archeology, we must not conclude with a kind of neopositivism concerning present archeology. Even though it is now as anxious about its methods of investigation as about the results it can claim, even though it provides an incomparably more precise image of the times of the birth of Rome than it did in the past, archeology now runs the risk, because of its own success and the volume of responses it has provided, of overlooking all the old and new questions that continue to be raised, in particular those regarding phases prior to the emergence of the city of Romulus. An attentive examination of these times can reveal to us, by way of comparison and contrast, some of the most innovative characteristics of the community that was taking shape on the banks of the Tiber.

[34] Other names are mentioned in L. Quilici, *Roma primitiva e l'inizio della civiltà laziale* (Rome, 1979), 12.

[35] G. Pinza, *Monumenti primitivi di Roma e del Lazio antico* (1905), vol. 15 of *Monumenti Antichi dei Lincei*.

[36] G. Pinza, *Storia della civiltà latina*, 4 vols. (1924).

CHAPTER 8

THE TEMPORAL ORDER

ROME DID NOT originate in a vacuum; the city was not an absolute beginning in Latium or in the rest of the peninsula. Before it, other forms of life flourished, and modern archeology is seeking to discern their traces. Rome even existed before Rome. Beginning in at least the fourteenth century B.C.E. (the date of the most ancient material remains identified on the site), people came to settle on the soil of what was then only a group of wooded hills along a great meandering river. But if nothing is lost and nothing created, how could Romulus have founded Rome, since it already existed? Must we abandon the legend without delay and return to archeology alone, the enormous progress of which allows for a totally new approach to prehistoric periods?

Let us try for a moment to reconstitute the development of Rome solely in the light of the lessons of archeology. What do we see?[1] A few extremely rare pottery shards for the most ancient periods (from the fourteenth to the eleventh centuries B.C.E.), then, for the following periods, a few tombs, the number of which never exceeds about ten, and then, traces of humble wood and cob huts, which apparently gave way little by little to more elaborate constructions. On the Palatine, the Capitol, and the Quirinal, hills so present in the narrative of origins, there is almost nothing. But we have to admit that beginning at a certain moment, a city existed, since we find, this time in greater and greater number, tiles, decorations in terra-cotta, and votive repositories, which attest to the fact that as of the seventh century B.C.E. at least, a large human community lived there, venerated gods for whom they built temples, and gathered in specially designed places, no doubt to debate "politics."

But how did they move from the first stage, characterized by settlements limited to a few rare hovels scattered over an immense space, to an apparently numerous and prosperous community concentrated around what is now the Forum? Even an extremely thorough examination of the few objects saved from oblivion and destruction offers no response to that question. Needless to say, these few things are a great deal, since thanks to them it is possible to have a relatively precise idea of the material conditions of existence and the natural environment that reigned during those so distant periods of the past. But it is

[1] See chap. 9 below.

only by turning to the "literary" tradition that we can ask those paltry objects questions they could not solicit by themselves. Archeology thus records a development (suggesting rather than demonstrating it) but cannot explain it. Nor can it respond to the "why"—the province of theology!—or even to the "how" of this development, that is, to its modalities. On a single site, for example (the Forum), archeology has identified tombs, which then gave way to other structures, huts or merely enclosures.

It is not that the literary tradition allows us to ask what are automatically good questions. But if we do not wish to reduce archeology to a kind of (devalued) natural science, noting, on the one hand, the given state of different elements, and, at the other end of the chronological axis, the displacements, extensions, and modifications of these elements, we must take into account the primordial legends. Not to do so would mean falling back, behind the apparent neutrality of a scientific "archeologism," into a form of determinism that dares not speak its name: "That's how it was at the beginning, that's how it is at the end, the beginning explains the end, and the end depends on the beginning." We must thus turn to the narrative of origins, but without believing that it in itself offers the solution to the questions raised, especially since human occupation of the site of Rome is attested to archeologically well before the eighth century B.C.E. (when the tradition places Romulus). By the very fact of its existence, this narrative is a question, but a question that deserves to be taken altogether seriously.

In fact, turning to the literary tradition as an instrument for investigation and reflection (and not as a ready-made solution) does not impoverish the archeological documentation by excluding or simplifying it. On the contrary, it makes that documentation appear more complex than it seemed at first sight, and enriches it with multiple possibilities. Conversely, turning to archeology, provided it is not used as a kind of trial by ordeal, leading directly either to an acquittal or to a death sentence for the tradition, can show the density and diversity of that tradition.

Nevertheless, the study of the Romulean legend is not sufficient to explain the advent of the city of Rome. To understand Rome, we must look earlier and elsewhere. The specificity of the Roman phenomenon will appear all the more clearly in contrast to conditions existing prior to the formation of an urban center. The lacunae in our documentation at the site of the city itself are enormous, and the list of what we know is infinitely smaller than the list of what is unknown to us. In fact, we cannot even make up that list because, in reality, we do not know what we do not know. Rome was long one center among others in Latium, at a time when people lived around bodies of water, paths of communication, or naturally fortified places, united among themselves by religious ties, and regrouped, following modalities difficult to analyze, into leagues regularly bringing together "peoples" (or their representatives) around a sanctuary of which they were members. That is why we will better understand Rome by first considering Alba, Lavinium, Gabii (or rather, Osteria dell'Osa), and Nemi, that is, the communities that were prosperous during the most remote times of the Latin federation, to which they, as well as the future Rome, belonged. Modern archeology came into being by moving away from the art object and toward the descriptive inventory of sets of objects; in the same way, it cannot confine itself today to the study of an isolated site, even if that site is Rome, but must aim to integrate it into a series of analogous sites, by analyzing it in terms of the territory of which it is part.[2]

While it may seem valid and worthwhile to illuminate the birth of Rome by examining other sites that, though they shared characteristics at the beginning, did not evolve in the same way, we must wonder whether the principle of that comparison can transcend criteria that are merely geographical (the same region), typological (same kind of site), and chronological (different sites analyzed for the same periods).[3] That is, can we go so far as to suppose the existence of ethnic factors? In other words, is it possible to speak of a shared "Latinness" in all the centers of Latium, Rome included? And on what might we base that "Latinness"? Is there a specifically Latin population in Latium, and if so, when did it begin?

In responding to that type of ethnic question, archeologists, and then historians, long believed they could use the concept of "culture," defined in archeological terms as the set of material characteristics proper to a given geographical area. Hence they built imposing systems on the basis of the complementary notions of culture, people (which progressively came to replace race), and influences, this last being conceived at the beginning of the century as brutal and massive invasions. Today, it is understood in a much more flexible and nuanced way as diffusion (hence the name diffusionism is sometimes given to this type of explanation).[4]

But as the particular discoveries have accumulated and led to more refined analyses open to diverse interpretations, the fragility of these great theoretical instruments, which served to elaborate the first surveys—and usefully served, let us not forget—has increasingly appeared. Let us place ourselves for a moment in the situation of archeologists from the future. Would they be right, in observing the frequency of restaurants called pizzerias on both sides of the Atlantic, knowing that the word is of "Mediterranean" origin, to conclude that there was an invasion of North America by Italy? Or, if they knew nothing about the word

---

[2] For an account of recent tendencies in protohistorical archeology, see the essays published in *Dialoghi di Archeologia*, 1986, issue entitled "Prospettive storico-antropologiche in archeologia preistorica." See also above, chap. 7.

[3] At least if we do not confine ourselves to noting simply the linguistic unity of Latium in the historical era.

[4] The different theories are presented and analyzed in J. Heurgon, *Rome et la Méditerranée occidentale jusqu'aux guerres puniques*, 2d ed. (Paris, 1980), chap. 1 and pp. 351–63, on "anti-invasionism and its limits."

itself (which is our own situation in regard to the most ancient stages of the cultures of central Italy), to believe the reverse was true? Yet historians have done nothing less in seeking for so long to reconstitute hypothetical invasions and influences based solely on the material indexes identified by archeology. Moreover, in my intentionally anachronistic comparison, I chose a particularly favorable case, in the sense that the parameter considered is still clearly particularized and easily identifiable; whereas, in protohistoric archeology, the parameters that define a "culture," considered in isolation in any case, remain, with a few happy exceptions, limited and difficult to circumscribe exactly. The evidence may be a similarity in the decorations on vases of very different kinds, or conversely, a similarity in vases with different decorations (rarely the two together); or it may be some kind of funerary object. Above all, in this notion of "cultures," the idea persists of closed and autonomous sets, totalities definable by the sum of a certain number of elements, active in a given geographical era and during a definite period of time. To move from one "culture" to the next, from the Villanovans to the Etruscans, for example, whose archeological traces are superposed on the same territories, historians had to resort to the hypothesis of discontinuity. In other words, at a time when the theoretical model reigning in the field of history was the causality of events, historians transposed the imperatives of that model, despite the absence of any solid foundation, to the prehistory of the peninsula, practicing a kind of archeology of the event. Thus they invoked invasions, massive migrations, and sudden shifts in populations whenever they needed to explain the shift from one culture to the next.

Nevertheless, the unity, efficacy, and, finally, the very pertinence of that notion of "culture" have largely been called into question, along with the associated notions of relation, influence, interference, and reciprocal reaction. Historians saw that the indexes considered could lend themselves to completely different conclusions from those that had first been formulated. Naturally, it was the extremely fragmentary nature of the documentation that led to, or rather required, constant efforts at complicating and refining the problematics and methods of approach. Thus, once the great classifications of the beginning of the century had been set in place, primarily in Montelius's footsteps,[5] historians became more sensitive to the ever increasing complexity of the facts, to the continuities in space and time between "cultures," which were revealed by the study of archeological "material." For a long time, for example, it had been noted that necropolises in Latium practiced both cremation and inhumation. Historians first explained this duality of funeral rites by pointing to ethnic factors, assuming that different rites corresponded to different peoples; later, they opted for a strictly chronological interpretation, considering inhumation a later stage than

---

[5] See O. Montelius, *Civilisation primitive en Italie depuis l'introduction des métaux*, 2 vols. (Stockholm, 1895 and 1920), long a reference work.

the practice of cremation. We now realize, however, that the two rites coexisted within a single chronological period, in accordance with complex modalities.[6]

Theories that had explained the peopling of Europe during the Bronze Age by the more or less brutal, more or less sudden, arrival of ethnic groups that were already constituted as such could no longer be maintained. Several decades ago, historians abandoned the attempt to interpret the existence of different cultures on ethnic grounds. Their efforts are currently directed not toward the ethnic question but toward the reconstitution of human behaviors, through the study, from an anthropological perspective, of archeological remains in their original context. In the place of "culture," they now prefer to speak of archeological "facies," a more neutral and more prudent concept.[7]

But although it was not possible to rediscover archeologically the traces of an originally Latin people, might it be possible to do so with the help of linguistics? After all, is not a language the most remarkable repository of history and prehistory? And linguistics has long recognized Latin as an Indo-European language. Thus it all seemed simple: Since they knew that the Indo-Europeans were originally located somewhere in central Europe, historians had only to identify, by means of archeology, the progression of a "culture" from the north to the south of the peninsula, in order also to find the traces of the descent of the future Latins, or rather of the Proto-Latins, toward their final destination. That effort was first made with the terramarae. Since then, historians have pursued all the great civilizations whose progressive displacement from north to south they believed they could reconstitute.[8] With time, the illusions and dangers of this type of linguistic geography have appeared more clearly. It was noted, for example, that in central Italy there was a Latino-Faliscan group and an Osco-Umbrian group, which, though resembling each other in general, also presented enormous differences. But how to interpret these contradictory characteristics? Was there a shared origin, namely, an Italic language, already detached from the Indo-European branch, or were the resemblances the result of long proximity?[9] Given the importance of structural kinships and of the fact that, as far as we can

[6] As shown by the example of the necropolis of Osteria dell'Osa, on the site of Gabii between Rome and Palestrina. The site was excavated by A. M. Bietti-Sestieri and her team.

[7] See the important preface to R. Peroni, *L'età del bronzo in Italia* (Rome, 1990).

[8] For example, the so-called Apennine civilization, which began in the fourteenth century B.C.E., or the so-called urn field civilization, apparently originating in Hungary/Transylvania, and active beginning in the twelfth century B.C.E. In the face of heaps of objects that, from one end of Europe to the other, resemble one another, there is a strong temptation to discover behind this mute (and deceptive) uniformity Indo-Europeans, whose necessary existence is postulated by linguistics.

[9] G. Colonna supports the view that the Faliscans originally belonged to the same group as the Latins, and that the progression of the Sabines shattered that unity. See his "Preistoria e proto-storia di Roma e del Lazio" (1974), 280ff. That essay offers indirect proof of the Sabine legend regarding Rome's origins. In contrast, other historians claim that even in the most ancient phases, Latins and Faliscans belonged to two different groups. See Poucet, *Origines de Rome*, 142.

tell, the differences seem to become more pronounced for the period for which we possess inscriptions (that is, the seventh century B.C.E.), the hypothesis of a shared Italic origin is more satisfying. This is especially true inasmuch as the example of Etruscan, a non-Indo-European language present for centuries in an environment that was completely different from it, demonstrates that influences can come into play only in relation to initial resemblances.[10]

Nonetheless, the multiplicity of exchanges, relations, and reciprocal influences that are visible as far back in time as we can go does as much harm to the hypothesis of a shared Italic language as to that of an original Indo-European. To explain the arrival of the Indo-Europeans in Latium, we must think less of a spreading wave than of a sequence of currents, extended over time, a multiplicity of infiltrations, a much more complex evolution in prehistory than was initially believed. At the beginning of the century, when two new Indo-European languages—Tokharian and Hittite—were discovered, it appeared that many of what had been considered early traits were in reality to be resituated at the end of a long evolution. The idea of a unique and originary Indo-European gave way to a much more nuanced vision. There again, the very notion of origin gradually dissolved. Under such circumstances, we cannot resist wondering whether Dumézil's trifunctional system, with the unified meaning and the clarity of line that characterize it, does not depend in the last instance on such a unitary conception of Indo-European, which was very marked by nineteenth-century invasionism. In addition, linguists have abandoned the idea of an original Latin language whose principal traits could be discerned through comparative linguistics. They are much more sensitive than before, in this and other fields, to the diversity of possible interpretations of a single fact.[11] If elements prove to be characteristic of one language (and analysis has identified a great number of these in Latin), are we to explain them as archaisms or as innovations? On the other hand, evolutions shared by several languages do not necessarily prove reciprocal influences but can sometimes originate independently from one another. And if better-defined indexes lead us to speak of influences, we still never know which language influenced the other. There is always the risk of taking the model for the copy or vice versa.

All these reasons, infinitely detailed in specific interpretations and commentaries, mean that, for the last few decades, historical linguistics has turned away from such risky speculations, explaining historical relations in the course of the first millennium B.C.E. based on the linguistic state observable from inscriptions, and then reconstituting the states immediately preceding. That reserve is

---

[10] This argument is mentioned in Peroni, *L'età del bronzo*, 388.

[11] On this matter, see the issues discussed by M. Lejeune in the collective volume *Mémorial des études latines* (Paris, 1943), regarding "the position of Latin in the Indo-European field." See also his essay in *Popoli e civiltà dell'Italia antica* 6 (1987), devoted to the languages and dialects of the peninsula before Roman domination.

praiseworthy and has been very productive; it would be a shame, however, to leave aside questions that in my view deserve to be asked, even if monolithic conclusions must be abandoned.[12] For example, the Umbrians of Gubbio excluded the peoples of Iapygia[13]—separated from them at the beginning of the Iron Age by hundreds of miles—from their celebrations, whose ritual has been transmitted to us by the engraved bronze tablets called the Eugubine Tables. It is therefore clear that the practice of linguistic geography remains not only valid but necessary, provided we do not seek ready-made solutions from it. After all, an increasing awareness of the complexity of the phenomena cannot mask the major fact that Latin belongs to the Indo-European language group, and that something therefore "happened"! Moreover, the process continued into the historical era and, as Massimo Pallottino rightly points out, the conquest of Italy by Rome was only the last act in the Indo-Europeanization of the peninsula.[14] Quite simply, it is important, in order to avoid past errors (at least those particular errors), to keep in mind the totality of available data. A few indexes may allow us to go into some detail concerning the time when the Proto-Latins (since, in the historical sense, there were no Latins as yet) arrived in Latium. Through archeology, we recognize a culture, or rather a specific archeological facies, in Latium, only in the tenth century B.C.E., with the most obvious sign provided by the famous hut-urns.

Are we therefore to fix the age of the earliest Latins in the first millennium B.C.E.? That would be forgetting that when archeology discerns the traits of a clearly defined regional entity, that entity is already at the end of a process of differentiation that had no doubt been proceeding for centuries. We must therefore situate the Proto-Latins even farther back in time. The example of Linear B, a language deciphered from clay tablets—some of which date to the fifteenth century B.C.E.—which has proved to be the direct ancestor of classical Greek, provides a precious point of comparison. Mycenean civilization supposedly began in the early part of the second millennium B.C.E. and lasted nearly a millennium, which shows how slow the evolutions can be. In the case of Latin, we have access only to an already advanced stage, however archaic it might seem to us. Another fact, which has value only as an index, also deserves to be taken into consideration. The civilization of the Lipari Islands and of Sicily, whose importance can be detected archeologically beginning in 1600 B.C.E., in its influence and extraordinary prosperity for some three centuries at least, indisputably

---

[12] See D. Sivestri's helpful comments in *L'etrusco e le lingue dell'Italia antica* (Pisa, 1984). See also A. Prosdocimi, "Lingua e preistoria: Appunti di lavora," in *Miscellanea di studi classici in onore di Eugenio Manni* (Rome, 1979), 1835–90.

[13] Eugubine Tables, table I 43, VI b 52–55. See Heurgon, *Rome et la Méditerranée occidentale*, 56. Heurgon opposes Devoto, who makes the Iapygians neighbors of Gubbio (see Heurgon, p. 88). For an explanation of this hostility in terms of much more recent issues, see the remarks in C. Ampolo, *Gli Etruschi e Roma* (Rome, 1981), 54 n. 33.

[14] M. Pallottino, *Storia della prima Italia* (Milan, 1984), 29.

played a major role in the evolution of the peninsula, to the point of being sometimes considered a vehicle of the Indo-Europeanization of Italy.[15] In that respect, let us not forget the place that the Siceli, the mythical inhabitants of Sicily, occupy in the legends and even the toponymy of Latium (according to Dionysius of Halicarnassus, a section of Tibur—that is, Tivoli—bore their name).[16]

All that should not make us forget what linguists call the Mediterranean substrata, the study of which, though it may have occasioned some excesses, has been unjustly abandoned. It seems all the more necessary now, since Latin seems to have retained a large part of its Mediterranean—or in any case pre-Indo-European—substrata.

Perhaps we shall find that all these questions lead to few certainties. Nonetheless, a continuing quest is necessary. Science originates in astonishment; uneasiness suits it well.

We possess numerous terms of comparison for raising these questions in relation to the data accessible for analysis. In many of their aspects, the properly historical phases continued for a long time to preserve characteristics already present in the periods prior to writing. Hence, when the Volscians seized a part of Latium in the fifth century B.C.E., and when Rome itself seized a city and deported its inhabitants to its own territory (as in the case of Velletri, a city in the Alban Hills, in 338 B.C.E.), how can we not recognize the illustration, within the historical period itself, of these movements of population that we glimpse only through a fog for more remote eras?

Can we know, then, who the first Latins were? In a certain way, we can give only a negative response, not only because of the gaps in our knowledge, but also because the very existence of the original Latins must be questioned. Whoever they were, the people who lived on the plains of Latium at the dawn of the second millennium B.C.E. were not Latins, but rather *became* Latins.[17] Exchanges, infiltrations, dispersions, influences, relations, displacements, invasions, raids—nothing ought to be excluded a priori in accounting for the emergence of a Latin ethnos. The analysis from either perspective—archeological or linguistic—reveals an ever more complex reality resistant to constants. Throughout the three millennia before the Common Era, there is not a shift from the particular to the general, an increasing uniformization of customs and civilization; on the contrary, the shift is from the general to the particular. There

---

[15] Ibid., 54.

[16] These traditions are studied in magnificent detail by E. Pais throughout his oeuvre (though he supposes too low a chronology). S. Mazzarino's innovative *Dalla monarchia allo stato repubblicano* (Catania, 1946) also sheds light on fundamental aspects of the question (pp. 27ff.). See also Heurgon, *Rome et la Méditerranée occidentale*; and Pallottino, *Storia della prima Italia*, 57.

[17] Hence they are called Proto-Latins. That said, the great continuity revealed by the archeological remains seems to exclude the possibility of massive outside influences, at least after 1600 B.C.E. See Peroni, *L'età del bronzo*, 388.

are many regional entities, but they appear only at the end of a process several centuries long. The vastly different cultures of Italy in the eighth and seventh centuries B.C.E., where the Etruscans, the Ligurians, the Latins, and the Osco-Umbrians can all be distinguished from one another, mark both the beginning of the history of the peninsula and the culmination of its prehistory. But, as the Mycenean example shows, that does not mean that the huge cultural groups of earlier phases[18]—the Paleoveneti (located in the region of Venice), the Villanovans (in present-day Tuscany and Emilia), or the southern Adriatics (east of central Italy)—were great dinosaurs with only a rudimentary organization. Who could have imagined the complexity of the Mycenean culture in considering only the archeological remains, without the decipherment of Linear B?[19]

The question of ethnic identity was long approached in relation to criteria that were not always made explicit. And, to tell the truth, between the warring theses of autochthony (which assumed the Latins were originally from Latium, and that their civilization thus emerged by spontaneous generation as it were) and of invasionism (which saw the Latins as invaders, thus situating the origin of Latin "civilization" to the north, in central Europe even), the choice was probably not a matter of indifference. Is it an accident that the theory of the terramarae, which considered the Po Valley the origin of the Latins, had so much favor in the newly unified Italy of the Piedmont monarchy?

All that should not lead us, however, to abandon totally the ethnic point of view in the study of the most ancient Latium. To eliminate it, as researchers have a tendency to do today, orienting their archeological investigation toward social anthropology (a necessary dimension, by the way), may amount to the same thing as considering it a self-evident truth, as was done in the past. In both cases, there is an impoverishment of the analysis. It is unquestionably a step forward not to consider the ethnic argument a response; but we must not stop envisioning it as a question.

Even apparently negative results in this area can prove to be of great scientific utility. Although we must give up the attempt to establish a relation of equivalence between archeological "culture" and ethnic populations, we must still attribute more than negative efficacy to that insight. Let us take the case of the Sabines, to whom the literary tradition, so often condemned as such, grants a major role in the foundation of Rome. The ravishment of the Sabines, Tarpeia's betrayal, the alliance between the Romans of Romulus and the Sabines of Titus Tatius, and, finally, the Sabine origin of King Numa are the principal episodes in a veritable Sabine chanson de geste, which is very present in the accounts of the primordia. And, among the countless arguments invoked to undermine faith in that set of traditions, the principal one, according to Jacques

---

[18] Which probably appear monolithic to us only as a result of the inadequacy of the documentation.
[19] See Peroni, *L'età del bronzo*, 23.

Poucet, is certainly that "until now, archeology has not been able to find any true confirmation of an important Sabine presence at the origin of the city."[20] For more than thirty years now,[21] everyone has rushed to repeat that argument, seeing it as proof that the tradition lied when it spoke of Sabines at the origin of Rome. Because the tradition was seen to be the product of a fabrication, researchers could justify a mythological analysis that appealed to Indo-European tripartition, or a literary interpretation. In fact, the two points of view shored each other up. Let us concede that "the original Sabines, if they did exist, left no perceptible archeological traces." Granted, but what does that prove? In other words, it is not possible to give that archeological absence the value of proof unless one postulates an equivalence between material culture and ethnic population, that is, unless one takes for indisputable a principle that the very progress of archeology has reduced to nil. The historicity of Sabine participation in the foundation of Rome is not proved by archeology any more than it was in the past.[22] But at the very least, we cannot say, and this is very important, that the result of the excavations passes definitive judgment on the texts.

We find an example a contrario in the Volscians, a people who conquered a part of southern Latium during the historical era. If we had possessed only the evidence of archeology for this period (the fifth century B.C.E., hence clearly later than primordial Rome), in the absence of the very rich literary tradition conserved regarding that episode, an essential part of the history of Rome and Latium would have remained forever inaccessible to us.[23]

The ethnic concept remains necessary for understanding early Latium and the beginnings of Rome, but it must not be erected into an absolute, and its historical dimension must be recognized. The existence of different peoples and, in this case, of a Latin ethnos is not a given that imposes itself ready-made for analysis. We cannot speak of Latins in remote prehistory any more than we can speak of a French nation in reference to the Celts, the Gallo-Romans, the Franks, or the Burgundians, who all occupied the territory that, well after them, was called French.[24] Over the centuries, with the help of outside influences and the resistance they provoked, the ethnos took shape and became aware of itself, posited itself in opposition to other groups.

"Let whoever belongs to the city of Tadinum, to the tribe of Tadinum, to the Etruscan, Naharcian, or Iapygian nation remove himself from our people,"[25]

---

[20] Poucet, *Origines de Rome*, 143.

[21] That is, ever since the archeologist Müller-Karpe showed, in his fundamental *Vom Anfang Roms*, that there is no Sabine specificity in the material revealed by the site of Rome, contrary to what had been maintained until that time.

[22] Some researchers, however, do not despair of identifying a Sabine specificity in the archeological evidence. See Colonna, "I Latini," 452.

[23] Here again, there may be a few tenuous indexes (Colonna, "I Latini," 519), but they would no doubt have remained in the shadows without the aid of the literary tradition.

[24] See Pallottino, *Storia della prima Italia*, 44.

[25] Eugubine Tables, table VI b 52–55.

proclaimed the bronze tablets discovered at Gubbio, expressing the wish to see the stranger "flee full of terror, dejected, buried, covered with snow, with water, beaten, wounded, on the ground,"[26] all for the greater glory of the community of Gubbio of course. This was true for all the great "names" (in Latin, *nomen* refers both to the people and to the nation) that shared domination of central Italy: Latins, Etruscans, and Umbrians. In the narrative of origins, Latinus, mythical king of Latium, strongly opposed the Etruscan Mezentius, a legendary expression of a more general relation, which archeology continues to uncover. In that sense, it is fitting to grant renewed attention to this entire jumble of traditions, rich in vanished place-names and peoples, where the ancients went in search of prehistoric times. But, of course, we must not take the traditions literally.

Where antiquity, and thereafter a good part of modern historiography, saw timeless essences, modern science reconstitutes slow processes of formation. In the end, there is no more a Latin people in itself than there was a Roman plebs in itself, opposed for all eternity to a self-identical patriciate. After the bankruptcy of all the theories that, from the beginning of the nineteenth century, attempted to explain the antagonism between plebs and patriciate in terms of conflicts of race, nation, or social status, historians have shown that such antagonism emerged only progressively in the history of Rome, and that neither the plebs nor the patriciate was definitively constituted at the time of the last Tarquin's departure.[27] Identity comes about only through opposition to others.

For the first time in history, then, it is possible for archeology to situate the evolutions that saw the future city of Romulus slowly come into being over the course of centuries. Although it is hardly possible to perceive archeologically the existence of a Latin ethnos before the tenth century B.C.E. (and even that is only a hypothesis), this does mean that that date is to be taken as an absolute beginning. Let us therefore rapidly pass over the more ancient phases of the prehistory of the peninsula.[28] After the Neolithic (from the sixth to the third millennium B.C.E.), after the Aeneolithic and the beginning of the Bronze Age (up to the first centuries of the second millennium B.C.E.), the civilization whose epicenter lies in the Apennines saw the arrival, in the middle of the Bronze Age (from approximately the sixteenth to the fourteenth century B.C.E.) of the first Myceneans—traders or settlers?—whose influence was especially visible during the phase immediately following, the "sub-Apenninne" period (thirteenth and twelfth centuries B.C.E.). But the background shared by Etruscan and Latial civilizations took shape particularly during the Protovillanovan phase, which lasted

---

[26] Ibid., table VI b 58.

[27] See H. Last's article in *Journal of Roman Studies*, 1945, and Momigliano's essays in *Roma arcaica*. See especially J.-C. Richard, *Les origines de la plèbe romaine: Essai sur la formation du dualisme patricio-plébéien* (Rome and Paris, 1978).

[28] For these phases, we borrow the enumeration provided by Pallottino in *Storia della prima Italia*, 49.

until the ninth century B.C.E.. That was the soil from which sprang the branch of an archeological facies proper to the region of Latium.

As of that time, it is even possible to delimit chronological sequences for the most ancient history of Rome that are much more refined than for preceding periods. This result was made possible primarily by the pioneering work of Pinza, who divided the evolution of Latial civilization into two great periods, and then by the exceptional developments in archeological research in the last few years.

Since the middle of this century, Rome, like every great capital, has gradually transformed the territories that surround it into suburbs. It is a peaceful conquest of course, unlike the incessant wars Livy recounts, but, unlike the result of those wars, it is also irreversible, completely and definitively transforming the landscape. For many years, unfortunately, that advance occurred without any archeological supervision and produced irremediable destruction. An account of that destruction would, alas, be quite long.[29] As people became aware of the interest of the scientific and cultural issues of Latial archeology (often considered until then as a local and poor-quality variant of Etruscan archeology), systematic and regular excavations, and "salvage yards," multiplied.

The first great turning point came about when, in 1955, excavations were undertaken in Lavinium, on the site where Roman legend placed the landing of Aeneas. These were overseen by Lucos Cozza and Ferdinando Castagnoli. Pursued since then without interruption, they have uncovered a major city of archaic Latium. But it was the beginning of the 1970s, characterized by intense urbanization, that opened a new era. At that time, there were discoveries or excavations in Decima (1971), in the necropolis of Osteria dell'Osa (1971), in Gabii (1976), in La Rustica (1975), in Ficana (1975), in Acqua Acetosa Laurentina (1976), in Satricum (1977), and, finally, in the temple of Sant'Omobono in Rome, which was explored for the second time (it was discovered at the end of the 1930s) beginning the same date.[30] Thus the contemporary return to Rome, of which the excavations of the Palatine are the most striking manifestation, was preceded and anticipated by almost twenty years of intensive research in the rest of Latium.

These excavations and the analyses they allowed serve to better shed light on the shared culture and, no doubt, the shared civilization that linked Rome before it *was* Rome to the rest of the Latial region.

To fix the chronology, we must by definition possess a point of anchorage that allows us to detail by successive deductions the unfolding of the entire sequence. As it happens, that initial reference point is missing for the most

---

[29] See Quilici, *Roma primitiva*, 15–18. See also the catalog *Civiltà del Lazio primitivo* (Rome, 1976), 377–81 (by S. Quilici Gigli).

[30] We borrow this list from Colonna, "I Latini," 424–25.

ancient periods of Latial civilization.[31] We know that the Mycenean civilization ended in the twelfth century B.C.E., and we have the sure reference point of Greek colonization for the eighth century B.C.E. (whatever the variations of interpretation in the details). But, in relation to these two "chronological pillars," we can date the first manifestations of a specifically archeological facies of Latium only through a chain of deductions and hypotheses.

We may thus fix the beginning of the first Latial civilization at the dawn of the first millennium B.C.E., conceding that it is probable that the process of regional differentiation began during the two or three preceding centuries.[32]

For the whole of Latial civilization to which Rome belongs, four great phases are habitually distinguished between the end of the Bronze Age and the end of the so-called Orientalizing period in the sixth century B.C.E., so named because it was marked by eastern influences. The second and fourth of these phases are themselves divided in two.[33]

Thus, after the first two phases, called I and II A, which run, respectively, from 1000 to 900 B.C.E. and from 900 to 830 B.C.E., forming a unified totality, there is phase II B, which began in about 830 B.C.E. and ended in about 770 B.C.E. Phase III spanned the years 770 B.C.E. to 730/720 B.C.E., and thus covered the period during which, as we know, the literary tradition fixes the reign of Romulus and the foundation of Rome. Finally, phase IV includes two parts, the first running from 730/20 B.C.E. to 640/30 B.C.E., and the second from 640/30 B.C.E. until the 580s B.C.E.

It goes without saying that these dates are only approximations, obtained through long research and a chain of deductions; it is out of the question to assign them the status of events. It is nonetheless true that they provide an analytic framework for the beginnings of Rome, a framework that is much more solid and precise than the broad periodizations to which prehistorians are condemned. This is no doubt still the long term, with its play of lengthy developments and background tendencies, but we can nevertheless sketch a picture for each period considered. From one half-century to the next and, toward the end of the cycle, from one quarter-century to the next, the variations become visible.

According to the traditional conception, the term "history" applies to societies that possess writing, while "prehistory" refers to those that do not. For the periods immediately preceding the invention of writing, however, the development of archeology and the extraordinary refinement of knowledge that results

---

[31] This is highlighted by M. Pallottino in "Sulla cronologia dell'età del bronzo finale e dell'età del ferro in Italia," in his *Saggi di antichità* (Rome, 1979), 1: 95–127.

[32] For example, A. P. Anzidei, A. M. Bietti-Sestieri, and A. de Santis do not hesitate to assert this in their archeological survey *Roma e il Lazio dall'età della pietra alla formazione della città* (1985), 139.

[33] In its essentials, this classification comes from the German archeologist Müller-Karpe.

from it (of which Latial archeology offers a magnificent example) have made it necessary to introduce a new concept, "protohistory." It designates those times that were formerly relegated to the obscurity of prehistory, but that are now increasingly well known owing to the progress of archeology, as the example of Rome brilliantly demonstrates.

PART 3

AND ROME BECAME A CITY . . .

CHAPTER 9

VILLAGES, LEAGUES, AND FEDERATIONS

G USTAVE FLAUBERT SAID that every age is an age of transition:[1] what great truths lie in received ideas! Let us keep this truth well in mind in the face of these clearly delimited, precisely defined, and well-arranged chronological tables that provide early Rome with a temporal framework everyone can agree on. Are such chronological divisions disputable, and should we replace them with others better adapted to archeological reality? For nearly fifteen years, that is, between the publication of Heinrich Müller-Karpe's first writings at the end of the 1950s[2] and the 1976 exhibition in Rome on primitive Latium,[3] which secured the victory of the German archeologist's system, the battle raged between the advocates of a low chronology of Latial civilization, defended by the Swedish school and especially by the great archeologist Gjerstad,[4] and the defenders of the high chronology set in place by Müller-Karpe. Must we renew the debate and conclude in favor of Gjerstad rather than Müller-Karpe, as is now generally done?

There is no question of that: the high chronology described in the last chapter, due essentially to Müller-Karpe, has taken root for reasons that resist criticism. But however valid that chronology may be, it is still true that reliance on such a classification, however convenient and indispensable, is not devoid of ambiguities. These ambiguities do not lie in the details but are linked to the very principle that grounds any effort of this type. From this perspective, it is hardly important that one classification was adopted rather than the other, since, in both cases, everyone agreed to recognize several differentiated and successive chronological phases in the analysis of archeological material.

Of course, that classification, which resulted from the relentless efforts of several generations of scholars (it began early in this century with the work of Pinza),[5] in itself constituted enormous scientific progress and has become an extraordinary instrument of research and interpretation.

---

[1] Gustave Flaubert, *Dictionnaire des idées reçues* (Lille, 1988), article "Epoque (la nôtre). L'appeler époque de transition, de décadence."

[2] See Müller-Karpe, *Vom Anfang Roms*; and id., *Zur Stadtwerdung Roms*.

[3] See the exhibition catalog *Civiltà del Lazio primitivo*.

[4] See Gjerstad, *Early Rome*, in which all the archeological material from the primitive periods found in Rome appears.

[5] Pinza, *Monumenti primitivi di Roma e del Lazio antico*.

But a summary glance at the controversy that long divided the specialists on the question should not lead to a positivist reading of the conclusions that resulted. If, between two clearly opposed chronological systems, one held sway over the other, it was not because one was "true" and the other "false," but because one accounted for the totality of the parameters to be taken into consideration *better than* the other. Müller-Karpe's system, the basis for the chronology now accepted, however useful and productive it may be for research, is still an approximation.

In the first place, it was established in the 1950s, that is, *before* the large new excavations that, for the most ancient periods of Latial civilization in particular, multiplied tenfold the available documentation. For a long time, in fact, the specialists, in their overly passionate debates regarding questions of chronology, could refer only to a few dozen tombs belonging to partially known necropolises and, with the exception of those where Boni had operated, more plundered than excavated during the last century. In Rome, for example, in the Forum, about ten tombs on the site of the Arch of Augustus (that is, near the temple of the deified Caesar, in the center of the plaza), twenty-five near the temple of Antoninus and Faustina, and then, on the Palatine, an isolated tomb, were nearly the only traces of the most ancient periods of the city. From them, archeologists and historians had to reconstitute the process of the birth of the city of Romulus, occasionally appealing to a few tombs that had appeared elsewhere in Latium as isolated and enigmatic witnesses. Moreover, the archeologists of the time had not mastered the techniques of analysis that would have allowed them to identify the traces of settlements, which are always more difficult to distinguish on the terrain.[6] Archeology counted up the dead, but the precise and concrete conditions of life remained obscure.

That disparity has certainly not disappeared, but it has been attenuated, and here and there, the silhouette of the villages and hamlets where people who were not yet Romans lived, on the site of a Rome that did not yet exist, can be seen emerging from the mists of prehistoric times. The available documentation has thus grown considerably, owing to excavations, first in Latium, and now again in Rome. To take only one example, Osteria dell'Osa,[7] on the site of the ancient city of Gabii, where, according to legend, Romulus and Remus were sent to complete their education, has been methodically explored for nearly ten years and has provided no less than six hundred tombs. Given that the documentation has increased to that extent, certain analyses, already outdated, must undergo some adjustments, even though the recent finds confirm them in their main lines.

---

[6] This point and its consequences for the knowledge of primitive Latium have been convincingly argued by A. Guildi in an article in *Rivista di Archeologia*, 1982.
[7] See the bibliography at the end of this volume.

Even in cases where we do not wish to refine the fixed chronological frame-work, we must remember that it is only a theoretical framework, a method of research, and not an objective reality established once and for all and imposed on the analysis from the outside. Chronology is for archeology what the Linnaeus classification is for botany: both exist only as instruments of elabora-tion and expression for their sciences. Thus a chronological classification must remain what it is: a necessary hypothesis that is both accepted as valid and called into question, in a double movement that is not contradictory but complemen-tary. A chronological grid is not only the condition for the interpretations archeologists and historians make by examining the archeological documenta-tion, it is also the product of theories that themselves depend on a given state of documentation, soon outmoded by the progress of new excavations. This point is often lost. Sooner or later, the time comes when the initial model is con-fronted by such a large number of variants that it becomes necessary to reevaluate it in its very principle.

To schematize the two systems in question, we might say that while the universally adopted high chronology of the German school grants decisive importance to statistically significant recurrences, notably in the associations of types of objects found in each tomb, the low chronology of the Swedish school is more sensitive to the diversity revealed by the pottery and to local variations in it. Broadly speaking, one chronology favors the move from the general to the particular, while the other, now abandoned, took the reverse course.

Of course, going back in time is out of the question, and it is clear that the low chronology, which has the history of the Roman site begin "only" in the eighth century B.C.E.,[8] is no longer well founded. But although the specific results of the method must be abandoned, it seems increasingly clear that some of the considerations that inspired it deserve to be taken into consideration once more. The framework of Müller-Karpe's chronology will be retained, but also revised and broadened.

One example will suffice to show the necessity of perpetually calling into question the received truth, a method that is characteristic of any truly scien-tific approach.[9] The necropolis of the temple of Antoninus and Faustina (or rather the twenty-five tombs found there, which were no doubt part of a more extensive necropolis) contained some inhumation tombs and some cremation tombs. Theories of the last century interpreted this duality first as the traces of different races, and later as those of different peoples. The Sabines were sup-posed to have buried their dead, and the Romans or Latins to have cremated theirs; that funerary dualism served to "prove" the Romano-Sabine duality of earliest Rome, so often at issue in legend. More recently, the duality was taken

[8] Gjerstad has the first phase of his periodization begin early in the eighth century B.C.E.
[9] For the following reflections, I have drawn inspiration from A. M. Bietti-Sestieri's fundamen-tal "I dati archeologici di fronte alla teoria," *Dialoghi di Archeologia*, 1986, 249–63.

as a sign of different archeological "cultures." In what was a great step forward, Müller-Karpe proposed a strictly chronological reading, with inhumation preceding cremation.[10] But the new excavations of Osteria dell'Osa show that these two funerary customs were not successive but simultaneous, and the explanation for their diversity is ritual and not chronological in nature.

This means that archeological investigation can no longer be focused solely on chronological objectives. In the preceding chapters, we have seen the shift from the priority granted the art object to a conception of more extensive totalities, notably tombs, with archeologists classifying every object, the number of which can reach as high as a hundred. The modalities of association between objects (one type of vase with one type of weapon) served as Müller-Karpe's ground in establishing his chronology. As science multiplied its parameters and refined its problematics, the constants, used as monads and intangible absolutes, were broken up and further divided. For contemporary archeology, which considers the *primordia Romana* among its fields of choice, there remains nothing more of the notion of race, which in the past reigned supreme (in the division between Indo-Europeans and Mediterraneans), very little of peoples, and less and less of "culture," which still flourished only a short time ago. Similarly, the supremacy of "the site," considered an archeologically significant totality, has increasingly given way to the notions of "territory" and "environment," so that, there again, the case of Rome can and must no longer be dissociated from the examination of Latium taken as a whole. Similarly, establishing a chronology, however refined, cannot be the archeologist's or the historian's ultimate goal. Researchers are increasingly led to take an interest in the study of behaviors and, from there, in social and legal structures. Gradually, the entire life of the large towns of early Latium and its numerous and restless Latin tribes (*populi*)—which long included the inhabitants of the future Rome—has emerged, owing to the efforts of modern science with its richly diverse and proliferating areas of specialization.

Paradoxically, it is the technological development made possible by the use of computers that has raised the risk of rigidifying this still necessary evolution. On the luminescent screens of these miraculous little machines, which archeology for good reason puts to great use, the date attached to each of the catalogued objects is stripped of its hypothetical character and acquires a legitimacy, an obviousness, an objectivity—the weight of reality in short. The computer user is always tempted to take words (or numbers) for things, theory for fact, appearance for essence. Indisputably, this effect of reification induced by computers is one of the greatest challenges confronting archeology. Moreover, these new techniques orient archeology entirely toward the revived hope of a finally complete

---

[10] See, for example, Müller-Karpe's comments on the Forum necropolis in his *Vom Anfangs Roms*, 33 and 34: "We believe that the archeological data can clearly be interpreted in accord with legendary data."

documentation, a horizon that is without a doubt as chimerical as positivist history's old search for definitive causality. To respond to these challenges, we must therefore remain attentive to the complex and constant interlacing between spatial and temporal continuities and breaks, between diversities and uniformities, which are revealed in the study of a material whose volume grows almost daily. Diversity is not necessarily to be interpreted chronologically; conversely, uniformity is not the sign of chronological identity. Frequently, archeologists find objects, and even sets of objects, which were used for very long periods of time. This means that the notion of "culture" can no longer be considered pertinent from the chronological point of view. And even when they find in two different places groups of objects composed and structured in the same way, it is increasingly clear that the objects were used in different ways and that they conceal different customs and ways of acting and thinking. Thus, despite very strong apparent analogies, the Roman necropolis of the temple of Antoninus and Faustina, and the necropolises uncovered on the site of Gabii, reveal very different rites and practices, at least on certain points. In Rome (though Rome as such did not yet exist), for example, cremation seems to have been reserved for women, whereas in Gabii (or more precisely, in Osteria dell'Osa and Castiglione), it seems to have been the prerogative of men. Only the anthropological analysis made possible by the new excavations, inaccessible in the last century with its exclusive concern for the art object, has allowed us to reach that conclusion. In that case as well, the data now in our possession were not available in 1950–1960.

The Swedish school insisted upon the idea of a great diversity of practices, in places sometimes quite close to each other. There is nothing in this idea that ought to surprise us. After all, in the middle of nineteenth-century France, with the Industrial Revolution well under way, Alexandre Dumas, arriving in the capital from his native Villers-Cotterêts, noted with humor, in reference to a youthful misadventure, that Villers-Cotterêts fashions were unfashionable in Paris.[11]

In reconstituting the image of earliest Rome, which can be done in large part only through comparison with nearby sites that are better known archeologically, we must not forget the infinite diversity of times, places, and beliefs, which the archeologist's and historian's rigorous and rigid classifications have a tendency to conceal. The narrative of origins, as the Romans of antiquity transmitted it from generation to generation, is also full of traps and illusions for anyone attempting to discern what Rome was before it was Rome.

The classical tradition as we find it in Livy, Virgil, and Dionysius of Halicarnassus places the foundation of Alba by Ascanius between the foundation of Lavinium by Aeneas, come from Troy to fulfill his destiny in Latium, and the foundation of Rome by Romulus. Lavinium, Alba Longa, Rome—three

---

[11] Alexandre Dumas, *Mes mémoires,* rev. ed. (Paris, 1986), 260: "I was at the height of fashion in Villers-Cotterêts, and at the height of last year's fashion in Paris."

names, three cities, three moments in the canonical history of origins. In Rome itself, legend has the Arcadian Evander precede Aeneas and settle on the site of the Palatine before the Trojan hero.

There remains almost nothing of this grandiose symphony in three movements. In fact, it is not even enough to modify the order of that series and place Alba or Rome first, for example. It is the very idea of such an evolution that must be challenged in its principle, in the light of several decades of archeological research and discoveries. First of all, in this artistically arranged triptych, one of the three tableaux has proved to be only a trompe l'oeil: Alba Longa, as we have already noted, existed as a city only in and through the mirages of a legendary composition intentionally and subtly retouched. When we reread without bias the numerous classical "witnesses" to the metropolis on Mons Albanus,[12] we can only be struck by the fact, extremely surprising at first glance, that they do not agree among themselves and reveal a complete ignorance (and for good reason) on the part of the ancient authors regarding the exact location of the mythical city. Sometimes, most frequently, they situate it on Monte Cavo itself, whose imposing mass dominates the waters of the lake in which its silhouette is reflected; sometimes they seem to locate it on the opposite shore, which is today occupied by the village of Castel Gandolfo; and sometimes, in fact, they do not allow for any identification whatever. The only truly precise text is by Dionysius of Halicarnassus, who writes in book 1 of his *Antiquitates romanae* (Roman antiquities) that "when this city was founded, it was built near a mountain and a lake, in the space between the two, which constituted ramparts as it were for the city, making its conquest difficult."[13]

It is curious that the most detailed classical text is the one whose evidence has been the least heeded, with moderns generally placing the city of Ascanius, son of Aeneas and founder of Alba according to legend, on the other side of the lake, facing the site described by Dionysius. On that site today, the summer residence of popes rises up, the successor to an imperial villa where Emperor Domitian made frequent stays, in a place neither too close to nor too far from his capital. The hesitations on the part of the ancients are amplified in the multiple proposals for the site made by moderns. None of these hypotheses has led to agreement, but each at the very least serves to shed light on the difficulties arising for the adoption of the others. To place trust in Dionysius, researchers have to set aside the most numerous and most ancient sources on the matter; if, on the contrary, they wish to follow these others, they cannot take into account the only complete description that has been conserved, that of Dionysius.

There is only one way out of this double bind, and that is to abandon the notion of reading the tradition literally, but without challenging it as a whole.

---

[12] In the following pages, I borrow the results of research published under the title "La localisation d'Albe," in *Mélanges de l'Ecole Française de Rome* 98 (1986): 47–90.

[13] Dion. Hal. *Ant. rom.* 1.66.

This means not hesitating perpetually between condemnation and acquittal, but rather taking into account the tradition as an element that is historically significant by its very existence, and seeking to explain it in terms of its progressive formation and elaboration. In legend, Alba emerges from the void only to immediately disappear once more; it is hardly mentioned except in reference to its destruction by Tullus Hostilius, king of Rome, which supposedly took place in the seventh century B.C.E. To understand that tradition without immediately rejecting it as false and historically unfounded, on the pretext that it does not seem to be archeologically founded, we must begin with one of the most important religious manifestations of early Latium, the most important perhaps. These were the Feriae Latinae, which for several days every year brought together Latin peoples on the summit of Monte Cavo. The mountain was occupied by the sanctuary of their common god, Juppiter Latiaris, that is, Jupiter of the Latiar, the great feast of the Latins. That grand solemnity was both religious and political, since on that occasion the participants reinforced their feeling of belonging to a common group, the *nomen latinum*, and established relations among themselves. These relations were facilitated by "God's truce," which was imposed on them during the festivities, celebrated throughout the history of Rome and until the end of the Empire. From the beginning to the end of Roman antiquity, the annual return of this holiday was one of the surest signs of the continuity of a civilization. When it finally stopped being celebrated, the Rome of Romulus did not have long to live.

But this great "national" gathering, which became the expression of Rome's power when the city on the banks of the Tiber conquered all of Latium (this was definitively achieved in 338 B.C.E.), had a humble origin. In prehistoric times, before the territory of Latium had any cities but was populated by mere villages and hamlets made up of a few wood and cob huts, the feast of the Latin god Jupiter, on the highest mountain of the region, was the nerve center of the Latin federation, regrouping in the same alliance all the Latin tribes, some of which occupied the site of the future Rome. With time, political ties loosened, and each component of the federation asserted its autonomy, though the religious ceremony was not abandoned. In other words, the federation dated from a time when cities did not yet exist in Latium. But the absence of urban life on such a religiously prestigious and important place did not fail to astonish the Romans of the classical age, who saw their magistrates and the entire population of the city going every year in procession to a place situated in the countryside. To their eyes, this isolated sanctuary could only have been the principal temple of a city destroyed by Tullus Hostilius.[14] Like nature, the mythic mind abhors a vacuum. When it found a holy place of federal and preurban origin, it invented a city, inferring its destruction so as to be better able to establish its existence.

---

[14] Note that Poucet, beginning from completely different methods and assumptions than my own, arrived at the same conclusion on this point. See Poucet, *Origines de Rome*, 295.

In fact, archeology seemed to confirm the lesson of the traditional narrative. Based on the tombs found near Castel Gandolfo, nineteenth-century archeologists believed they could restore a unique and central site corresponding to the seat of the mythical metropolis. The actual remains of Alba were never identified, despite several centuries of investigation in the field, but that was merely additional evidence of the veracity of the tradition, which held that Alba had been completely destroyed by the Romans of Tullus Hostilius, with the exception of its temples. In that way, the absence of archeological evidence was simply one more piece of evidence for a fideist reading of the narrative of origins.

What we now know about the inhabitants of primitive Latium and earliest Rome suggests another reading, which cannot be reduced to hypercritical negation. On the contrary, it entails giving historical value to the legend, but a value that does not conceal the legendary dimension. That reading is no longer immediate and literal but is grounded in a hermeneutics attentive to the particular characteristics of the source.

Since 1816, the date of the first finds near Castel Gandolfo, discoveries have multiplied and spread. Above all, other analogous sites have been explored, including the site of Rome, inasmuch as that was possible. The lives of the early Romans, at a time when they did not yet bear that name, are incomparably better known to us now than they were even a few years ago, owing in particular to nearby and similar sites such as Gabii (Osteria dell'Osa), Lavinium, and Ficana.

What does a study of these sites show? That in the most ancient phases of Latial civilization, generally from the tenth (or eleventh) to the eighth century B.C.E., there did not exist an urban center anywhere, in whatever sense we wish to give to the word "urban." There were still only groups of dispersed huts (modern archeology has been able to identify settlements, which was not possible in the last century) near bodies of water or natural paths of communication. Alba was not destroyed, because it never existed as a city. But that does not at all mean that it had no historical reality. Rather, it was a federation, not a city; and Rome also experienced that phase of development. The memory of these primordial forms of society was conserved for religious reasons by the Romans, who continued to participate in the Feriae Latinae. But, in being conserved, that memory was also transformed to fit the dominant model of the city. In fact, Rome became a city, which was then to be *the* city par excellence, whereas Alba, its legendary metropolis, did not get beyond the stage of federation. It would be wrong to call that stage preurban, since, in that case at the very least, it did not lead to the formation of an urban center, in contrast to what happened in Rome.

In fact, the memory of that ancient federation persists in the very name of Alba, which was that of the zone where, on the banks of Lake Albano, settlements were dispersed at a distance of a few kilometers from each other and shared a life in the shadow of their federal sanctuary. The legendary city founded by Ascanius bore the name Alba Longa not, as Livy believed, because of "its position the entire length of a hillside,"[15] which would have made it a kind of prehistoric road village, but rather because it was a group of hamlets, both topographically dispersed and religiously and politically united, in a zone stretching out *lengthwise,* Alba *Longa,* around the lake and at the foot of a mountain evoked by the root of the place-name Alba (which we frequently find used to designate peaks—for example, in the name of the French "Alps"). Alba Longa, the site of a sparse and fragmentary settlement, was never a city. Cicero, in a famous passage of *Pro Milone,* speaks simply of "regions" (*regiones*), "sacred Alban hills and woods." That zone, consecrated and, so to speak, "fossilized" over the centuries by the perpetuation of very ancient religious ceremonies, was traversed by a road called the *via Latina,* which led to the sanctuary of Jupiter. That name is not the name of a city, as is the case for other Roman roads, but rather of a region, because there never was a city near Mons Albanus, and the mountain must logically be considered the heart of the most ancient Latium. Hence Alba Longa and its lake were the crucible in which Latium forged its unity and its identity, in accordance with a process similar to that which saw Switzerland come into being around the Lake of the Four Forest Cantons.

But in that case wouldn't it be simpler to take the legend literally? Not really, since we would then have to take from Castel di Decima and Ficana what we grant to the example of Alba. For these two centers, and especially Ficana, the classical literary tradition, which speaks of destruction by the Romans, is contradicted by archeology. These sites were still vital *after* the date of their supposed destruction. If we wish to maintain a fideist reading of the tradition, we must decide that, in one case, it is to be reinterpreted (Ficana), and, in the other (Alba), taken literally. In other words, the "destruction" of Castel di Decima and Ficana would be understood in an exclusively metaphorical sense, whereas the "destruction" of Alba, attributed by legend to Tullus Hostilius, would have to be accepted as a fully historical event. This means that the fideist exegesis of the tradition does not even have the merit of simplicity and coherence, compared to what we consider an indispensable hermeneutics. In reality, it is necessary to reckon with the entire complexity of the legend in each particular case.

Moreover, how could we accept the Lavinium-Alba-Rome schema set in place by the narrative of origins, when we see that Roman soil has provided remains that hardly differ from those found elsewhere in Latium, on the sites mentioned, including remains with a striking resemblance to those of the Alban Hills? Identical archeological material exists in both cases, on the banks of Lake Albano; the remains, if not of a city then at least of a preurban center on the banks of the Tiber, would thus have to be interpreted simply as the traces of a few isolated settlements. Not only must the legendary image of an Alban

---

[15] "Ab situ porrectae in dorso urbis" (Livy *Ab urbe condita* 1.3).

metropolis be reinterpreted and not accepted as such, but the anteriority of Alba and Lavinium in relation to Rome, though asserted by the literary tradition, has not been proved by archeology. There was no city of Alba, and Rome is as old as its two so-called metropolises.

Must we then abandon legend and definitively take our leave from it? No, since even when it lies, legend continues to tell the truth. Confronted with a religious and federal preeminence that, as time went on, became incomprehensible and inexplicable in any other way, legend, under the influence of Greek historiography no doubt, translated it into chronological and colonial terms. Lavinium and Alba were placed *before* Rome, and Rome was seen as a colony of these two "metropolises."[16] Thus legend transformed the original elements (names in particular) of a vanished reality more than it misrepresented them.

Owing to recent discoveries made elsewhere in Latium, we can retrace the image of the site of Rome before Rome existed, provided we take our distance from nineteenth-century hypotheses overly marked by the urban model. Too often, historians linked evidence uncovered at some site of the modern city directly and without hesitation to an early entity granted the expanse and unity that characterize the city in historical times. That entailed forgetting that although they emerged from Roman soil, these remains were not Roman. For the most ancient periods, they attest to the existence not of a great unified totality, but of villages independent from one another, separated at times by waterways, at other times by valleys. Since antiquity, the growth of what is now a capital city has transformed these natural features into paved streets lined with buildings. Originally, the *via Sacra,* for example, was very probably only the bed of a small torrent whose waters came down from neighboring hills, which were markedly steeper than they are today.[17]

Where were the most ancient vestiges of these first Roman villages found? It goes without saying that this question has no meaning or usefulness unless we take into account the historical development of the Eternal City and its archeological consequences. When nothing is found in a particular place, it is not always because it was uninhabited; it may be because no one ever found out about what was exhumed, sometimes from antiquity on. In this area more than others, what specialists call the argument *e silentio* must be handled with care.

This became very clear when, for several years, people believed they could safeguard the relative chronology of Lavinium, Alba, and Rome postulated by the literary tradition based on the absence of archeological evidence in Rome for the periods prior to the initial phases of Latial civilization. True, in the Forum, Boni's discoveries had revealed tombs full of hut-urns similar to those

---

[16] This was also Heurgon's interpretation in *Rome et la Méditerranée occidentale*, 75.

[17] As recent studies have shown, that was the case, for example, for Velia Hill. See N. Terrenato, "Velia and Carinae: Some Observations on an Area of Archaic Rome," forthcoming in *Papers in Italian Archaeology*.

brought to light in the Alban Hills, but the site of Rome did not seem to have been inhabited before the age to which these remains belonged, unlike other sites of Latium, Lavinium in particular.[18] There, excavations identified "sub-Apennine" shards at the end of the 1960s. It thus became very tempting to see in that apparent chronological gap a confirmation of the antecedence of Lavinium over Rome, postulated by the narrative of origins.

We now know, however, that the site of Rome was inhabited as early as Lavinium: practicing the archeology of archeology mentioned earlier, specialists have recently realized, in reexamining the product of excavations executed a few decades ago at the site of the Regia, or "royal palace," located in the Forum, that in the most ancient stratigraphical layers were pottery fragments of the "sub-Apennine" era, going back to the Bronze Age.[19] As a result, the legendary chronological priority of Lavinium has to be reinterpreted, no doubt in religious terms. Subsequently, as yet incomplete excavations begun in 1987 have confirmed the existence in the zone occupied by the Regia and the temple of Vesta of a settlement going back to the first phases of Latial civilization (tenth century B.C.E.) and occupied until the seventh century B.C.E.[20] In reality, its presence could already be inferred from the necropolis that Boni found near the temple of Antoninus and Faustina, which includes twenty-five tombs dating from the first two periods of Latial civilization, in other words, from the tenth and ninth centuries B.C.E.

Not far from there, a study of the remains found earlier under what is called the Arch of Augustus[21] (that is, on the right flank of the temple of the deified Julius Caesar in the center of the Forum, on the site where the dictator's body was carried on a pyre by a mad and weeping crowd) shows traces dating back to the Late Bronze Age (that is, the thirteenth century B.C.E.). Much later, that same site contained a necropolis, beginning in the tenth century B.C.E., in other words, during the most ancient phases of Latial civilization properly speaking. If these are truly vestiges of an early village, which is far from certain, that substitution can be explained solely by natural causes; for the valley of the Forum was at the time subject to strong floods caused by the nearby Tiber.

Nevertheless, the very length of time that the site was abandoned before then (at least a century) could lead us to think, in accord with an inference made

---

[18] See P. Sommella, "Lavinium, Rinvenimenti preistorici e protostorici," *Archeologia Classica* 21 (1969): 18–33.

[19] See R. Peroni, "L'insediamento subappenninico della valle del foro e il problema della continuità di insediamento tra l'étà del bronzo recente e quella finale nel Lazio," *Archeologia Laziale* 2 (1979): 171–76. Cf. A. J. Ammerman, "On the Origins of the Forum Romanum," *American Journal of Archeology* 94 (1990): 627–45.

[20] See R. I. Scott, "Regia-Vesta," *Archeologia Laziale* 9 (1988): 23. Scott speaks of "the hut settlement of the Forum where this summer [July 1987] a limited number of trustworthy new traces were found farther to the south, toward Vesta." He then analyzes material dating from Latial phases I and II.

[21] Peroni, "L'insediamento subappeninnico," 173–74.

by the archeologist Renato Peroni, of "causes independent of natural events," in other words, of human intervention, part of the long, complex, and tortuous process that led to the birth of Rome. The question then arises of where to situate the settlement corresponding to the tombs of the Arch of Augustus, which date from the beginning of Latial civilization (that is, the tenth century B.C.E.). Some considered the Palatine, and to be more precise, the Germalus, but in that case, the reasoning has to confront the absence of documentation—an absence that, let us repeat, is not conclusive in the case of Rome. If we truly wish to restrict ourselves to the archeological facts (but they are no less fragile than the historical "facts," whose theoretical consistency fell apart under the blows of the Annales school), we might consider the remains of huts near the temple of Vesta and the Regia. In that hypothesis, however, the necropolis of the temple of Antoninus and Faustina finds itself without a corresponding settlement . . .

Only recently, more precious evidence of the first villages on the Roman site have come to light. At the base of the Capitol, looking out over the Forum but integrated into the mass of the hill, there is an austere edifice, constructed by the Romans during Sulla's time to serve as an archive repository (*tabularium*), whose beautiful archways, recently restored, provide a majestic backdrop for the Arch of Septimius Severus. Of these archives, which consisted of bronze tablets, nothing has survived (except an insignificant military diploma found in the 1920s), and the archways of the Tabularium now shelter only the great void of dead centuries. But, in another way, the Tabularium has guarded the Roman archives well. A few years ago, archeologists found in its foundations a few pottery shards from the very beginning of the Iron Age (about the ninth century B.C.E.), shards that very probably belong to a village situated on the Capitol.[22]

Below it, at the foot of the Arch of Septimius Severus, where Boni discovered the Lapis Niger, later investigations by Pietro Romanelli[23] (conducted in 1955–1956 but published only in 1984) revealed, beneath the level of the famous archaic inscription, a natural basin where the waters descending from the neighboring hills collected. Other bodies of water of that nature existed at the time in the valley of the Forum, some of which persist, such as the Pond of Curtius or the Spring of Juturna; but the basin clearly played the role of a great drinking trough, where herds of pigs, sheep, and cattle (identified by the remains of bones left on the site) gathered. Yes, history is eternal return, for at the origin, the Forum Romanum was what it became again centuries later, after the end of the Roman Empire and the retrenchment of medieval Rome: a cattle ground or Campo Vaccino. Old engravings have left us a depiction of the place, with, precisely, a drinking trough two steps from the Arch of Septimius Severus!

---

[22] See A. M. Sommella, "L'esplorazione archeologica per il restauro del Tabularium," *Archeologia Laziale* 6 (1984): 159–63.

[23] See *Monumenti antichi pubblicati dall'Academia dei Lincei* (Rome, 1984), vol. 52.

The most ancient traces of occupation left on the site of Rome are the vestiges collected during the various excavations executed near the church of Sant'Omobono, one of the richest sites of archaic Rome (the remains of a great temple have been uncovered there, apparently one of the two that the tradition attributes to King Servius Tullius on that site). There is evidence going back to the beginning of the Middle Bronze Age, in other words, to the *sixteenth* century B.C.E.[24] Since they appear in clods of dirt brought in from elsewhere, these shards cannot indicate the existence of a settlement at the precise location where they were found, that is, at the bottom of the Capitol. They are to be linked, in fact, to a village situated on the Capitol itself, on the spurs facing Tiber Island and at the curve in the river at that point in its course. To limit ourselves to the archeological realities themselves, the most ancient vestiges of settlement on the site of Rome during the protohistorical era were found there and nowhere else.

Let us now attempt in a few words, based on the evidence just described, to retrace the region's evolution, from this first human settlement in the Middle Bronze Age to the constellation of villages that immediately preceded the foundation of Rome by Romulus.

Given what we have said about the Roman site,[25] it is probably not surprising to note that the first stable settlement took shape, to judge in any case from the existing indexes, near the river and the island that made Rome a "first bridge" city, that is, one that offers anyone coming from the coast the first possibility for crossing the river. The settlement may have been that of a sedentary population, but it is more probable for that period that the site was occupied only intermittently by a population of seminomadic herders. We can reasonably suppose, however, that the Capitol Hill was more or less continuously occupied during the following periods, since remains going back to the beginnings of the Iron Age can be linked to it. This is not the side of the hill facing the Tiber, but the part that dominates the Forum, and there was not just one settlement covering the entire hillside, but several hamlets distinct from one another.

After the Capitol, human occupation seems to have extended toward the valley of the Forum beginning in the thirteenth century B.C.E., with the vestiges of the Arch of Augustus and of the Regia dating from the "sub-Apennine" era. These vestiges may have also come from the nearby hills. A period of abandonment followed: at the beginning of the tenth century, at the dawn of Latial civilization, the Forum was a space for the dead. But we must not think, as some have done even very recently, that this funerary practice was exclusive, since, beneath the Regia and the temple of Vesta, archeologists have identified traces of huts, some of which go back to the initial phases of Latial chronology (that is, to the tenth century B.C.E.). There again, we must look to the neighboring hills,

---

[24] See the proceedings of the colloquium entitled "Lazio arcaico e mondo greco" in *La Parola del Passato* 35 (1974) (essay by L. Daminato).

[25] See above, chap. 6.

the Velia and the Palatine, for the settlements corresponding to the tombs; but again, it is not necessary to think that the hills were entirely occupied by those villages. For the Palatine, for example, the discovery of a tomb from the Iron Age (tenth century B.C.E.) under the House of Livia, of a tomb that was probably not isolated but part of a necropolis, in other words, of a space necessarily apart from the spaces reserved for the living, implies that the villages that may have been located on the hill were separated from one another. This is indicated by the fact that ancient toponymy differentiated between several peaks for each of Rome's hills.[26] As far as we can judge from an analysis of the horizontal stratigraphy of the Forum necropolis (that is, from a study of the spatial distribution of tombs by their date), it seems that the progression of what was not yet Rome moved from west to east, beginning at the Tiber (and the Capitol) and heading toward the Velia. Such are the conclusions we can draw from a complex, confused, and fragmentary documentation, endlessly divided as we are between the need to restrict ourselves to the actually observed facts and the no less pressing need to make adequate inferences and generalizations.

Considering that evolution as a whole, we are struck by the fact that the site of Rome was continuously occupied; and, indisputably, such continuity could only have been intentional, even though Rome as a unified organism did not yet exist. Hence the birth of the city of Rome came about on a site that had already been occupied for a very long time. Settling first along the natural paths of communication, the inhabitants regrouped on the hills, no doubt fleeing the frequent floods (attested to archeologically by numerous layers of alluvion), and probably also searching for better security (the weapons appearing in the tombs at the end of the Bronze Age are an index of the importance of war for these small communities). On the Capitol, the Palatine, the Velia, and soon the Quirinal,[27] villages of wooden huts were set up, sheltered by more or less summary enclosures. Each evening, members of a small number of families gathered, each family under the authority of a clan leader, who protected the community, the possessions, and the animals from outside dangers.[28] Certain cities in Latium and nearby Etruria retained the trace of this system of sparse settlements not yet integrated into a single organization; this trace persisted even into the historical era, in the plural form of the cities' names. Such was the case, for example, for Gabii, Veii, Tarquinii (Tarquinia), Bovillae (near Lake Albano),

---

[26] That was the case for the Capitol, the Palatine, and the Quirinal.

[27] In fact, the two tombs from the Iron Age discovered near the Forum of Augustus indicate the very probable existence of a settlement on the nearby Quirinal. See Gjerstad, *Early Rome*, 2: 269 and 4: 39. At another settlement on the Quirinal three tombs were found near the Church of Saint Sylvester.

[28] The recent excavations of Osteria dell'Osa allow us to know the precise conditions of life in this type of hut village. See A. M. Bietti-Sestieri, *Preistoria e protostorica nel territorio di Roma* (Rome, 1984), 160–95; and the Turin exhibition catalog *Ricerca su una comunità del Lazio protostorico* (1980).

and Velitrae (Velletri). In fact, that was also the case for many Greek cities, in particular Athens (Athenae), whose inhabitants in the third century B.C.E. still remembered that their ancestors had lived in towns and small separate villages ("pagatim habitantes in parvis illis castellis vicisque," wrote Livy)[29] before joining together into a single city.

The toponymy, or more exactly the liturgy, of Rome also retained traces of that plurality and that dispersion of primitive settlements. In the holiday called Septimontium, which the Romans continued to celebrate even in the historical era, a certain stage of Rome's development was reflected. In Rome, the future city was still made up only of villages and hamlets distinct from one another, but maintaining neighborly relations, as is natural, leading to gatherings and exchanges during regular holiday times, placed under the protection of shared deities. Modern scholars have been able to establish that the Septimontium was a procession, probably designed to purify the territory it delimited.[30] The feast of the "seven hills" (*septem montes*)[31] does not correspond, as was later believed,[32] to the canonical seven hills of Rome (that is, the Palatine, the Quirinal, the Viminal, the Esquiline, the Caelian, the Aventine, and the Capitol), but to a more limited group. The identity of these seven hills was established by the research of scholars of antiquity, who were eager to shed light on a very old ceremony still taking place during their time.[33] We thus know that the Septimontium comprised the Palatine, the Velia, the Fagutal, the Subura, the Germalus, the Caelian, the Oppian, and the Cispius, or, in other words, three main hills—the Palatine (with its western part, the Germalus), the Velia (the hill that disappeared in great part in the 1930s as a result of the Imperial Fora road cut through it), and the Esquiline (with its three faces, Oppian, Cispius, and Fagutal)—and one valley (the Subura). Ancient authors also tell us that a sacrifice called Palatuar was celebrated on the Palatine and the Velia. That is all we can know a priori about what was for a very long time, in classical Rome, only a fossil holiday, evidence of a completely vanished state of affairs. Other indexes, however, allow us to know just a little more about that Rome of villages, the memory of which is conserved in the Septimontium.

When are we to situate the Septimontium? It goes without saying that the question has meaning only if we take into account the continuity of occupation

---

[29] Livy *Ab urbe condita* 21.30.

[30] See C. Ampolo, "La città arcaica e le sue feste: Due ricerche sul Septimontium e sull'equus october," *Archeologia Laziale* 4 (1981): 233–40 (with bibliography); and A. Fraschetti's essay in the journal *Studi Storici* (1984): 35–54.

[31] It seems that the prefix *septi-* in the name of the Septimonium holiday is not to be understood as a passive participle signifying "enclosed" (*saepti*), contrary to what was long believed. See L. Najo's argument in the *Actes du Colloque international: E. Benveniste aujourd'hui* (Paris, 1984).

[32] For example, Varro, who wrote that "the day of the Septimontium is called that after the seven hills where the city is located" (*Ling.* 6.24). See also Lydus *Mens.* 4.155.

[33] See Festus *De verborum significatu* 458 and 476.

we have noted on the Roman site and the fluidity it necessarily implies. A religious holiday cannot be dated like a battle, since it is the expression of a given stage of civilization, not an event. That holiday brought out peasants from the hills, not citizens: "A holiday not for the people, but only for the folk from the mountains."[34] That remark, attributed to Varro, a great Roman scholar of antiquity, assumes all its meaning when we remember that "people" (*populus*) is the precise and technical term used to designate the citizens of the city constituted as a group, that is, a new form of society, whose unity and organization contrasted with the diversity and autonomy of the populations that had remained faithful to older ways of life.

At a time close to the origin of the Septimontium, the Romans, or more exactly, those who inhabited the site of the future Rome, were not citizens, members of a unified community aware of itself. They were only *montani,* folk living on hills (*monte*), who, of course, knew one another and had regular relations among themselves but did not yet follow a common destiny. In particular, the fact that the Palatine did not appear in the Septimontium as a single and unique place points to a period prior to the foundation of Palatine Rome and the new unity that resulted from it.[35] Historians long believed that the Palatine foundation could only have been an original stage (that was the opinion in the nineteenth century), and that is why they felt obliged to place the Septimontium *after* the foundation of Rome, but all the same *before* the truly urbanized Rome, which the tradition traces to the end of the regal period. We now know that the Palatine foundation was in no way an absolute starting point; moreover, new elements seem to show that, in accordance with the tradition, it can be placed at the midpoint of the eighth century B.C.E. It thus becomes both possible and necessary to push the date of the Septimontium back by an equal number of years; it should be placed *before* the foundation of Rome properly speaking. Afterwards, in fact, there is no reference to Septimontium, but only to Rome. And the fact that the list of the seven hills includes Caelian and Esquiline is the sign not of a primacy definitively assured the Palatine and already extended to neighboring hills, but, conversely, of a preeminence that is only in the process of formation and that allows zones on the margins of what was not yet the heart of the system (Palatine-Velia) to assert themselves. At that stage, it would be wrong to define these zones as mere satellites, since at the time they were only at the beginning of their development. The Palatine and the Velia already played a role more important than the other hills, since they were apparently the only ones where the sacrifice of the Palatuar was celebrated, but this was in no sense an exclusive role.

Under such conditions, during what period can we place the Septimontium? Or rather, what stage of development of the Roman site does the Septi-

---

[34] "Feriae non populi sed montanorum modo."
[35] We borrow a remark from Momigliano, *Roma arcaica,* 24. See also pp. 60 and 80.

montium symbolize? It was a phase when the settlements were on the hills; when, of course, the Forum had not yet appeared as such; and when, beginning from the Palatine-Germalus pole, in contact with the approaches of the river, a system took shape that was oriented toward the northeast, made up of the Caelian and the Esquiline (which includes Fagutal, Subura, Cispius, and Oppian). The tombs of the Forum date from the first two periods of Latial civilization, and these tombs are linked to settlements situated primarily on the Palatine and the Velia. Afterwards, beginning at the end of the ninth century B.C.E., the valley of the Forum no longer welcomed anything but children's tombs next to huts; conversely, the first tombs began to appear on the Esquiline, at the site of what would be the large necropolis of archaic Rome.[36] Between these two concomitant phenomena, despite what has sometimes been said, it is difficult not to establish a relation of cause and effect. The development of the Esquiline necropolis must no doubt be interpreted as the index of the existence of a new entity, already vaster and more substantial than the Septimontium (which included none of the hills situated beyond the Cispius and remained within relatively modest limits). The attempts at reconstitution by modern scholars focus on an area of about 125 acres.[37] The Septimontium procession did not pass through the territory of a city; it ignored the distinction between the sacred space constituted in antiquity by any city and the rest of the world, where the civic community relegated its dead, so as not to taint the city by their presence. That distinction became fundamental later on and took on material form with the pomerium attributed to Romulus. But at the time of the Septimontium, that essential separation, which translated into the placing of tombs on the Esquiline, had not yet occurred; both tombs and huts, it seems, were adjacent to the Forum.

Thus it was not yet a city developing in the territory of the future Rome, but rather a league establishing ties between its members, ties that did not rule out a great freedom of action. It is therefore no accident that the sacrifice celebrated by the *montani* on that holiday was called the Palatuar, a name that so closely evokes the Latiar of the peoples of Alba. Moreover, we must no doubt consider the inhabitants of the principal villages of the Septimontium to have been the Velienses, who we know participated in the oldest Feriae Latinae.[38] The Septimontium league included neither the Capitol nor the Quirinal,[39] two hills that were nonetheless inhabited from the beginnings of Latial civilization. That is precisely because the foundation of Rome had not yet taken place, a foundation whose principal characteristic, according to tradition, was to unite in a single group communities that until then had been separate, hostile, and

---

[36] On the Esquiline necropolis, see the catalog *Civiltà del Lazio primitivo*, 125ff.
[37] See Ampolo, "La città arcaica," 234.
[38] According to Pallottino's hypothesis. See *Saggi di antichità*, 1: 239–41.
[39] As Dominique Briquel reminds us in *Histoire de Rome* (forthcoming).

rivalrous. There may be no direct archeological proof of a Sabine specificity to the origins of Rome (in any case, there is never any direct archeological "proof"), but the insistence of the literary sources in presenting the Capitol and the Quirinal as typically "Sabine" hills, combined with the absence of these hills on the list of the Septimontium, does not appear to be fortuitous. Before the fusion of Latin and Sabine elements, or, to set aside any allusion to the legend of origins, before the inclusion of the Palatine, the Capitol, the Quirinal, and the Esquiline in a single entity, Rome was not a city but a league, and the Septimontium was not the first manifestation of a future city, but a celebration at the end of the sowing season, in December of each year.[40] Modern science, with its concern for distinctions that did not even exist in ancient reality, has decreed that the solidarity expressed by that holiday was "political" in nature. And in fact, as time passed, the constellation of villages that at the time occupied the site of an eternal city that did not yet exist fell sway to forces of attraction and gravitation that, one day, finally gave birth to a new totality, to which the name Rome could be given for the first time.

---

[40] Wheat and barley were sown in November, beans in December. A Latin agronomist tells us that "pars ultima [sementi] quae septimontialis satio dicitur" (a part of the [bean] seeds must be thrown toward the middle of the sowing season and another part at the end. This second sowing is called septimontial" (Columella *Rust.* 2.10.8).

CHAPTER 10

BIRTH OF THE CITY

"WE MUST NOT FORM our idea of the city of Rome in its beginnings based on the cities we see today." More than two and a half centuries after Montesquieu wrote these words at the beginning of his *Considérations sur les causes de la grandeur des Romains et de leur décadence* (Considerations on the causes of the greatness of the Romans and of their decadence) (1734), they are charged with new weight and significance, in the light of the most recent excavations and research on the origins of Rome, whose foundation was attributed by tradition to Romulus. Rome is called an eternal city, but it ought rather to be known as a city eternally rebegun and refounded, endlessly taking on new forms throughout its history of many millennia. It is easy to accept the fact that the Rome of Michelangelo and that of Victor Emmanuel II were profoundly different from each other. But we too often forget that between the Rome of the "Romulean" period and that of the time when the temple dedicated to the Castores was built in the Forum by the dictator Aulus Postumius Albinus, there were equally significant differences, as well as a similar elapse of time.[1] Consider, then, the half-millennium that separates the first huts found near the Arch of Augustus[2] from those brought to light by the archeologist Vaglieri on the Palatine at the beginning of this century.[3] The ancients were obscurely aware that the history of their city consisted of such perpetually new beginnings. They evoked new foundations, referring to one or another of Rome's successive masters—Camillus, Sulla, or Octavius, for example. Octavius even chose to name himself Augustus, in a reference to Romulus and the augurs, the divine investiture attached to the founding king; and like Romulus, Octavius chose to fix his residence on the Palatine.

---

[1] There are three centuries between Michelangelo and Victor Emmanuel II: the first died in 1564, and the second in 1878. There is hardly less time between the middle of the eighth century B.C.E., when legend places the foundation of Rome, and 484 B.C.E., when the temple was built in honor of Castor and Pollux.

[2] It matters little whether the huts were located on that site or whether the remains are debris from somewhere else, as seems more probable.

[3] Vaglieri found the remains in 1907 but interpreted them as the remains of a necropolis. This led to a polemic with L. Pigorini and put an end to the excavations. See the catalog *Civiltà del Lazio primitivo*, 143–44 (essay by C. Ampolo).

That "inspired hill" of the Roman site and of the legend of the city's origins is indissociably linked to the gesture of Romulus. The cradle in which the twins were placed on the order of their great-uncle, the usurper Amulius, who wanted them to perish in the waters of the Tiber, ran aground at the foot of the Palatine. And it was on the Palatine that, in the classical age, a hut, said to have been that where Romulus and Remus lived among herders who had saved and sheltered them, was piously and regularly maintained. And, while his brother Remus chose the Aventine, Romulus placed himself on the Palatine to observe the favorable flights of birds (vultures!), whose appearance signified the approval of the gods for his plan to found a city. Thus it was on the hill which the twelve vultures had flown over that legend depicts him founding a city, to which he gave the name Rome. Rome was born on the Palatine, and, if we are to believe legend, it is there we must seek the archeological signs of the advent of the city.

Excavations still under way have revealed evidence that seems to lean in that direction, evidence that had long been sought, but in vain. For the first time in the history of Roman archeology and of research into the most ancient history of the Eternal City,[4] there are material remains from the heart of Rome, on the very site of its mythic foundation, remains capable of dissipating somewhat the legendary mists that, until now, have enveloped the birth of the city of Romulus and hid it from view. But before turning briefly to the result of new excavations undertaken beneath the Palatine, let us consider the terms of the debate about the birth of the Roman city that have existed until now.

Very often, historians have abandoned the idea of precisely explaining the birth of a "Romulean" Rome or have simply denied the existence of a community deserving to be called a city before the sixth century B.C.E. and the Etruscan presence.[5] In many Roman histories, even those devoted to the *primordia urbis,* Rome was there from all eternity because, finally, it could not not have been. Researchers hastened to note a supposed Palatine primacy in order to move on to the archeologically and historically easier task of studying Rome in the seventh, and especially the sixth, centuries B.C.E.[6] For those making the effort to reconstitute the primitive development of the *urbs,* two diametrically opposed models of interpretation were possible, but neither provided a definitive solution. Was Rome born by joining distinct villages, or rather

---

[4] Even apart from the initial confusion regarding the interpretation of the hut foundations found in 1907, the identification of a small settlement on the Palatine would not have sufficed to prove the topographical unity of the hill, to which the wall now brought to light seems to attest.

[5] "Politically, the Etruscans were the first to give Rome a central government. As they had founded the city of Rome, so they created the Roman State" (Homo, *Primitive Italy,* 112). Recently, this point of view has been represented by R. M. Ogilvie in his significantly titled *Early Rome and the Etruscans* (Atlantic Highlands, N.J., 1976), 30.

[6] A significant example is Alföldi's famous *Early Rome and the Latins,* which moves without transition from the Latin league (chap. 1) to the problem of the Etruscan presence in the city on the banks of the Tiber (chap. 2).

by expanding progressively from an original kernel? In other words, did the city of Romulus result from the conjunction of communities that had been separate, independent, and sovereign until then, in short, through what is called synecism, a term borrowed from Greek historians? Or, on the contrary, was it born from the nuclear and linear development of a single settlement?

What, finally, was the birth of Rome? An equality between autonomous villages or the primacy of an original kernel? A plurality of constitutive elements or a primordial unity? An alliance between distinct entities or the growth of an initial mass? The aggregation of several centers or the enlargement of a single group? A sudden advent or a progressive evolution? A datable event or the unfolding of a slow process? A historically and archeologically definable moment or a phenomenon of the long term? Conjunction or extension? Revolution or evolution? Fusion or diffusion? Formation or foundation?

The debate, which was very keen until the 1970s, has been tempered a bit since the thesis defended by Müller-Karpe in 1962, in the book given the significant title *Zur Stadtwerdung Roms* (The urban development of Rome). That thesis seemed to have definitively triumphed over the view of a Rome born of synecism, as the Swedish archeologist Einar Gjerstad presented it.[7] The latter hypothesis, that the Roman city owed its origin to the union of communities different from one another, appears to result from a conception of history (and in this case, of protohistory) as a series of events, implying the idea of a temporal unfolding characterized by breaks, faults, and abrupt changes. At the time the thesis was advanced, however, the conviction that history was before all else the realm of the long term, of slow transformation and progressive evolution, was taking root everywhere, among historians of every persuasion. Moreover, the archeological vestiges in Rome for these periods were very rare and extremely fragmentary. Beginning with the Roman Republic and the Roman Empire, the evidence of the origins was reduced to the state of ruins, covered over by other ruins and often effaced. Under such conditions, modern archeological investigation, making a virtue of necessity and relying on the void, so to speak, had no trouble reaching the conclusion that the emergence and development of primitive Rome came about "naturally" from a starting point that had only to be identified. This recourse to the long or very long term was stripped of reference points to events, which only a civilization regularly practicing writing could have provided. It led historians to give priority to the processes of formation and evolution in preference to any idea of break or foundation, in short, to prefer continuity to discontinuity. But that meant facing the paradox of a time that had become almost motionless by being diluted and stretched over the long term. The emphasis given to permanence no longer allowed historians to conceive of the transition from one state to another. In the end, time was conceived as a history without history. The only thing left to do was to record and classify

---

[7] See the successive volumes of Gjerstad, *Early Rome*.

the archeological vestiges provided by Rome's soil. But they were few in number and stripped of any meaning in themselves, lending themselves to the most divergent interpretations. This positivism led to determinism: Rome was born because it could not not have been born. Nonetheless, other sites, bearing the names Ficana, Decima, and Osteria dell'Osa, have taught us that "natural" development does not suffice as an explanation.[8] Something else had to exist in order that, from a few wooden huts, a city came into being that was capable of dominating the entire region, before one day becoming the capital of the world.

Thus, long wishing to reconcile the naturalism proper to archeology and the respect for literary sources, in the absence of a secure chronology (which, as we have seen, was fixed only recently), researchers wandered from one hill to the next, randomly considering a few sparse finds, with the goal of identifying the original and first site of the Eternal City, but with the secret wish to stop at the Palatine and recognize the priority granted it by the literary tradition.

In 1928, at a time when the Palatine had not yet offered any "primordial" remains that could be assigned a sure date,[9] the authors of the very authoritative *Cambridge Ancient History* wrote that the "issue is whether the first settlers on the site of Rome, whose cremation tombs are found in the Forum, lived on the Palatine or elsewhere." In this anxious quest, the near absence (at the time) of any archeological proof did not prevent the authors from concluding with the assertion that "the ancient view that on the Palatine the beginnings of Rome should be sought seems to find every confirmation in consideration of general probability."[10] This conviction (or belief?) was universal, already shared by de Sanctis (who wrote at the beginning of the century that "the tradition that considers the city on the Palatine to be primitive Rome must be true"),[11] by his rival Pais (who noted that "the Palatine lent itself particularly to the formation of a civil and political center"),[12] and, a little later, by Homo. Homo based his argument on the hut foundations discovered by Vaglieri in 1907, near the temple of the Magna Mater (still visible today), which for several decades constituted the most ancient remains identified on the Roman site as a whole. Homo wrote that "the Palatine does, in conformity with tradition, really represent the original nucleus of the city."[13]

Historians once believed that the literary tradition spoke of a "foundation" of Rome by Romulus because it had transposed the actual supremacy and priority of the Palatine phenomenon onto the mythical plane, adapting it to the schema, borrowed from the Greek world, of the creation ex nihilo of a city by a

---

[8] This was very clear in the case of Ficana (see above, chap. 6).

[9] Vaglieri's excavations, interrupted after the polemic with Pigorini, were taken up only after World War II (1948 and 1949). On that polemic, see Gjerstad, *Early Rome*, 3: 45.

[10] *The Cambridge Ancient History*, 7: 354 (chapter written by H. Last).

[11] De Sanctis, *Storia dei Romani*, 1: 194.

[12] Pais, *Storia di Roma*, 1: 42.

[13] Homo, *Primitive Italy*, 75.

founding hero. Hence the idea of a "foundation of Rome" represented only the way the ancients imagined the birth of Rome, unable to picture it in any way other than this mental schema of the *ktisis* (foundation) familiar to Greek historiography.[14]

But that did not in any way imply the historical truth of the Romulean legend. Through that interpretation, which acquired the force and popularity of a veritable Vulgate, the tradition of Palatine primacy was safeguarded. As for the notion of a "foundation of Rome," it persisted only transposed, devitalized, stripped of any concrete value as event and, in a word, as history.

It was only on that condition, in fact, that historians could opt for the hypothesis of a nuclear and linear development from an original center, while safeguarding the preeminence of the Palatine recognized by the literary tradition. In other words, they conserved everything that could be conserved of the notion of a "foundation" but radically eliminated that of synecism, to which it was nonetheless indissociably linked by the tradition. The idea of a "foundation of Rome" was thus reduced to the expression of a habit of thought on the part of the ancients and to the translation, into ritual and chronological terms, of an actual priority of the Palatine Hill in earliest Rome. Inevitably as well, the recognition of a Palatine supremacy, combined with the rejection of the idea of synecism, led to a significant depreciation of the Sabine element in the legend of the *primordia urbis*. Since the birth and development of Rome were interpreted as the expansion of a settlement originally concentrated on the Palatine, there was no question of conserving as such the traditional image of a Rome born from the fusion of two communities, one Latin and the other Sabine. In one way or another, it became necessary, if not to deny all validity to legend,[15] then at least to displace in time the formation of the Sabine component in relation to a Rome considered to be already in existence.

That, then, was what historians believed they could infer from the examination of the known archeological facts, or rather, that was the general framework into which they believed they could insert the new data gradually uncovered in Roman soil.

But the facts, as we well know, are stubborn. And, as we saw in the last chapter, they show that the Palatine was not the site in Rome that revealed the most ancient traces of occupation. Elsewhere, in the valley of the Forum in particular, and also at the base of the Capitol, remains older by several centuries than those of the Palatine emerged from the depths of the Eternal City's substratum. To confine ourselves to the facts, it is thus the Capitol and not the Palatine that might claim to be the first hill of Rome. Of course, we could always appeal to the traditions mentioning the establishment in mythical times of a Saturnia, a

[14] See, for example, T. J. Cornell, "The Foundation of Rome in the Ancient Literary Tradition," *Papers in Italian Archeology* 1, *British Archaeological Reports*, Suppl. 41, 1 (1978): 131–40.

[15] See J. Poucet, *Recherches sur la légende sabine des origines de Rome* (Louvain, 1967).

city dedicated to Saturn, not far from the place where, much later, the great temple of Jupiter would be built. However, the archeological data relating to the early periods of Latial civilization (eleventh or tenth century to eighth century B.C.E.) do not allow us to conceive of a nuclear development from the Capitol, inasmuch as the most ancient shards on the Roman site, those of Sant'Omobono (which belong to the embankment areas and thus come from somewhere else), are linked to the Capitol only by means of a plausible hypothesis, not a certain one. In any case, to remain with the archeological facts (in an uncertain interpretation, it is true) the valley of the Forum may also have been occupied before the Palatine.[16] All that logically led the great archeologist Müller-Karpe, anxious not to make the archeological data say something they were not saying, to the conclusion that "one cannot prove and it is not even plausible that the settlement of the early Latial periods began on the Palatine and around it, as the product of a single act of foundation."[17] He took care to add, however, that "the Romulean tradition concerns the beginning of Rome as a city, not as a settlement," a last homage rendered to a literary tradition open to all interpretations.

For historians who wished to preserve the hill of Romulus as the foremost place in the protohistory of the Roman site, two solutions were possible. They could place the emphasis on the archeological traces found on the Palatine that were prior to the eighth century, since there were a few of these, dating from the first Latial phase (tenth century B.C.E.) in the layers situated under the foundations of huts discovered by Vaglieri.[18] That is, they could preserve, with a minimal adjustment, the antecedence and exclusivity of the Palatine in the process of Rome's birth. More radically, they could extend the surface of the original center (a procedure with the advantage of better taking into account the dispersion of the oldest archeological data in the valley of the Forum particularly) and shift the founding date of the *urbs* backward. For example, they could choose to identify that foundation with the formation of the Septimontium, which could even be linked to the chronology transmitted by the Greek author Timaeus, who situated the foundation of Rome in 814 B.C.E.[19] The two solutions had in common the fact that they abandoned any reference to the traditional date of the beginning of the Roman city, which Varro fixed as 753 B.C.E. In short, to save the Palatine, they decided to sacrifice Romulus!

Today, however, through unexpected and unhoped-for developments, the figure of the legendary founder of Rome has returned to the foreground and has again taken on substance, thanks to discoveries that introduce items of exceptional interest into the debate we have just traced.

---

[16] See above, chap. 9.
[17] Müller-Karpe, *Zur Stadtwerdung Roms*, 77.
[18] See the catalog *Civiltà del Lazio primitivo*, 144.
[19] See, for example, *Civiltà del Lazio primitivo*, 106.

In 1985, Andrea Carandini was entrusted by the Archeological Superintendence of Rome with the task of exploring an area situated at the foot of the Palatine, in the Forum, between the Arch of Titus and the House of Vestals, that is, a surface area of about an acre that until then had remained relatively apart from excavation operations. Already, the structures revealed on that occasion have revived and thoroughly renewed debate about the birth of Rome. But let us review the topographical and literary factors before turning to the description of the remains brought to light.[20] Although the modern visitor may have the impression that this sector is fully part of the Forum, we need to recall that for the ancients this zone belonged not to the great plaza of the city, but to the hill that ran along one side of it, that is, to the Palatine.[21] The rise in the valley floor was caused first by a large-scale operation, executed toward the end of the seventh century B.C.E.,[22] and then by the superimposition of successive buildings, and the reshaping of the Romulean hill due to the gigantic terracing project carried out for the construction of the emperors' residence. These gradually eliminated any continuity between the valley of the Forum and the Palatine, whose slopes originally encompassed areas that are now dominated by a veritable brick cliff made up of the buttresses and ruins of the imperial palace.

Below these slopes, then, recent explorations first uncovered the remains of houses dating from the middle of the republican era (second and third centuries B.C.E.), whose walls, rebuilt after a fire in 210 B.C.E., rested on foundations going back to the archaic era. Subsequent excavations were to show that during a period in the middle of the sixth century (about 530–520 B.C.E.), several large dwellings (at least four, but probably more) were constructed, each containing a vestibule (*atrium*), a garden, and everything that later characterized the houses of the Roman aristocracy. The remains of these dwellings were recognizable under the cellars of republican houses.[23] As they proceeded with their exploration (that is, as they continued to descend), archeologists realized that these great archaic dwellings all rested on a gigantic earth platform, about two meters deep, whose construction had occurred in two stages: as the great archaic houses

---

[20] My sources for the description of these excavations are the two lectures given in Paris by Carandini, on 16 and 18 February 1989, and the provisional publication found in the exhibition catalog *La grande Roma dei Tarquini*, ed. M. Cristofani (Rome, 1990), esp. 82 and 97–99, in anticipation of the detailed publication of "Palatino, pendici settentrionali: Campagne di scavo 1985–88," in *Bollettino di Archeologia* 2 (1990). I would like to thank Professor Carandini and the entire team, especially Nicola Terrenato, for their courtesy in allowing me to visit the site and for the interviews kindly granted me. It goes without saying that the interpretations that follow—and any errors they might contain—are my full responsibility.

[21] See Coarelli, *Il foro romano*, 1: 24.

[22] See Ammerman's fundamental "On the Origins of the Forum Romanum," 627–45.

[23] The excavations of these structures were made public in A. Carandini, M. Medri, M. Gualandi, and E. Papi, "Pendici settentrionali del Palatino," *Bulletino della Commissione Archeologica Communale in Roma* 91 (1986): 429ff.; reprinted in A. Carandini, *Schiavi in Italia* (Rome, 1988), 359–87.

were being built, the *via Sacra,* situated beneath them, was repaved, thus suggesting something like a relation of cause and effect.

These traces were already sufficient to lead researchers to ask important scientific questions in completely new ways, such as the problem of the acts of the last kings of Rome, or that of the origin of the Roman house. But the platform on which the Romans (or Etruscans?) had built prestigious constructions in the sixth century B.C.E., with stone walls and tile roofs, had not been built on virgin soil, as some might have thought. To the great astonishment of the excavators, even older traces appeared under these.

Where the slope of the Palatine had originally ended, upstream from the bed of a waterway—now vanished—which had established a natural boundary between the Palatine Hill and the Velia Hill, excavators' trowels gradually revealed traces of a system of fortifications lining the bottom of the Romulean hill, between the presumed site of the Curiae Veteres (ancient curiae) and that of the Sacellum Larum (or Larundae, chapel of Lares). One after the other, superimposed traces of three successive walls were uncovered, walls that had been built in nearly the same place. The most recent one, built parallel to the preceding one (at a distance of a meter and a half) and following the same technique, may be dated, it seems, between 550 and 530 B.C.E. It had first reused the defense provided by a trench dug for an earlier wall, but the trench was subsequently filled in. Before that fortification from the middle of the sixth century B.C.E., two other ramparts had been built (each with an artificial trench), one in about 600 B.C.E., constructed out of large regular blocks of tufa, the other in about 675 B.C.E., made of the same material, but less elaborate.

Indisputably, in these excavations, the most innovative, the most surprising, the most revolutionary find, precisely because it was also the most "traditional," was the discovery beneath these three walls of an even earlier wall, following the same path—with a few minimal irregularities—as those that had later taken its place. Made of a foundation of reddish tufa and probably clay and wood beams for the most part, this wall, about 1.40 meters wide, had been erected directly on virgin soil. The most extraordinary good fortune in the entire discovery was that, in its tufa foundations, a small number of fibulae and vases, well known to archeologists as essential dating instruments, were also found. The examination of the fragments of three vases and two fibulae (that is, brooches made of bronze, with which men and especially women of that time fastened their clothing) allowed archeologists to propose a date for the construction of this first wall, a date that is obviously not exact to the year or even the decade, but that nonetheless constitutes a scientifically necessary and plausible hypothesis.

That date lies between 730 and 720 B.C.E. and can be linked to another characteristic of the site explored.[24] In addition to the wall in its first state, a

---

[24] According to Colonna, whose fundamental surveys on the archeology of early Rome and primitive Latium are cited in the bibliography.

wooden fence had been built about fifteen meters downstream. The fence itself could not be recovered, of course, but its posts had left their imprint in the soil, and marks were visible (at the time of the excavations) in two places, each about ten meters in length. The fact that the marks occurred in two places, as well as the straight line they followed, prevented archeologists from envisioning simply hut foundations, as had been identified elsewhere, on the Palatine in particular. The most curious thing was that between this fence, carefully maintained subsequently and rebuilt on several occasions, and the walls already mentioned, there was a piece of ground that seems to have remained free of all occupation between the eighth and sixth centuries B.C.E. At that time, as we have seen, the entire site was covered over by a large terrace designed to provide the foundation for an entirely new region.

On such a dense site, so decisive strategically and occupied so early, the respect and upkeep of a strip of land—between the fence and the wall—safeguarded from all construction constitutes a most striking peculiarity. Contemporary in their realization and their use, the fence, the wall, and the neutral space they delimited were obviously all part of the same system, the elements of which, to be understood, must not be dissociated.

Under such conditions, how can we not think of the foundation of Rome by Romulus,[25] a foundation that the literary tradition illustrated and symbolized through the setting in place of the pomerium, the fortification that established the sacred boundary of the new city? How can we not link the date inferred from the archeological remains discovered by the recent excavations—730 B.C.E.—to the date attributed by tradition to Romulus's initiative, 753 B.C.E.? Between the two locations and the two chronologies, those of archeology on one hand and of the tradition on the other, the correspondence is more than surprising. It is astonishing, haunting even, and, to tell the truth, almost shocking! "One can deny the existence of Romulus in a university in Germany; it is more difficult when one sees with one's own eyes a wall that could only be the wall of the little Rome of the Palatine," exclaimed Jean-Jacques Ampère at the beginning of his *Histoire romaine à Rome* (Roman history in Rome), published in 1862.[26] The ruins that inspired such eloquent indignation at the time turned out to be merely remains that were more recent than was at first thought.[27]

But what are we to say in the face of this new "Romulean" wall? For, unlike Ampère and his contemporaries, we can rely on an archeology that is sure of its

---

[25] On Romulus, see the indispensable entries by J. B. Carter (1909) in N. H. Roscher, *Ausführliches Lexikon der griechischen und römischen Mythologie* (Leipzig, 1884–1932), 164–209; and by A. Rosenberg in Pauly-Wissowa, *RE* 1.A1: 1074–104. For recent bibliography, see C. Ampolo's commentary to Plutarch's *Life of Romulus* (Milan, 1988).

[26] J.-J. Ampère, *Histoire romaine à Rome* (Paris, 1862), 1: 7.

[27] These walls were discovered in 1847 above the Church of Saint Anastasia, later dated from the republican era. See Lanciani, *Ruins and Excavations*, 122. It would seem that archeologists are now returning to an earlier date.

methods and dating practices. However paradoxical it might seem, two and a half centuries of historical exegesis and criticism have left the modern researcher bereft, almost disarmed before the shock of such a revelation. Over the years, the centuries, and the patient achievements of scholarship, researchers had learned to distinguish carefully between history and legend; they had understood that the gesture of Romulus was to be interpreted in a metaphorical and symbolic sense. And now, a few stones, a few scoops of earth, put them face to face with the most brute materiality, the most literal presence of an "event" situated on the Palatine and dating from the eighth century B.C.E.

At that date and that place, how are we to interpret these trenches and walls, if not by raising the question of the pomerium?[28] Until now, historians often considered texts mentioning the primordial furrow traced by Romulus around the Palatine as pure falsification, scholarly reconstruction, fairy tales of erudition to delight the imagination of scholars from the end of the first century B.C.E., who were infatuated with archaisms. Indisputably, we must carefully distinguish between the reality of the pomerium, if such a reality exists, and what has been imagined and dreamed in that regard, from the time of Augustus particularly, when the prince claimed to be Rome's restorer and Romulus's successor. Nor can what moderns have supposed and inferred be confused with that possible reality, which now appears to us only through the prism of their successive visions. It is nonetheless true that, henceforth, the vestiges discovered beneath the Palatine oblige us to look again at the a priori condemnation of sources disdainfully called literary (we shall see in the next chapter what is to be made of that modifier). Only a short time ago, Poucet wrote with some justification that "the traditional date of 754/3 does not mean very much archeologically speaking."[29] Some may even argue in the future that "archeology does not allow us to take a clear position," insisting on how early and how continuously the Roman site as a whole was occupied, or on the difficulty and fragility (which are undeniable, by the way) of the interpretations to be attempted based on new discoveries. But let us admit that, in the past, if the most resolute of the tradition's accusers had been asked what kind of proof they required to overturn, at least in part, the almost unanimous condemnation of which the Romulean tradition was the object, they would have demanded nothing more than what has been brought to light from the bottom of the Palatine slopes![30]

[28] I have approached this question in a preliminary manner, as it arises in the light of recent excavations of the Palatine, in an article forthcoming in *Table ronde internationale du CNRS sur la divination dans le monde étrusco-italique* 4. See A. Grandazzi, "Tacite, Annales XII, 24: La question du pomerium." I summarize the conclusion of that article here.

[29] Poucet, *Origines de Rome*, 137 and 139. Momigliano writes that "until now, archeology has revealed no inscription or other sign pertaining to the act of foundation, if there ever was one (as the tradition asserts, a fact that is not without importance)" (*Roma arcaica*, 15).

[30] In 1985, Poucet noted, regarding the period of the Etruscan kings, and hence, in the first place, of Romulus, that "the absence of real archeological confirmation is rather troubling" (*Origines de Rome*, 160).

This is especially true in that the indexes that lead us to recognize these vestiges as the traces of the Romulean foundation are numerous and do not all
come from the literary tradition or from the Roman context alone. Far from it.

It has long been accepted and very generally recognized that, in the definition of an urban or preurban space, the notions of limit, of confines, and of
boundary take on fundamental importance, not only in Rome but everywhere
else in central Italy. The famous bronze tablets found in Gubbio, Umbria, the
text of which describes an ancient liturgy in minute detail, mention on several
occasions "the augur stones" at the "boundaries of the city";[31] and we cannot
help but think at this point of the inscribed stones (*cippi*) that, Tacitus tells us,[32]
delimited the territory of the city of Romulus. In the same way, archaic Etruria
was full of boundary *cippi* (called *tular* in Etruscan), at least some of which
served to indicate urban borderlines. Hence the sanctified delimitation of the
territory of a "city," as the Romulean pomerium defined it, enters the order of
facts noted in places other than Rome and not only in Etruria.

This last point is of particular importance. One of the most commonly
advanced arguments against any possible historical substance to the Romulean
legend was the Etruscan origin of the founding rites it represented.[33] And the
Etruscans did not arrive in Rome until the seventh and sixth centuries B.C.E.,
according to the tradition itself. As a result, the Etruscan character of the establishment of a borderline such as the pomerium would be precisely the best
demonstration of its legendary and nonhistorical aspect. The Romans would
have simply linked their rites of origin to those being practiced when they
founded a colony. Such reasoning, which in appearance obeys the most rigorous
logic, is still nothing but a condemnation of legend by . . . legend. For who
asserted that the founding rites were Etruscan? A certain number of ancient
authors,[34] and, it is true, a number of modern specialists after them, among
whom we are not surprised to find a majority of Etruscologists. But other
ancient authors (and not the least important) do not breathe a word about it—
out of national pride, it is said, or out of hostility toward the Etruscans. Yet
nothing is less sure: in reality, the example of Gubbio even seems to prove the
reverse, unless we see it as the result of Etruscan influence. But that is disputable.
If we therefore stop interpreting the Roman situation as the product of Etruscan
influence, we realize that we are dealing with a ritual proper to the whole of central Italy in the archaic era. The delimitation of a pomerium is no doubt not
specifically Roman—Tacitus and Cato did not assert it was in any case—but it
is not specifically Etruscan either.

[31] Eugubine Tables, especially table VI a.

[32] Tac. *Ann.* 12.24.

[33] See the objections of F. Casganoli, based on foundations different from my own, in *Parola
del Passato*, 1977, 243.

[34] A list of them can be found in D. Briquel, "I riti di fondazaione," in the collection *Tarquinia:
Ricerche, scavi e prospettive*, ed. M. Bonghi Jovino and C. Chiaramonte Treré (1987), 171–90.

Why, then, did the ancients (though not all of them) often describe them as such? Undeniably, they had a tendency to link everything concerning the rites of divination, including the pomerium as the sacred limit defined by augurs, to the ancient and mysterious Etruria. Hence we must give a more general import to that question: Why was there this Roman tendency to attribute to the Etruscans the rites of divination practiced in the city? In my view, the response can be found in a piece of evidence recognized half a century ago, when the unity of culture and civilization that characterized the center of the peninsula in archaic times was brought to light by archeologists and historians (especially with the pioneering studies of Santo Mazzarino).[35] Rome and Etruria originally had many points in common, on the religious level especially; but with time, the initial similarities gave way to increasingly extensive processes of differentiation, and practices that continued in Etruria, for historical and social reasons I shall not analyze here,[36] gradually ceased on the other side of the Tiber. Thus the Romans came to consider typically Etruscan what was only typically archaic. That is why Etruria seems to have played such a role in ancient Roman religion, and why, conversely, the Etruscan religion seems so Roman in certain ways!

The two religions, emerging at the same time but distant from each other, and by that very fact developing differently, ended up being attributed, according to the conception of the ancients (and moderns), to different times. The rites of the Etruscan religion were defined in relation to the Roman as a relation of anteriority, that is, of origin. All things considered, this is somewhat the same mental process Racine pointed to in the preface to *Bajazet*—a tragedy in which he chose to translate the subject matter's distance in time (antiquity) by distance in space (the Orient)—when he wrote that "people do not really distinguish between what is, so to speak, a thousand years from them and what is a thousand miles."

Under such conditions, attributing an Etruscan origin to a part of the pomerium tradition should not lead us to reject the identification of the recently discovered vestiges (whose material reality, in any case, cannot be denied) with the Romulean boundary, or to date the Etruscan presence in Rome any earlier. Once more, the legend turns out to be neither true nor false, but, in its very emergence, the product and the expression of a complex and plural history.

Another temptation, which is even more appealing, since in giving in to it we have the impression we are denying ourselves all satisfaction, is to try to interpret these vestiges as mere remains of fortifications, from a purely positivist and factual point of view. But to this we may respond that, at least in its first phase, the wall, situated at the bottom of the slope of the Palatine (and not at the top as might rather be expected, if it were to meet purely defensive

---

[35] See Mazzarino, *Dalla monarchia allo stato repubblicano*.
[36] See M. Torelli, *Storia degli Etruschi* (Rome, 1972).

objectives), does not seem to have constituted a true fortification.[37] In fact, its meaning appears more ritual in nature. The legend says nothing less, after all, when it shows Remus leaping over the enclosure traced by his twin brother.[38]

Conversely, some might refuse to recognize the wall as the pomerium, arguing that it served to delimit a city, and that in the eighth century B.C.E. there was obviously not yet a city of Rome as we understand that word. To respond to these two objections, let us consider what archeologists sometimes call the Villanovan revolution,[39] the synecisms that, in a relatively restricted time period, were observed at the beginnings of the Iron Age, on a large scale and over an immense territory, more or less covering Latium north of the Tiber and present-day Tuscany. Where Etruscan cities from the historical era would later be located, dense settlements came together, and all around them hamlets and villages were abandoned. Modern archeology interprets that gigantic mutation in terms of economy, the intensification and concentration of exchanges, and the spatial redistribution and arrangement of the territory. But in ancient societies, the "political" element (in this case, the decision, whether forced or not, to fix one's residence at a given site) cannot be separated from the religious element. How, then, are we to believe that such an upheaval could have occurred without being accompanied and expressed by rites and religion? In a protohistorical society such as earliest Rome, the establishment and reinforcement of a community in what was to become a center, in relation to what was becoming a periphery, implied and required a distribution of territory between the inside and the outside, between what was to be "hostile" (foreign) and what was "friendly," in short, a definition of what was "urban" and what was not. In Rome, the instrument for that distribution and definition was none other than the pomerium.

Conserved in the extraordinary fossil layer of Roman religion are numerous signs that show both the unity and the isolation of the Palatine Hill in relation to its environment. In its immediate vicinity, even in the classical age, stood chapels of small and obscure deities; modern specialists have demonstrated that these deities were associated with notions of protection and of boundary. Thus, all around the Palatine, the gods Aius Locutius, Angerona, Tacita-Muta, and Acca Larentia kept watch. They were deities of silence, of the dead, of "the beyond" in every sense of the word (recall that, with the definition of the city by the pomerium, the dead were buried outside its territory), particularly present

---

[37] Beginning in about 650 (or 675) B.C.E., however, the wall did have an artificial moat. See A. Carandini in *La grande Roma dei Tarquini*, ed. Cristofani, 97.

[38] "'The enemy will easily jump over your wall, and so do I!' and he jumped over it." Dion. Hal. *Ant. rom.* 1.87; cf. Plutarch's *Life of Romulus*, in *The Lives of the Noble Grecians and Romans*, trans. J. Amyot and T. North (New York, 1941): "In the end for a mockery [Remus] leapt over his wall" (p. 69).

[39] See, for example, G. Bartoloni, *La cultura villanoviana* (1989), chap. 4: "La rivoluzione villanoviana."

along the marsh of Velabrum, which surrounded both the Palatine on the Tiber side and a part of the Forum.[40]

Hence the boundary, whose traces have been discovered and whose establishment the "literary" tradition attributes to Romulus, sanctified, on the site that was beginning to be Rome in the eighth century B.C.E., the particular and pre-eminent status of the Palatine. Until quite recently, the very idea that the Romulean legend could have corresponded to anything historical was articulated only to be immediately and resolutely rejected by historical criticism, which had grounded its legitimacy and ambitions in the total rejection of "fable." But thirty years of archeological research in Latium ought to make the data provided by recent excavations less unthinkable and less "scandalous" than in the past.

In places of Latium outside Rome, thus in the same area of civilization, other walls, also dating from the eighth century B.C.E., have been unearthed in recent years. In Castel di Decima (in the Pomptine Marshes), in Ficana, on the hill of Acqua Acetosa (today surrounded by the suburbs of Rome along the *via Laurentina*), in Lavinium, perhaps in Ardea, and no doubt in other lesser-known sites, archeologists continue to identify defensive structures going back to the eighth century B.C.E., at least in their first state.[41] In that way, the paths of Latial archeology lead us once more back to Rome. Conversely, the importance that the Roman literary tradition attaches to the pomerium suggests that the fortifications found in Latium were charged with a sacral meaning, for the pomerium is a religious notion as much or more than a material reality (Mommsen, who devoted a famous essay to it, spoke of it as a "Begriff," that is, a "concept").[42] To see these fortifications simply as defensive projects (which they were *as well* of course) would be to establish a radical alterity between the spheres of the political and the religious, that is, to introduce an anachronism into those archaic societies, leading to a reversal in meaning.

In Rome, then, the establishment of a pomerium line in the 730s B.C.E. attests to the existence, beginning in that period, of a community that was aware enough of itself to wish to establish between its territory and the external world a boundary that, if not uncrossable, was at least very clearly percepti-ble.[43] Under these conditions, can we not believe that, with these last discoveries and all those that preceded them, we finally have the response to the great debate mentioned a moment ago? Is it not now clear that Rome was founded on the Palatine by a founder who can be situated in the eighth century

---

[40] See Coarelli, *Il foro romano*, 1: 255–76; Carandini, in *La grande Roma*, ed. Cristofani, 82 and 84.

[41] See Carandini in *La grande Roma*, ed. Cristofani, 178 (Ficana), 184–86 (Lavinium and Castel di Decima), 171 (Laurentina Acqua Acetosa), and 194 (Ardea).

[42] See T. Mommsen, *Römische Forschungen* (Berlin, 1879), 2: 23ff.

[43] In any case, the top of the hill seems to have had, at least from the sixth century on, walls that served both as support and defense. See the remarks of P. Pensabene in *La grande Roma*, ed. Cristofani, 86.

B.C.E., in substantial agreement with legend, and to whom we will be less hesitant than in the past to give the name Romulus? Is it not equally clear that Rome resulted from the progressive expansion of a primitive kernel, which it is appropriate to situate on the Palatine Hill, where recent excavations have brought to light the major role it played in the advent of the city of Romulus?

Thus ought not the old hypothesis of synecism be definitively abandoned, in favor of a development of an original settlement, situated, precisely, on the Palatine?

Despite appearances, however, the new discoveries do not suddenly put an end to this great debate by awarding the definitive victory to one thesis over the other. In reality, they complicate the debate, enrich it, and, in short, provide the means for transcending it.

In fact, the choice between the two hypotheses, synecism or progressive expansion, that is, foundation or formation, is no more obvious than it was in the past. True, for the theory that views Rome's emergence to be the result of synecism, in other words, of a unification of villages that had been separated until that time, the primacy seemingly granted the Palatine by the newly discovered walls is very troubling. According to that same theory, these villages found their "natural" place for exchanges and relations in the valley of the Forum. And the foundation of Rome through a fusion of their respective communities would have marked the endpoint of these relations. But, as studies still under way show in increasingly clear terms,[44] the Forum in its natural state was only a low plain traversed by waters, regularly flooded by the nearby Tiber, in short, a drainage basin, a swampy and muddy shoal, and, apart from a few protrusions, not at all a ready site for the birth of a city, which historians have often wanted to see in it. Its construction (as the American archeologist Albert J. Ammerman has shown) required a gigantic effort of filling in and terracing, which could have been realized only by a society that was already numerous and organized, in other words, by a civic community. Hence, in that case, the hypothesis of synecism takes the effect for the cause and supposes the problem solved as soon as it is raised. As a last resort, the hypothesis may then argue the probable existence of other fortified systems protecting and isolating the other hills of Rome, notably the Velia, from the eighth century B.C.E., thus attesting to the existence of a plurality of villages on the Roman site.[45] But, apart from the fact that, at the current state of

---

[44] Studies by the American archeologist A. J. Ammerman. See his "On the Origins of the Forum Romanum," *American Journal of Archaeology* 94 (1990): 627–45. This article is based on a complete reexamination of the most ancient archeological remains found at the site, and on depth soundings designed to give information about the geomorphological configuration of the valley of the Forum in the tenth century B.C.E. See also id., "Morfologia ed ambiente del'area del Foro Romano," forthcoming in *Archeologia Laziale* 11, which anticipates a monograph on the question.

[45] See especially Terrenato, "Velia and Carinae." I am extremely grateful to the author for sending me the manuscript.

the research, there are only indexes and not proof of such an assertion, the primacy of the Palatine is not suggested solely by the results of recent excavations. Without speaking of the particular nature of the deities established all around the Romulean hill, which, as we have seen, manifest in negative, so to speak, its importance and preeminence, we cannot forget that the Palatine included some of the places that were the most organically linked to the myth of the origins of the city, such as the mysterious Roma Quadrata or the cave of Lupercal, where, it was said, Romulus and Remus were sheltered by the kindly she-wolf. The Palatine was also the hill that the procession of victorious generals marched around before ascending the Capitol to the temple of Jupiter. The Palatine was where, each year, the procession of the Luperci (wolf men) marked the city's limits by tracing a protective and purifying circle around the primordial hill. And it was on the Palatine that the seats of the curiae, those very ancient forms of association, more ancient no doubt that Rome itself, were regrouped.[46]

Do not all these signs obviously show that it was from the Palatine that the creation and expansion of Rome occurred, with recent discoveries in the end only confirming the hypothesis of a progressive development from an initial kernel located on the Romulean hill? Hence archeology and legend illuminate and reinforce each other, finding the place of their definitive reconciliation on the Palatine.

But in spite of everything, that would be to forget that, if we look closely, the theory of the formation of Rome by nuclear expansion from the Palatine can be adopted only at the expense of a certain number of objective data that are difficult to integrate into such a framework. First, the recent excavations, in bringing to light fortifications that were constructed and inaugurated at a "historical" moment that can be situated in time with relative precision, imply, in whatever manner they are interpreted, a break, an "event" so to speak, which the dominant nuclear model had the function and the advantage of avoiding. How, in fact, can historians say that the development of Rome occurred "naturally" from the Palatine if one of the most obvious signs of that "natural" preeminence of the Romulean hill is precisely the evidence of an intervention, situated in time and space, of human, and by that very fact, historical, origin? It will always be possible, of course, to believe that the intervention only sanctified a preexisting state, but that is nothing but one interpretation among others that are equally plausible.

Moreover, we have seen that, to restrict ourselves to the existing archeological remains, the Palatine does not appear to be the cradle of Rome.[47] In addition to a tomb found under the House of Livia, the most ancient tombs of Latial civilization (which began, let us recall, in the eleventh or tenth century B.C.E.) are

---

[46] The *curia Saliorum*, gathering place for the Salii, ancient priests of Mars, was also located on the Palatine. A tradition claimed that Romulus's augur staff (*lituus*) survived the Gallic fire intact.
[47] See above, chap. 9.

those of the necropolis of the *via Sacra,* near the temple of Antoninus and Faustina, and they are linked to a settlement located in all probability on the Velia rather than the Palatine.[48] As for the first evidence on the Roman site, that stemming from the "sub-Apennine" age of protohistory, it is no doubt to be linked to a hamlet situated on the Capitol. Far from the Palatine and predating the first evidence found on its surface, other remains thus call into question the antecedence granted to the Romulean hill by the nuclear model.

The preceding remarks thus lead us to the paradoxical realization that the Palatine was not, archeologically speaking, the first hill of Rome (in any case, such a claim is not *proved*) and that it was nonetheless distinguished from all those that surrounded it by an indisputable primacy that was "literary" (legendary) as well as institutional and religious. To explain the birth of the Roman city, we can thus ground ourselves neither in the hypothesis of synecism nor in that of nuclear development.

Thus we are led back to the central question of this book: What was Rome in its beginnings? Once more, the overly simplistic theoretical constructions have disintegrated when confronted with the "facts" and with unresolved difficulties.

It is clear, of course, that each of the two schemata mentioned offers not a full and definitive solution but its share of truth—precious and disputable, irreplaceable and provisional. Rome did not come into being *stricto sensu* through synecism or through nuclear expansion, through formation or through foundation, but was the product of a process of development that supposes at one and the same time the joining of dispersed forces and the growth of a center that had become primary. That process participates in the long term but is also marked by key moments that can be interpreted as true events.[49]

Nothing is born from nothing. The Romulean foundation, the traces of which have now been uncovered, after being sought in vain for so long, could not have occurred except because, on the whole of the Roman site, a gigantic and complex movement was under way, embracing the most diverse elements and putting into play dynamics that were sometimes contradictory, sometimes convergent, leading gradually to a rise in the density of human activity and occupation in these places that would one day be Rome.

Archeologists date the beginnings of what was later (in the seventh and sixth centuries B.C.E.) to be the large necropolis of archaic Rome on the Esquiline Hill, from the ninth century B.C.E. (Latial period II B). It is difficult not to place that date in relation to what was observed at about the same period in the

---

[48] As Heurgon shows in *Rome et la Méditerranée occidentale,* 84.

[49] That is the solution generally arrived at. See Heurgon, *Rome et la Méditerranée occidentale,* 88; M. Pallottino, "Le origini di Roma: Considerazioni critiche sulle scoperte e sulle discussioni più recenti," *Aufstieg und Niedergang der römischen Welt* 1, 1 (1972): 36; Torelli, *Storia degli Etruschi,* 128–30; Momigliano, *Roma arcaica,* 16.

Forum, where the necropolis ceased to be used, and the area welcomed dwellings. It may well be that this was still a private space, and that the Forum— at least the spur seemingly formed by the natural platform, where the Regia (royal palace) and the temple of Vesta would later be established[50]—did not in any way constitute the public space it would later become.[51] This occurred only when the large natural basin, its center marked by the placement of the equestrian statue of Domitian, was filled in and leveled. It is nonetheless true that the two phenomena (end of the Forum necropolis and beginning of the Esquiline necropolis) seem to be part of the same system and attest to the existence, if not of a city, then at least of a federation of villages in the process of unification.[52] The Septimontium seems to reflect that transitional state (but is there such a thing as a fixed state?), which saw the protohistorical league evolve into the city of historical times. In the last century and at the beginning of the present one, that Septimontium league was often interpreted as a second stage in the development of Rome, in relation to the Palatine phase marked in legend by the foundation of Romulus. Since the territory defined by the Septimontium extended well beyond the Palatine Hill itself, it was thought that it resulted from the expansion of the primitive kernel first constituted by the hill. Behind this schema, which recent studies have totally reversed, is concealed the weight exerted by the model of a nuclear, "natural," and linear development. In reality, the Septimontium did not yet bear the name Rome for the very simple reason that Rome did not yet exist when the holiday was celebrated, in an area whose epicenter was located around the Palatine, of course, but also around the Velia. Only the conviction that the Palatine foundation constituted an absolute starting point could have led historians to make the Septimontium into Rome, to which the name given by Romulus at its foundation was nonetheless lacking.

Hence those who, in about 730 B.C.E., established around the Palatine an enclosure that was never forgotten by tradition chose a site that had already been occupied for a very long time. The Palatine foundation, whose reality in my view can be neither denied nor minimized, was possible only because, throughout the territory of the future Rome, a process of formation was under way whose tenuous but indubitable signs modern archeologists have brought to light.

Formation or foundation? The debate, posited in the exclusive terms of one or the other, is inadequate to account for a complex reality, and the problem of

---

[50] Ammerman seems to rule out the presence of settlements on the Forum before the end of the seventh century B.C.E. ("On the Origins of the Forum Romanum"), but excavations under way near the Regia and the temple of Vesta appear to attest to the presence of huts before that date. See Scott, "Regia-Vesta."

[51] See C. Ampolo, "Die endgültige Stadtwerdung Roms in 7 und 6 Jahr. v. Chr.—Wann einstand die *civitas*?" in *Palast und Hütte* (1982), 319–24.

[52] We could interpret that concomitance as the expression merely of a sociological and cultural tendency (and not a political one in the exact sense of the term), but, nonetheless, it shows that "something" was under way.

the anteriority of the Palatine, formulated as a function of the hypothesis of nuclear development alone, is in great part a false problem. Neither a pure and simple synecism nor a pure and simple formation, the birth of Rome proceeded from both at once. The indisputable symbolic and religious primacy of the Palatine has been interpreted as the sign of a priority on the level of facts, based on a theoretical model of nuclear development. But the facts themselves turn out to be less and less compatible with this model, so that the notion of a foundation must today be rehabilitated, but without the notion of formation being abandoned for all that.

What is the Romulean foundation in fact, whose material traces the newly discovered walls have restored to us? It now appears that it constituted, on the basis of an attraction already at work on the whole of the Roman site, the canalization, the recuperation, the unification, and the concentration in favor of the Palatine alone of energies that until then had been scattered among a constellation of villages and hamlets. For the weak and intermittent links that characterized the leagues of the old Latium, it substituted the ritually sanctified, grounded, and defined coherence of a new organization. To the federal plurality of the past, it opposed the (pre)urban unity of the future. The league of the Septimontium had already held one of its sacrifices (but not the only one) on the Palatine, namely, the Palatuar, which closely evokes the Latiar of the Feriae Latinae. In appearance, nothing changed when Romulus (for the sake of convenience, let us give that name to the builders of the Palatine walls) chose the Palatine as the place to trace the pomerium. Nonetheless, that visible continuity also expressed a profound break, because, between the Palatuar and the pomerium, there is a difference in degree that is also a difference in nature. The Palatuar was the point of a convergence of forces come from elsewhere, yet the pomerium became the radiating center of a monad that, before it began to expand, was first the site of a formidable concentration of density, in accordance with a process we can now call the foundation of Rome. Hence it is only because there had already been that first development of a central element (Palatine and Velia) that there could be a synecism, and it is only because there was synecism that a nuclear development could assert itself subsequently as it did. The birth of Rome resulted from a foundation that itself supposed a formation already under way. It was translated into an event, datable in time (the eighth century B.C.E.) and locatable in space (the Palatine), an event that was itself part of the long-term phenomenon of the emergence of cities in archaic societies. Not only, then, did foundation not exclude formation, but the latter was even necessary for the former to be possible. A starting point toward new horizons, the foundation of Rome was also the end point in an age-old process.

The growing multiplicity and complexity of the archeological data not only oblige us to invalidate the old hypotheses but also lead us to rethink even the conceptual instruments that structure and condition any interpretation. In this case, if we move beyond the old dilemma of synecism versus expansion and take into account long-term evolutions brought to light by archeology, we can restore to the notion of foundation, until now devalued and devitalized, its role as an "event," its contingency. In short, we can reintroduce the historical into history.

For Rome, this means that the Palatine concentration, that is, the Romulean foundation, came about by eliminating satellite communities (however that was done). Known and identified by archeologists at many sites of protohistorical Italy, this phenomenon can be examined more closely in Rome. The tradition, in fact, shows Romulus combating the neighboring cities of Fidenae, Veii, Crustumerium, and Antemnae, and even destroying a center called Caenina, of which nothing is now known.[53] Despite obvious anachronisms (which could, moreover, be of very ancient date), it is difficult not to establish a link to what can be observed on the Roman site. What does the regrouping on the Palatine of the seats of the curiae mean, in fact, if not the subjugation of the plurality of forces, which until then had been dispersed throughout the entire space of a federal system, to the advantage of a now unique center of development? The Romulean pomerium sanctified a primacy that was not only natural (whatever indisputable advantages the Palatine owes to its geographical position) but was also conquered by force of arms. In these communities, war was a daily reality from the appropriately named March to October, as the mute but eloquent evidence of Latial tombs from the ninth and eighth centuries B.C.E., rich in both defensive and offensive weapons (often miniature ones), confirms with each new discovery.[54]

In societies that were almost completely unfamiliar with technological progress, and where commercial relations were still very modest, war was almost the only means for a rapid accumulation of wealth.[55] That is why any attempt to calculate the resources available to the communities of protohistorical Latium must take into account this incomparable factor of progress and development constituted by war in its various forms (periodic raids, endemic conflicts, etc.). The Romulean foundation of Rome, then, far from being simply the self-evident expression of the geographical supremacy of a hill fated above all others, actually implied the elimination (whether physical or simply "political") of neighboring and rival communities.

[53] As Ampolo underscored in his commentary to Plutarch's *Life of Romulus* (17.314), there is at least a topographical logic to that tradition, since Fidenae, Crustumerium, and Antemnae were all located along the ancient *via Salaria*, whose role in the emergence of Rome we have already examined.

[54] In the ninth and eighth centuries B.C.E., women's tombs were curiously more numerous than men's sepulchres (which alone contained weapons). See *Dialoghi di Archeologia*, 1980, 90. This imbalance has often been interpreted as a difference in the funeral ritual. In my view, it could be explained by the fact that the warriors who fell elsewhere on the battlefield were not buried in the necropolis of their native village.

[55] See, for example, J. Cels Saint-Hilaire and C. Feuvrier-Prevotat, "Guerres, échanges, pouvoir à Rome à l'époque archaïque," *Dialogues d'Histoire Ancienne* 5 (1979): 104–36. For the organization of the Roman city as a function of war, see T. J. Cornell's essay in the proceedings of the colloquium *Alli origini di Roma*, ed. E. Campanile (Pisa, 1988).

That first correlation can be read transparently in the tradition whose value was underscored by Mommsen,[56] that linking any extension of the pomerium to the growth of the territory of the Roman state. Conquest and the sacral delimitation of the territory of the city are linked, not secondarily, but organically and originally.

Later on, the tradition, as it did in the case of Alba Longa, translated that religious primacy of the Palatine, which was also the mark of a political, which is to say, historical, hegemony, into the terms of chronological priority. Modern research attempted to follow that schema of Rome's beginnings, but to no avail; it tried to show that the legend did nothing but transport to the plane of religion and myth the primordial supremacy of the Palatine. In reality, as in many of the centers of Villanovan Etruria, the Romulean foundation, of which the pomerium is the sign, supposes first of all a displacement, a "recentering." In Rome that recentering was "internal" so to speak, since it operated on the same site as that of the other concurrent hills. In Etruria, conversely, it could be called external, since it operated through large-scale transfers of populations over distances that sometimes reached several dozen kilometers.

In fact, this Romulean foundation of Rome, the existence of which is manifested in the remains recently brought to light, already appears in what we know of the oldest institutions of Rome. Regarding the three primitive tribes of the *urbs,* the Tities (or Titienses), the Ramnes (or Ramnenses), and the Luceres, we know very little of course, except that they did not correspond to ethnic divisions, despite modern efforts at exegesis in that sense (such an interpretation was in favor in the nineteenth century), or to territorial or family divisions. Explanations in terms of the Indo-European functional tripartition have fared no better, as Georges Dumézil himself was led to abandon them.[57] But in the correspondence of their names to what appear to be the three primitive centuries (subdivisions of the cavalry, which were later doubled) and of their number to the thirty curiae, we might already be tempted to recognize the silhouette of a masked founder as it were.[58] With the new discoveries, that silhouette has become clearer, which does not mean we can speak simply and directly of an individual named Romulus, nor of course of another named Remus. But if the foundation of Rome was truly the establishment and sacralization of the hegemony of one community over its neighbors, what other legendary schema could better illustrate that relationship, which was both identity and difference, alliance and opposition, than the fratricidal struggle between twin founders?

[56] See Mommsen, *Römische Staatsrecht*, 6: 2.

[57] See the remarks in Poucet, *Origines de Rome*, 101–3. The institutional questions that can be raised regarding the classical data were formulated by Momigliano, *Roma arcaica*, 42 and 93ff. See also L. R. Menager, "Les collèges sacerdotaux, les tribus et la formation primordiale de Rome," *Mélanges d'Archéologie et d'Histoire de l'Ecole Française de Rome* 88 (1976): 455–543.

[58] See Momigliano, *Roma arcaica*, 23, 99, and 100.

Hence the idea of a founder of Rome must be fully rehabilitated, for it has been revived with an archeological, and as a result historical, content, which could never have been imagined even a few years ago. "There is no archeological confirmation of, and some evidence against, the traditional date of the foundation of Rome in the eighth century," observed Arnaldo Momigliano in the survey he wrote at the beginning of the 1980s for the new *Cambridge Ancient History*.[59] In wishing to reduce the notion of foundation to a spontaneous process of development, through recourse to an archeology practiced as a variant of the natural sciences, and in wishing to reduce history, that is, culture, to nature, proposing the model of a nuclear and original expansion from the Palatine, Momigliano encountered insurmountable contradictions (which, of course, did not escape his exceptionally shrewd mind), which could be resolved only by abandoning the notion of foundation, a notion that constituted the crux of the Romulean legend. Regarding the huts discovered on the Palatine, agreement was almost universal. At first, historians underscored that their chronology (dating from the eighth century B.C.E.) agreed with that of the Romulean foundation of Rome. But when, a little later (in 1954), they discovered, under the site of the House of Livia,[60] an adult's tomb dating from the tenth century B.C.E., it soon became obvious that an immediate and "fideist" reading of the tradition was becoming impossible. The presence of a tomb, belonging no doubt to a vanished necropolis, implied that the Palatine had been occupied before the time of the legendary Romulus. It also implied, though historians paid less attention to this fact, that the simple nuclear model was problematic and that it was not enough to assign it an earlier date in relation to the legendary chronology. In fact, since a necropolis could exist only outside a settlement, it followed that the tomb by itself was enough to indicate that, at its date, the unity of the Palatine had not been accomplished and was then occupied by several distinct villages and not by a single "city." In addition, the list of "hills" that participated in the Septimontium still distinguished between the Palatine and the Germalus, which is nothing but the western part of the Romulean hill. A few years later (in 1959), Gjerstad's reexamination of embankment earth exhumed in 1935 near the Church of Sant'Omobono in the Forum Boarium, and the identification of fragments of sub-Apennine pottery, to which new finds (from the Tabularium) were then added, demonstrated the ancientness and even perhaps the priority of the Capitol.

These new discoveries on the Palatine thus illustrate—and this is not their least paradoxical contribution—the need to go beyond a mere archeological inventory in order to understand the evolution of Rome on the basis of archeology. The new elements provided by these recent excavations show once more that no taxonomy, however complete, can dispense with a work of interpreta-

---

[59] Now in Momigliano, *Roma arcaica*, 16.
[60] See the catalog *Civiltà del Lazio primitivo*, 121.

tion. That fact has nothing to do with the classic (and tired) debate about objectivity versus subjectivity in history. It is simply that, considered in their most objective truth, lined up to proclaim the obviousness of their existence, the data revealed by archeology concerning the emergence of the Roman entity turn out to be contradictory and incomprehensible when measured by the yardstick of the theory of a nuclear and linear development. And in such a case, there is obviously only one thing to do, and that is to change the theoretical model.

The foundation of Rome is now archeologically perceptible, and that is a totally new development. But even as its long-contested reality manifests itself, we can understand why it remained hidden until now. Let there be no doubt, the disputes and denials will continue (along with the inevitable concessions), since that reality is not archeological in the first place. For a long time, historians interpreted the development of the Roman entity using the analogy of a living organism, whose growth occurred from an initial cell (in this case, the Palatine). That schema, with the place it reserved for the ideas of determinism and progress, has to be abandoned.

The very notion of a foundation discovered and restored to the history of Rome turns out to be more complex than once thought. The model of Rome's development through formation from a primordial kernel undoubtedly enjoyed favor for so long because it rested on the idea of a foundation understood as an absolute, invisible, and original beginning, given for all eternity, timeless, and, so to speak, metaphysical (situated beyond memory and evolution). Reread in the light of new discoveries, the known archeological elements on the Roman site as a whole show that it was, in contrast, an *event*, datable, situatable, (partially) visible, in short, historical and memorable. Like any event, the foundation thus had a past and was rich in future developments. It was a break, but it was also continuity, a starting point but also a destination, a foundation but also a formation.

Formation *and* foundation, foundation *because* formation. The two processes, then, are not contradictory and exclusive, but complementary and concomitant.

This formulation obviously does not in any way constitute a compromise between two theses, which I might feel obliged to reconcile, impelled by some spirit of compromise. This is not reconciliation but transcendence, a way of accounting for a "reality" as best I can, a reality whose growing unity and complexity have exploded the too rigid frameworks within which they had been confined. The major, the literally fundamental, importance of the notion of foundation is clear in the Roman conception of history and time.[61] Until the end of antiquity, in Rome and a good part of the Roman Empire, time was counted and recounted *ab urbe condita* "from the foundation of the city" (though, in fact, that dating method was later practiced particularly by educated

[61] Underscored by Pallottino in "Le origini di Roma," 22–47, esp. 33.

people and scholars). It is also clear why, in so many of its features, the new city continued the ancient leagues of protohistory, even as it constituted something radically different from them. Hence the thirty curiae of Rome recall the thirty tribes (*populi*) of the Latin league (*nomen latinum*). The she-wolf, before becoming the symbol of the *urbs,* was the totem animal for the Latial populations of prehistory.[62] And there was a dictator in Rome just as there had been at the head of the Latin league. But it was in Rome and only in Rome that the old "words of the tribe" were charged with new meaning.[63]

If the notion of foundation must be revised and stripped of its false simplicity, the same is true for the notion of city. It is to a great extent because that word came to mean the reality it connoted in the classical age, that historians, finding no traces of that reality at the time of Romulean Rome, denied not only all existence but even all possibility of existence to a foundation of Rome in the eighth century B.C.E. There again, we need to historicize, that is, to relativize the general idea designated by the word "city," an idea so general that it often loses all concrete substance.[64] It is obvious we cannot denote, with what has become the all-purpose term of our own urban civilization, both the reality of the eighth century B.C.E. and that of the first century C.E. and after. Needless to say, we would seek in vain a forum on the Palatine resembling those public squares that later became the radiating center of classical cities. We would seek in vain the temple of Vesta, the public hearth that symbolized the permanence and even the life of the community. The Forum, when it came to exist, developed at the bottom of, and hence outside, the Palatine, and we now know that such a development did not occur before the second half of the seventh century B.C.E. Under such conditions, many believed it logical and necessary to place "the foundation of Rome" not before that period, thus depriving what was becoming a process not only of its chronology but of its compactness and exactitude.

In reality, the Forum and the sanctuary of Vesta do not seem organically linked to each other except in a topography that itself resulted from historical evolution. It is no paradox to say that the temple of Vesta was not located in the Forum, but that the Forum developed within its environs. The fire of the city,

[62] As A. Alföldi shows in *Die Struktur des voretruskischen Römerstaates* (Heidelberg, 1974), 84. Note that we do not know the provenance of the famous bronze she-wolf that can now be seen in the Palazzo dei Conservatori on the Capitol. In any case, it seemingly cannot be identified with any of the monuments mentioned by ancient authors. At least we can assert that it is an archaic statue (fifth century B.C.E. at the latest), and thus necessarily of Etruscan origin. See Cristofani, ed., *La grande Roma,* 145.

[63] On that continuity between the league and the city, see M. Torelli, "Rome et l'Etrurie à l'époque archaïque," in *Terre et paysans dépendants dans les sociétés antiques,* proceedings of the 1974 Besançon colloquium (Paris, 1979), 251–311.

[64] For a comprehensive view of the urban phenomenon in antiquity, see F. Kolb, *Die Stadt im Altertum* (Munich, 1984).

when it began to burn for perennial Rome, during an era that the most ancient objects of the votive repositories of its sanctuary allow us to place toward the end of the eighth century B.C.E.,[65] did not constitute the center (a center that, moreover, seems curiously decentered) of a public square, which may not yet have existed. Rather, in the shadow of the nearby Palatine, it marked the link between the Romulean hill and the opposite hill of Velia, where, and this is no accident, objects discovered in the votive repositories attest to an occupation that also goes back to at least the eighth century B.C.E.[66]

In fact, certain specialists do not rule out the possibility that the cult of Vesta had a first form of existence on the Palatine itself, and I wonder if Augustus's decision, when he became Pontifex Maximus, to establish a chapel dedicated to Vesta in his "palace," which was located on the Romulean hill, did not rest on a tradition of that kind that was later forgotten. In doing so, this new Romulus, as Augustus saw himself, reestablished ties with the time of origins, when the Vestals were none other than the daughters of the king, and the hearth they honored that of the royal residence (Regia, later occupied by the Pontifex Maximus).[67] And since we know from the very ancient ritual of the Argei[68] that there was a place on the Palatine considered both the house and the sanctuary of Romulus (significantly, the same Latin word is used in both cases, *aedes*), it is legitimate to infer, since the tradition linked to that hut does not appear to be artificial, that a "common hearth" could have existed on that spot, before that of the Forum.

But, above all, the Forum itself could not have existed as such until after an intervention whose scope appears more and more clearly in the eyes of present-day archeologists.[69] Far from being the place of the ("natural") birth of Rome, the Forum presupposes and requires its existence, even though Rome was not yet what we ordinarily understand by the word "city." In other words, it is not because there already existed a community organized and regrouped on the Palatine that the Forum could have been transformed into a public and central

[65] See Cristofani, ed., *La grande Roma*, 62. The round shape of the temple of Vesta recalls, more than that of the most ancient huts, that of a hearth itself, of which the temple is the symbolic hypostasis. That consideration ought to allow us to relativize the eternal debate on the supposed form of the most ancient huts of Latium (round or square?). If, moreover, the analogies between the first period of Latial civilization and of Aegean civilization suggested by Müller-Karpe are truly confirmed, we would then be justified in proposing a link between Vesta and Hestia on new grounds. See also Poucet's comments on the myth of Tarpeia (*Origines de Rome*, 228).

[66] Cristofani, ed., *La grande Roma*, 105.

[67] See Coarelli, *Il foro romano*, vol. 1. The Vestals were placed under the authority of the Pontifex Maximus, whose residence adjoined their sanctuary. In having the perpetual fire brought near him, Augustus could thus remain on the Palatine. Of course, we do not intend to give to the proposal that follows any value but that of a working hypothesis.

[68] Varro *Ling.* 5.54: "apud aedem Romuli." The Argei was a religious ceremony that consisted in carrying twenty-seven wicker effigies in procession throughout the city, before throwing them into the Tiber.

[69] On this, see Ammerman, "On the Origins of the Forum Romanum."

square, to the point of becoming the "Forum *Romanum*," that is, the place where Rome asserted its identity and power in view of everyone. In order for the Forum to be able to become the new center of the *urbs*, the city had to undergo its first developments and become aware of itself on the Palatine. The Romulean hill, as we have seen, is rich in symbolic and mythic places that appear as so many indexes of sovereignty. In addition to the cave of Lupercal and the home of Romulus (*casa* or *aedes Romuli*) just mentioned, there was also the sacred dogwood tree—born, it is said, from the lance of the founder—the fig tree Ruminal, the Roma Quadrata, and the *mundus,* the center of the city and of the world. These same signs of sovereignty reappear in the valley of the Forum, near the Comitium, the mythic site of the reconciliation between Romulus and the Sabine Titus Tatius. There is another fig tree Ruminal; Roma Quadrata is evoked there; and ancient authors also situate the *mundus* at that site. In these duplications, where nineteenth-century hypercritics saw only confusion and errors in the sources, we can now detect the mark of an extension of the Palatine city and of a transfer of signs of sovereignty and "urban" identity that resulted from it.[70]

Although it was not a city in the classical sense of the term, the city founded by Romulus and designated by a word—*urbs*—that is of neither Indo-European nor Etruscan nor Greek origin (as was noted long ago),[71] already constituted an entity conscious of itself and revealed to itself through a complex set of signs, "memory sites," and legends.

In that entire evolution, we see to what extent the Palatine was in a privileged position, both in relation to the first emergence of Rome, which occurred around the Forum Boarium and the passageway and dock it represented, and in relation to the expansion toward the other hills and beyond the Forum Romanum, which characterized the city's history afterwards. In reference to both these axes of development, the Romulean hill enjoyed a central situation.

In the first system, it was of course in competition with the Aventine, which also dominated the valley of the Forum Boarium; but the Aventine was so closely linked to the hinterland, descending toward it in a gentle slope, that it was virtually indefensible. Romulus, who chose the Palatine, thus won out over Remus, who had wanted to found Rome on the Aventine. If the presence of the twins makes any sense, apart from the well-attested symbolic value that the myth of divine twins has always had in folklore (signifying violence and power, in a complex manner that combines positive and negative aspects), it may lie in the topography the myth represents.

---

[70] This explanation was presented with the discovery of the Lapis Niger, by E. Pais (taking the lead from Jordan), in an appendix to *Storia di Roma*, vol. 1. See also D. Briquel, *Histoire de Rome*, forthcoming. I am extremely grateful to the author for having sent me her manuscript.

[71] See the remarks of the linguist C. de Simone, in the proceedings of the colloquium *Alle origini di Roma*, 31.

In the second system, only the Capitol, whose mass even today dominates the Forum Romanum, could have been a serious rival for the Palatine. But the Capitol suffers from the reverse peculiarity. It is certainly defensible, but so much so that it is inaccessible; its slopes are extremely steep, extremely high on nearly every side; moreover, its surface area is much smaller than that of the Aventine or the Palatine. Yet the presence of another "home of Romulus" (*aedes Romuli*) on the Capitol, affirmed in the sources, retains the trace of that probable rivalry.

Expansive but naturally delimited, defensible but accessible (on the Velia side especially), dominating the course of the Tiber but also the valley of the future Forum—which, before becoming a site fixed for encounters and exchanges, was still only a border zone—situated beyond the gates (called *fores* in Latin, in which we recognize the word *forum*) of the Forum's enclosure, the Palatine was thus the place for the foundation by Romulus. That is, it was a place of residence (but the contemporary example of Ficana shows that the hill was far from completely covered with huts, and that large spaces were left vacant), of refuge (for those who lived on neighboring hills, the Velia especially), of gathering and of prayers, on the part of a community conscious of itself, of its identity, of its unity, which recognized and discovered itself in the name Rome, a name that would henceforth be its own.

We thus cannot reduce "urbanization," that is, the birth of Rome, to the construction of monuments, which took place only later (in the seventh century B.C.E., to be precise). Modern attempts to place the foundation of Rome in the ninth century B.C.E., on the pretext that something had already happened before the eighth century, or, in contrast, in the seventh century B.C.E., on the pretext that the first great monuments on the Forum were not built prior to that date, are in fact symmetrical and must both be rejected.

Yet we must not for all that deny the past and future realities. The foundation of Rome can and must be placed at the time assigned it by legend, which until now has been condemned and scorned. This foundation represents what we could call the crystallizing point of a process whose complete evolution extended over the long term, beginning in about the ninth century B.C.E. and ending in the seventh, and over a large space, involving from the beginning the Roman site as a whole. But within that duration and that space, it took shape at a given moment and a precise place. Of course, if we liked, we might retain the word "foundation," but give it the insipid and transposed sense it has assumed, to describe the initial and final stages of this long movement. But we can no longer deny that as it was used in the tradition of the origins of the city, the term "foundation" designated a precise reality limited in time and space. That reality, however, did not exhaust the notion of foundation, which is mental and ideological as well as factual and historical. Commemorated in the narrative of origins, the foundation became a perpetual celebration and a new beginning in the history of Rome.

Does the very name of the community of *Roma,* which asserted itself on the Palatine in the eighth century B.C.E., tell us something about it? Legend says that Rome was named after its founder, Romulus. As always in such a case, we must of course invert that schema: Rome preceded Romulus, who was none other than "the Roman" par excellence. The name Rome was long considered Etruscan, at a time when the study of the origins of the *urbs,* abandoned somewhat by hypercritical historians, tended to become an auxiliary and provincial field of the flourishing discipline of Etruscology. Even recently, there has been a desire to find confirmation for that Etruscan origin in the inscriptions found here and there, in Orvieto and Bomarzo especially,[72] which noted a clan named Rumelna or Rumlna. But if these inscriptions—which do not go back farther than the sixth century B.C.E.—prove anything, it is not the Etruscan origin of the name, but its later diffusion in Etruria, which is quite a different matter. Since the equivalence between the Latin and Etruscan forms of the name has been demonstrated, as is the case even for advocates of an Etruscan provenance, why suppose that "Romulus" was only the transposition of "Rumelna/Rumlna," rather than the reverse?[73]

In reality, the noun "Rome" is an old word of Italic origin: farther to the south of the peninsula, in the interior, lies the territory of the Hirpini people, whose name indicates that, like the first Romans, they had the wolf as a totem animal (in the Oscan language, the wolf was called *hirpus*). And, among the centers inhabited by this people, we find mention of a Romulea, whose name closely recalls "Rome" and "Romulus." There was even a mountain called Romola in the area; if its name was original, it would further reinforce the value of that link.[74] In these names, we are thus inclined to recognize an old word such as *ruma* (or *rumen*), by which the Latin language designated the teat of an animal. In this case, it would allude to the *mamelons* of the hills on the Roman site, which we also discover in the name of the fig tree Ruminal, in whose shade, according to legend, the she-wolf suckled the twins. We might also think of a very old name for the Tiber, *Rumon,* an explanation that is no different from the last, except in appearance, for the river acquired that name either because of the mountains from which it came, or from the reliefs it crossed, above, precisely, the site of "Rome."

Thus that name, before being limited to the city founded by "Romulus," was that of an entire zone, and we must believe it preexisted the initiative of the

---

[72] See C. de Simone, in the journal *Glotta* 53 (1975): 134 n. 22. The inscription of Bomarzo is published and dated by G. Colonna in the proceedings of the 1979 colloquium of Rome, *Gli Etruschi e Roma* (1981), 169–72. See also de Simone, in *Glotta,* p. 201.

[73] For all the data on the question, see Ampolo's commentary on Plutarch's *Life of Romulus* in *Le vite di Teseo e di Romolo,* ed. C. Ampolo (Milan, 1988), 33: "Non è necessario pensare che *Romulus* e *Roma* derivino dall'etrusco" (It is not necessary to think that "Romulus" and "Rome" derived from the Etruscan).

[74] Suggested by E. T. Salmon in "The Hirpini: Ex Italia semper aliquid novi," *Phoenix* 43 (1989): 225–35.

legendary brother of Remus. Across the entire expanse of the site of the city to come, there is evidence of toponyms of similar formation. There was a Remoria (on the Aventine), a place called Remona, and an *ager Remurinus*.[75] The foundation of "Rome" consisted not in creating ex nihilo a name that did not exist before (such was the classical schema of the "imposition of names," obviously implausible both linguistically and historically), but rather in limiting its application to a precisely defined and henceforth delimited place, in this case, the Palatine. Subsequently, parallel to the rise in power and the expansion of the new entity, the name Rome extended to all the neighboring hills.

As for the name Romulus, one of the surest accomplishments of modern linguistic research, which, however, has been insufficiently exploited, is to have shown long ago that it was not an artificially fabricated diminutive, but an authentically archaic name, on the same order as Rutulus (the people that occupied the territory of the city of Ardea) or Volsculus (the Volscian people, long the blood enemies of Rome). Then, like the French François, the term designating membership in a community became a family (or given) name. The archaic singularity of the name Romulus and the nonexistence of its legend elsewhere than in Rome both prove the age and authenticity of the Romulean tradition.

All this allows us to arrive at the question we had not wished to ask before, but that now can no longer be avoided, even though it is so simple, so crude as it were, that we would almost like to be able to elude it, since the reality that emerges from the excavations and the new questions they continually elicit appears endlessly more complex, both more clear and more obscure.

"The truly clear things do not forget the shadow from which they come," wrote Claude Roy, an essayist and also a remarkable poet.[76] Do the new excavations on the Palatine prove that an individual named Romulus really existed in the eighth century B.C.E.? Despite appearances, this too simple question calls for an answer that cannot be simple. It goes without saying that, until now, we have spoken of Romulus, founder of Rome, adopting the legend as such only as a matter of convenience. We did not intend to offer a solution to a problem that we could not yet raise in its true terms. We first had to clarify the very notion of the foundation of Rome. For all that, does the reality of that foundation authorize us to postulate the reality of a founder?

Yes and no. In looking closely, we find at least five possible hypotheses.

The first is represented by the famous essay Mommsen devoted to "the legend of Remus" in 1881,[77] in which he strategically chose to emphasize the most difficult part to grasp in the Romulean legend, that concerning the brother

---

[75] Not to mention the Porta Romanula on the Palatine, if it really refers to a toponym beyond the Romulean hill, in accord with Colonna's convincing hypothesis in "I Latini."

[76] Claude Roy, *La fleur du temps, 1983–1987* (Paris, 1988), 309.

[77] T. Mommsen, *"Die Remuslegende," Hermes* 16 (1881): 1ff.

eliminated by the founder. Mommsen concludes by making the tradition of the twins a late creation, dating from the fourth century B.C.E. Even during those hypercritical times, the end of the nineteenth century, it was not possible to fix the date at a more recent era (for otherwise you can be sure it would have been done), because we know from Livy that, at the beginning of the third century B.C.E., monuments were erected in Rome to illustrate the legend of the twins and the she-wolf.[78] Mommsen thus interprets that legend as a fabrication designed to provide a model for the duality of power represented by the two consuls under the Republic. In the end, that theory raised insurmountable difficulties, since critics were quick to realize, not only that hatred of royalty, *odium regni*,[79] was a constant of the Roman mentality from the advent of the republican regime, but also that it would have been a curious and peculiarly dangerous constitutional model, since, in the end, Romulus killed Remus . . .

A second hypothesis stems from the fact that the name of the founder can be found in Rome itself, among a tribe and a *gens* (that is, a family, in the broadest sense of the term), the *gens Romilia*.[80] Neighboring Etruria provides an appealing model: cities such as Volsinii or Tarquinia apparently took their name from a *gens* that no doubt exerted a decisive influence at the time these inhabited centers took the form of a city. However, for Rome, objections are not lacking: In the canonical succession in which tribes were listed according to what seems to have been an order of precedence, the Ramnes (or Ramnenses) came only after the Tities (or Titienses). And even that assumes that Romilia can be linked to Ramnes, which cannot be done without difficulty. As for the *gens Romilia* itself, its only distinction in the history of the city lay in its obscurity! Finally, "Romulus" seems to be the name of an ethnic group much more than that of a *gens*.

The example of the history of archaic Greece suggests a third interpretation of the legendary figure of Romulus, which again does not in any way imply that an individual named Romulus actually existed. There might have been a civic cult, dedicated to a fictive heroic character, whose function was to legitimate, by mythic antecedence, the settlement reestablished in the eighth century B.C.E. As Anthony Snodgrass notes in *Archaic Greece*,[81] during that century in Greece, "from shortly after 750 B.C., in the regions of Attica, Boiotia, Phokis, the Argolid, and Messenia . . . we begin to find the almost entirely new practice of making dedications in, or otherwise showing reverence to, tombs of the Bronze Age." In almost all cases, he adds, "these are of the Mycenaean age—that is to say, of a period about 500 years earlier than the institution of the cult." On the basis of this hypothesis, we would have to suppose that, in Rome in 730 B.C.E.,

---

[78] In 269 B.C.E. by the Ogulnii brothers. See Livy *Ab urbe condita* 10.23.
[79] See P. Marin, *L'idée de royauté à Rome* (Clermont-Ferrand, 1982).
[80] See, for example, C. de Simone's essay in *Studi Etruschi*, 1975, 145 and 148.
[81] A. Snodgrass, *Archaic Greece* (Berkeley, 1980), 38–39.

on the Palatine, a tomb from the beginnings of Latial civilization or from the "sub-Apennine" period became the object of a similarly deferred veneration. To judge from the existing archeological evidence, such a schema appears neither impossible nor implausible. As in Greece, it is clear that the establishment of such a civic sanctuary was related to the shift to agriculture and the institution or development of private landed property. The rest of the tradition also seems to point to this, insisting on the distribution by Romulus of a lot of individual land (called *heredium*)[82] to all new Romans.

Of course, the most adequate location for this first heroic cult would have been the *aedes* (or *casa*) *Romuli,* whose presence on the Palatine we have already noted. The legendary place of Romulus's death, which was identified as the site of the Lapis Niger in the Forum, is another possibility. But in both cases, objections could be made. Romulus's hut on the Palatine was never depicted as a tomb, but, on the contrary, as the place where the founder first lived with his brother under the tutelage of the shepherd Raustulus. And, conversely, although it is true that significant traditions situate the founder's death in the valley of the Forum, the archeological remains discovered at the site, in particular in the votive repository, do not reveal any sacral construction in the zone before the beginning of the sixth century B.C.E. (or the end of the seventh).[83] In any case, according to that hypothesis, the individuals at the origin, when the wall was established in the eighth century B.C.E., remain unknown, even though they existed historically. Under such conditions, could not the foundation itself have been merely a community becoming conscious of itself, at the initiative of one or several of its leaders, at an already advanced stage of its civic, political, and social organization? That would be possible only if the establishment and consolidation of that community on the Palatine resulted from a natural and spontaneous evolution. But as we have seen from the dispersion of the archeological traces for earlier periods, that was not at all the case.[84]

There is thus a fourth hypothesis, which is not to be confused with the previous one. The legendary figure of Romulus might have been invented after the fact, not this time by the wall's builders, but by their successors, to explain the presence of a large number of remains on the Palatine and in its environs, which

---

[82] See Dion. Hal. *Ant. rom.* 2.7; Varro *Rust.* 1.10; Pliny *HN* 18.2, etc. That tradition, which is often disregarded even in specialized entries on Romulus, is at the center of the essays that were part of the 1980 colloquium published as *La formazione della città nel Lazio*, ed. C. Ampolo; see also the work of L. Capogrossi-Colognessi, especially *L'età arcaica*, vol. 1, *La terra in Roma antica: Forme di proprietà e rapporti produttivi* (Rome, 1981). The emergence of a Roman community was inseparable from the constitution of a territory, the *ager Romanus antiquus*. See J. Scheid, "Les sanctuaires de confins dans la Rome antique: Réalité et permanence d'une représentation idéale de l'espace romain," in *L'urbs, espace urbain et histoire* (Paris and Rome, 1987), 583–95.

[83] See Cristofani, ed., *La grande Roma*, 53.

[84] To avoid confirming the tradition by the tradition, I do not include the literary sources in this argument, even though, in fact, their existence and the concentration of the legendary corpus around the Palatine appear to be significant elements.

modern archeological investigation has dated, at least in the case of the enclosure and a few huts, from the eighth century B.C.E. According to that interpretation, the Romulean legend can be dated *after* the eighth century (a date that the material reality of the wall obliges us to keep, if not as a reference point, then at least as a guide). Other archeological indexes in other places, and especially in the Forum, where the site of the Lapis Niger was the object of particular veneration, suggest we cannot move the date any later than the sixth century B.C.E. Of course, we might want to call that veneration "non-Romulean" in nature, but then we would have to explain the presence among the votive objects of the remains of a vulture sacrificed there.[85] It is difficult not to think of the vultures announcing Rome's fortune in the augury scene of the twin founders.

However appealing these last two hypotheses might be, they do not so much solve the problem raised by the tradition of a Romulean foundation as displace it. They account for the formation of the tradition, not the causes that made it necessary, that is, the foundation of Rome, which they surround with a protective and prudent fog, reducing it to a long-term process, of which the legend would simply mark the end and the now conscious perception. But if there was an end, it is to be placed in the seventh century B.C.E. (I shall not return to the conclusions of recent studies on this point)[86] and is located in the Forum, not on the Palatine. In short, from this perspective, the place and date of the Romulean legend continue to pose difficulties.

There remains a fifth hypothesis, the least credible today, the most revolutionary, the most disconcerting to be sure, but perhaps also the most plausible, the most "traditional" in any case, and finally, the most simple . . .

It is the hypothesis that an individual named Romulus really existed in the eighth century B.C.E. and was at the origin of the remains that have come to light concerning the nucleus of a first organization, which we glimpse in the institutions of the city, the preeminence of the Palatine Hill, and the legend whose development we can read in the classical authors. That is not certain, of course, but it is possible and perhaps even—yes, why not?—probable . . .

Eliminate if you like that last qualifier and conserve a share of uncertainty to ensure good scientific method. But such uncertainty, so dear to Beaufort, can no longer be adopted from the outset as a prejudice but must simply be understood as the space open for a conclusion. We must admit that the wall on the Palatine (to speak only of that one piece of "data") was built after a human intervention (an obvious matter too often forgotten). As a result, although it is only one vestige among others (as those who wish to see it as only an "insignifi-

---

[85] See Cristofani, ed., *La grande Roma*, 58.

[86] See Ampolo, "Die endgültige Stadtwerdung Roms"; and id., "Le origini di Roma e la 'cité antique,'" *Mélanges de l'Ecole Française de Rome* 92 (1980): 567–76; Coarelli, *Il foro romano*, vol. 1, *Periodo archaico*; and G. Colonna, "Aspetti culturali della Roma recente," *Archeologia Classica*, 1964, 1–12.

cant" piece of evidence, meaning little in terms of the foundation, will no doubt say), we still need to understand why there exists a tradition that, with the pomerium, grants so much importance to the notion of limit, placing its establishment precisely at the midpoint of the eighth century and its location precisely at the foot of the Palatine.

In any case, even if it is true that we shall never know whether an individual called Romulus existed, we can only conclude that a "Romulean moment" was real, factual, that it was, in other words, a historical event that can no longer be denied or concealed or dissolved in the immemorial immobility of the long term.

Hence Rome was founded toward the second half of the eighth century B.C.E. on the Palatine Hill. Different causes contributed to this first advent of a city that would never again leave the world stage, causes that are all well known to archeologists and historians, who long ago shed light on the importance of the eighth century. In the first place, there was the process of demographic densification and aggregation, which we saw at work in the Septimontium, a process that was itself part of a widespread evolution, observable during the same period in Greek territory.[87] Second, and in direct relation to this phenomenon, came the influence of the civilizing currents from Greece or Magna Graecia, much earlier than was once thought, before the archaic inscription dedicated to the Dioscuri, which was discovered in Lavinium in 1959,[88] and before the Greek vases that, beginning in the eighth century B.C.E., were present on the site of Rome.[89] Along with other contributions that ought not to be forgotten, especially those made by Phoenician traders,[90] and the shock waves emitted by the great mutation under way during the same period in nearby Etruria, these led to the intensification of exchanges, to a progressive specialization of artisanal activities,[91] to the assertion of an aristocracy that acknowledged itself as such and regrouped behind charismatic leaders (Romulus, for example?). They led, in short, to the event of the foundation of Rome.

[87] See Snodgrass, *Archaic Greece*. That simultaneity of evolution is extremely odd and indirectly shows the early date and the intensity of the exchanges throughout the Mediterranean basin.

[88] For recent bibliography, see M. Fenelli, *Lavinio: Bibliografia topografica della colonizzazione greca in Italia e nelle isole tirreniche* 5 (1990).

[89] See especially E. La Rocca, "Due tombe dall'Esquilino: Alcune novità sul commercio euboico in Italia centrale nell'VIII sec. a. C.," *Dialoghi di Archeologia* 8 (1974–75): 86–103; id., "Ceramica d'importazione greca dell'VIII secolo a S. Omobono: Un aspetto delle origini di Roma," in *La céramique grecque ou de tradition grecque au VIIIe siècle en Italie centrale et méridionale* (Naples, 1984), 45–84.

[90] See R. Rebuffat, "Les Phéniciens à Rome," in *Mélanges de l'Ecole Française de Rome* 78 (1966): 7–48; and M. Gras, P. Rouillard, and J. Teixidor, *L'univers phénicien* (Paris, 1989).

[91] See, for example, A. M. Bietti-Sestieri and A. de Santis, "Indicatori archeologici di cambiamento nella struttura delle comunità laziali nell'8o sec. a. C.," *Dialoghi di Archeologia*, 1985, 33–45.

One question remains, no longer prejudicial like the others, but conclusive. How was the tradition of the foundation conserved for so many centuries? By what paths did the memory of the origins of the city reach Rome's first chroniclers, before finally reaching the scholars, historians, and poets of the classical age, who transmitted it to us, but in a form that was orchestrated, transfigured, perpetuated, and, through the magic of their art, recreated each time?

CHAPTER 11

THE PATHS OF MEMORY

I N THE SUMMER of 390 B.C.E., Rome went up in flames. Invaded by the Gauls, plundered but not subdued, Rome watched its own ruin from the top of the Capitol, where its final defenders had taken refuge. For several months of a long siege, ancient historians tell us (Livy and Plutarch essentially), hordes of Celtic horsemen, who had just crushed the Roman legions in the bloody and thereafter memorable battle of the Allia, pillaged the homes and monuments of a city that did not yet know it was eternal. It would take more than the doubtful victories of the Roman Camillus, probably invented by later historians anxious to restore the prestige of their city; it would even take more than the rumors of invasion threatening the invaders' homeland farther north. In fact, it would take all the gold the Romans could give to the Gauls of Brennus: "Vae vicitis!" "Woe to the vanquished!"

For the historian of the Celts, that temporary occupation of Rome is only one episode among many others in a great movement of migration that had begun much earlier and whose effects extended far into space and time. For the specialist in the Etruscan world,[1] that successful descent of the Celtic bands into the territories of a formerly prosperous people merely confirms the irremediable decline of a civilization then prey to slow social disaggregation and to the blows of its external adversaries: the Gauls, the Greeks, and the Romans. For the historian of republican and imperial Rome, the sack of Rome represents only a momentary reversal in the prodigious history of a city that finally came to represent the world.

But for anyone attempting to read the true history of the beginnings of the city of Romulus in what Michelet termed "the old novel of origins," the "Gallic catastrophe," as scholarship of the last century called it (Mommsen wrote a famous essay by that name in 1848),[2] traditionally raises a major difficulty of method, an insurmountable obstacle, a wall that criticism, far from seeking to scale, has long undertaken to build ever higher and to fortify ever more.

---

[1] On all these aspects, see the exhibition catalog *I Galli e l'Italia* (Rome, 1978).
[2] See Mommsen, *Römische Forschungen*, vol. 2.

In reading the classical sources, we have the impression that nothing could have escaped the destructive furor of the Celtic invaders. At the beginning of book 6 of his history, Livy, referring to the earliest times of Rome, speaks of

> events obscured less by their great age, comparable to the distance that nearly obliterates distant landscapes, than by the rarity of written testimony for that period, the only faithful guardian of historical events, and by the destruction in the city fire of most of the evidence that may have been contained in the registries of pontiffs and other public and private documents.[3]

Plutarch echoes these discouraging words in his *Life of Numa,* abandoning the task of establishing an exact chronology, since "the ancient registers of the city of Rome were lost when it was taken and sacked by the Gauls, and those which are extant at this day may not be true but were only made by men desirous to gratify certain people who have forced their way into the ancient houses and families of the first Romans, and are not at all about those they meant to represent."[4]

Since the early eighteenth century, these considerations and a few others of the same type have been at the center of the debate on Rome's origins. In its continued effort to distinguish the true from the false—history from legend— modern historical criticism has seen that episode as one of the major reasons for denying any historical foundation to the tradition of Rome's beginnings. It is no exaggeration to say that a good part of the scholarly exegesis of the primordia, as it was practiced until a recent date, consisted in extending ever farther the limits of that primordial void indicated by the classical texts. In an echo of Livy's remark, amplified to the dimension of the dominant mode of scholarship at the end of the nineteenth century, a historian thus exclaimed, at the beginning of a history of republican Rome published in 1873: "The Gallic fire is the decisive criterion in the question of sources, and allows us to cast our gaze on the credibility of the most ancient historical representation and on that which followed, a gaze that is lost in a disheartening void."[5]

Today, nearly a century after the discovery of the Lapis Niger in the Forum, and after more than three decades of almost uninterrupted archeological finds, we might think that such words no longer carry much weight. That would be to forget that scholarship, even hypercritical scholarship, is faithful to its own traditions. Thus we see a historian as informed as Finley, in a distant echo of Henry Dodwell—who even in the early eighteenth century had submitted the narrative of Rome's origins to a severe critique—wondering where Livy and Dionysius of

---

[3] Livy *Ab urbe condita* 6.1.

[4] Plut. *Life of Numa Pompilius,* in *Lives,* p. 177 [translation modified].

[5] Clason, *Römische Geschichte* (1873), 4: 10. Clason was Schwegler's successor; Schwegler died in 1857 before he could finish his history of Rome, which appeared beginning in 1853 and remains a reference work.

Halicarnassus had gotten their information, immediately responding that "no matter how many older statements we can either document or posit—irrespective of possible reliability—we eventually reach a void. But ancient writers, like historians ever since, could not tolerate a void, and they filled it in one way or another, ultimately by pure invention."[6]

Clearly, if ancient historians could not tolerate a void, modern historians for their part feel an indisputable fascination for it, to the point of forgetting the real progress that has occurred in our knowledge of the *primordia Romana*! In a certain way, some can always claim that we know nothing or will never know anything, and Finley himself was well aware of this. But although this type of analysis was an instrument for incomparable advances in the interpretation of literary sources in the eighteenth and nineteenth centuries, today it is no longer appropriate. The task facing the historian of the primordia is now to interpret the mass of new data that in recent years has increased if not our knowledge, then at least the questions we can ask of the legends of origins. Hypercritical exegesis performed an epistemological function, which was not made explicit, but which appeared clearly in the writings of Beaufort. It established the uncertainty of the most ancient Roman history and, according to the felicitous expression of an English admirer of Beaufort, it drew "the boundary line of authentic history."

What may have been an innovative and founding discourse in the past, however, no longer corresponds to the new scientific landscape of the primordia. Even looking with the most skeptical eye possible, we see something very different from a void.

Merely in the field of epigraphy, a science that was one of the great achievements of ancient history in the nineteenth century, when it was granted foremost epistemological status, we possess several inscriptions dating from the archaic period. In recent years, they have granted individuals that had been attested to only in the literary tradition, if not an existence, then at least historical plausibility. Thus archeologists have discovered the name Aulus Vibenna written on stones and vases; according to legend, his brother Caeles played an important role beside King Servius Tullius (giving his name, for instance, to one of the hills of Rome, the Caelian). Further, they have found the names of two members of the *gens Tolumnia*, whose importance for the history of Veii, then a great rival of Rome, is suggested in the sources. Also discovered a few years ago was the name of Publius Valerius, which it is tempting to read as "Publicola,"[7] to whom the literary sources ascribe a large role in the beginnings of the Republic.

---

[6] Finley, *Ancient History*, 9.

[7] Despite what Finley says (or does not say!) about it in the chapter entitled "The Ancient Historian and His Sources," where the example of Satricum occupies a significant place but is finally qualified as a "cul-de-sac." We do find one allusion in a footnote, devoted to an inscription that deserved better. See Finley, *Ancient History*, 28 and 111 n. 30.

More recently, archeologists have discovered an inscription bearing the name of Mezentius,[8] who until then was attested to only in the *Aeneid,* where Virgil makes him the relentless adversary of the Trojans who landed in Latium. The name Aeneas itself can be read on an inscription found not far from the site of ancient Lavinium,[9] and elsewhere, other names, such as Tallos Tyrannos, present in the legend of origins,[10] have been discovered or exhumed from ancient epigraphic compendia after a long (and significant) oblivion. Such is the case for Hustileia,[11] which evokes the name of the third king of Rome, Tullus Hostilius, a name considered by hypercriticism to be one of the surest signs of the fabricated nature of the narrative of origins (because it was seen as an artificial creation from the word *hostis,* enemy). In addition, there is the name of Tarchunies Rumach ("Tarquinius of Rome"), long ago identified on the walls of the François tomb,[12] which was discovered in Vulci in 1857, and that of Servius, legible on a divining stone[13] that also mentioned Fortune. The latter can refer only to King Servius Tullius, whose reign the texts place under the protection of that goddess. The François tomb also attests to the name by which Servius Tullius was known in Etruria—Mastarna—and makes him the adversary of Tarquinius of Rome,[14] as the literary tradition indicates.

One of the direct consequences of the discovery of these inscriptions, which, significantly, have multiplied since archeologists have begun methodically to seek them out, is to rehabilitate the information given by ancient authors on the monuments they said they had themselves seen.[15] What was long considered only fabulation and inexactitude can now be recognized as a documentary source, which should be carefully distinguished from the literary tradition into which it has been incorporated. Thus, Dionysius of Halicarnassus could see the text of a treaty between King Servius Tullius and the Latins in the temple of Diana, or another between Rome and Gabii conserved in the temple

---

[8] The exact references to these inscriptions (Aulus Vibenna, Tolumnius, Valerius, and Mezentius) are given in D. Briquel's essay in *Revue des Etudes Latines* 67 (1989): 79. For others, see the notes that follow.

[9] References in Momigliano, *Roma arcaica,* 322.

[10] Example signaled by Poucet, *Origines de Rome,* 89.

[11] First signaled by C. de Simone and republished by G. Colonna in *Mélanges de l'Ecole Française de Rome,* 86. The inscription dates from the seventh century B.C.E.

[12] See the exhibition catalog *La tomba François di Vulci.*

[13] Published by M. Guarducci (1951), it is dated to the fourth century B.C.E. by Coarelli in *Il foro boario,* 302, and to the second century B.C.E. by A. Maggiani, in *La grande Roma,* ed. Cristofani, 20.

[14] The tomb frescoes depict a mythic Greek cycle facing a historical Etrusco-Roman cycle. For an illuminating interpretation, based on the schema Etruscans = Greeks, Romans = Trojans, see F. Coarelli, "Le pitture della tomba François a Vulci: Una proposta di lettura," *Dialoghi di Archeologia,* 1983.

[15] The list of archaic documents that ancient historians recorded is presented and commented on in C. Ampolo, "La storiografia su Roma arcaica e i documenti," in *Tria corda: Scritti in onore di A. Momigliano,* ed. E. Gabba (Como, 1983), 9–26.

of Sancus. Cicero could still read the treaty concluded between Spurius Cassius and the Latins, not far from the place where legend claims Romulus dedicated a brass quadriga and his own statue—"on which he had the list of his exploits inscribed in Greek"—to Hephaestus (that is, to Volcanus). This last precision comes from Dionysius of Halicarnassus: since the sanctuary of Volcanus, that is, the Volcanal, is next to the Comitium, though not included within its enclosure, it is very possible that Dionysius, in using the expression "Greek characters," may have been describing an inscription actually written in archaic Latin (visually very close to Greek).[16] In that case, it would be none other than the Lapis Niger discovered by Boni two thousand years later.

That is also the reason we can no longer doubt the historicity of the treaty concluded between Rome and Carthage at the end of the sixth century B.C.E., the text of which has been transmitted to us by the Greek historian Polybius. As a matter of fact, the plausibility of that treaty was long ago suggested by the splendid Oriental-style tombs of Palestrina.

It is in fact difficult to identify consistent archeological traces of the Gallic fire on the terrain;[17] the fire was thus probably not the catastrophe scholars of the last century imagined. They may have been thinking of the ravages of Vesuvius in Pompeii or Herculaneum. Even there, however, fire, lava, and ash left countless inscriptions intact, and modern excavators have been able to uncover them. In fact, what indexes did hypercritics put their faith in to make the sack of Rome an apocalypse without remission? In the tradition, quite simply. That is not the least of the paradoxes of such an interpretation, which undertook to impugn the evidence of the literary sources concerning the beginnings of the city while at the same time grounding itself in those same sources and what they said about the Gallic fire. Inevitably, those texts, written centuries after the event, could be validated only by appealing to the oral tradition, however much it was spurned by hypercriticism! In a footnote, Mommsen himself had to suppose that "many details could travel by word of mouth across centuries."[18]

In my view, it is not impossible that the example of the terrible sack of Rome in 1527, so eloquently described by Ranke, that is, by the man considered by his contemporaries to be the greatest historian of the nineteenth century,

---

[16] Coarelli, *Il foro romano*, 176. The passage cited is from Dion. Hal. *Ant. rom.* 2.54. See also de Sanctis, *Storia dei Romani*, 1: 26.

[17] On this point, see the catalog *I Galli e l'Italia*, 226–30. Perhaps the houses of the archaic era uncovered at the foot of the Palatine above the "Romulean" wall will offer a few archeological traces of the Gallic fire. On the Palatine, at the site of the huts discovered by Vaglieri and Puglisi, a layer of embankment earth containing a large quantity of ash, hypothetically attributable to the fire of 390 B.C.E., has been found. See the catalog *Civiltà del Lazio primitivo*, 144. F. Melis and A. Rathje are about to publish a comprehensive study on the archaic houses identified along the *via Sacra*, in *Opuscula romana*.

[18] Mommsen, *Römische Forschungen*, 2: 331 n. 78.

influenced specialists in antiquity in their perception and description of the Gallic plunder of 390 B.C.E.[19]

Before the arrival of the Gauls, there was time to secret away sacred objects. And since, by its very nature, the content of a treaty is obviously conserved by the two contracting parties, nothing was easier, after the invader's departure, than to recopy the text from the copy conserved outside Rome. The Gauls may have overturned the bronze column on which the text of the treaty of Spurius Cassius was engraved, but we know from the example of the Vendôme column, reestablished after the Commune at the costs of the unfortunate Jean Courbet, that damaged columns sometimes find their place again, when they have a strong symbolic value for the city.

It was the great merit of the historian de Sanctis, at the beginning of this century, to show that in reality the traditions regarding the Gallic fire represented a myth of etiology, elaborated by the Roman annalists and historians from the third and second centuries B.C.E. to explain the rarity of documents prior to the sack of Rome by the Gauls.[20] In a similar way, the ancients, noting the narrowness and irregularity of the streets that characterized Rome before it was destroyed by the fire of 64 C.E., explained them by the haste with which the city was rebuilt after the Gauls' departure. Yet, as has recently been noted,[21] if this urban disorder proves anything, it is that Rome had grown over the preceding centuries to meet its own needs, without ever experiencing the upheaval and reorganization that a large-scale catastrophe would have inevitably brought. This does not mean that we must reduce the sack of Rome to an event without importance, however. On the contrary, we need to see that, through the distress it caused, and through the unexpected nature and the felicitous and unhoped-for outcome of the adventure, it occasioned a great work of the collective imagination, which wove festoons of legends, miraculous episodes, and marvelous anecdotes around the initial framework of real events. Of this process, which no doubt began at the very moment the Gallic bands invaded, the myth of the great devastating fire was one of the most elaborate products.

In the nineteenth century, when the field of history, with the study of antiquity occupying the first ranks, sought to assert itself as a science, the tradition of the Gallic catastrophe met with a particularly favorable welcome. Clio now had pretensions to found a scientific discipline, and it was of the utmost importance to be able to ground history's legitimacy in a recognized method

---

[19] For example, L. von Ranke writes: "Never did a richer booty fall into the hands of a more terrible army: never was there a more protracted and more ruinous pillage. The splendor of Rome fills the beginning of the sixteenth century; it marks an astonishing period of developement of the human mind—with this day it was extinguished for ever" (*Ecclesiastical and Political History of the Popes* [London, 1840], 1: 108–9).

[20] See G. de Sanctis, "La légende historique des premiers siècles de Rome," *Journal des Savants*, 1909.

[21] See Coarelli, *Storia di Roma*, 133ff.

and on criteria that could not be disputed. Faced with the results of reflections conducted since the seventeenth century by champions of "diplomatics,"[22] history as science made the notion of the *document* the building material for the new edifice it intended to construct. The choice between what belonged to the field of history and what had to be excluded from it was now based on the presence or absence of original documents, in other words, of written evidence contemporary with the periods to be analyzed. That explains the privilege granted epigraphy, and, conversely, the hypercritical orientation in the exegesis of the primordia. In the footsteps of historical Pyrrhonism, but with completely different objectives, historians thus defined the "Gallic catastrophe," in relation to the study of Rome's origins, as an epistemological and almost ontological break between history and legend, in other words, between shadow and light, being and nothingness.[23]

That is why, in the study of the city's beginnings, the question of sources has traditionally been a preliminary and prejudicial question, always treated at the beginning of specialized works. Even before introducing the subject matter, the author explains at length the many things blocking scientific knowledge of the period, a thousand and one reasons presented as so many variations on a single theme—namely, the absence of contemporary documents. At a time when archeology was confined to the search for art objects,[24] and continually vacillated between uncertain and divergent dates for the oldest eras, there existed for the study of Rome's origins nothing but a set of literary texts (and the adjective "literary" was in no way a compliment from the scholarly perspective), which historians had to analyze by the strict criteria of a rigorous philology, identifying and dating authors and extracting variants. Had they been contemporary with the events they related, that is, with the time of origins, the texts would have been documents; but since they were subsequent to them by several centuries, they were no more than "fictions" (as Niebuhr and Schwegler called them), "novels" (as Michelet said), "loathsome chatter" (the expression used by a philologist from the beginning of the nineteenth century, with reference to Dionysius of Halicarnassus).

Certain scholars, however, Johann Bachofen in particular, attempted to escape that narrowly philological perspective by showing the intrinsic and substantial value of the narrative of origins. But in the absence of any external reference points to that tradition, the approach of such scholars could not get

---

[22] See B. Barret-Kriegel, *Les historiens de la monarchie* (Paris, 1989), 4 vols., and his edition and commentary of J. Mabillon, *Brèves réflexions sur quelques règles de l'histoire* (Clermond-Ferrand, 1990).

[23] On this question and the developments that follow, see my "La notion de légende chez les historiens modernes des Primordia Romana, de Louis de Beaufort à Andreas Alföldi," in *La Rome des premiers siècles: Légende et histoire*, Actes de la Table Ronde en l'Honneur de Massimo Pallottino (Paris, 1990; Florence, 1992).

[24] See above, chap. 7.

beyond paraphrase and grandiloquence. As Mommsen noted, not without cruelty, reviewing the first tome of Bachofen and Gerlach's *Römische Geschichte*: "Livy writes better and more succinctly than Mr. Gerlach." We know that Bachofen, leaving the book uncompleted, was to return to the narrative of Rome's origins, taking the path of comparatism and anthropology, of which he was one of the pioneers (in addition to James Frazer and his *The Golden Bough*) in his master work, *Die Sage von Tanaquil* (1870).

Today, the Archimedean lever that was so long missing in the exploration of origins exists. It is the exceptional set of discoveries presented and analyzed in this book (though I make no claim to exhaustivity). How, then, can we not see that the increasing flow of archeological data, and of the at least apparent "confirmations" they provide for the narrative of origins, makes a complete change in perspective necessary? When no source of information external to the literary tradition could explain or correct the image tradition provided of earliest Rome, it was indisputably legitimate and useful to ask, preliminary to any research, about the very possibility of knowledge. Now that the elements external to the literary tradition have multiplied, however, to the point of showing if not the truth of the tradition (we have seen that often that term is inappropriate), then at least its value, its complexity, and the need to take it seriously, what was in the past an indispensable preliminary will become in the future not only an outmoded postulate, but an obstacle to any real analysis of the legend of origins. To those who denied that movement was possible, science has responded by walking.

"Why do we know nothing?" The evolution of research and the number of clear new discoveries have brought no response to that question of hypercriticism but have rather made it pointless, obsolete, inoperative. In fact, it was less a question than an initial prejudice, orienting all research from the outset toward the "void" of origins. But where historians of the past saw only an empty sky, we now see not a solid mass, of course, but a medium traversed by elements (sometimes reduced to mere particles) unknown in the past, influxes of matter that were unobservable a little while ago. We must, then, not ask, in a preliminary and negative manner, why we see nothing, since we certainly see something. We must rather take care to discern the exact outlines of the objects observed, in order to ask, as a function of the results obtained, where they come from and how they have reached us. In short, we must leave behind a question that has become not simply useless but counterproductive and replace it with an inquiry without which the new discoveries would remain literally unthinkable. By what paths has the memory of these obscure centuries been conserved and transmitted? How do we know what we know? Such an inquiry does not have the objective of delimiting, a priori and a contrario, the territory of a discipline, since that territory can emerge only once the value (which is not necessarily the truth) of the literary sources has been established, in the singularity of the particular research project and in relation to the new data provided by archeology.

That is why, in this book, I chose to reverse the usual order of exposition for the investigation of early Rome, placing these reflections at the end.

To answer hypercriticism by claiming that, in spite of the Gallic fire, there are still archaic documents, and that a breach can thus be made in the epistemological wall long constituted by the Gauls' sack of Rome, would be to situate ourselves once again within a field that was chosen and delimited by hypercriticism.

We must go a step farther, and to do that, we must call into question the very definition of the document—a definition proposed by nineteenth-century scholarship with reference to the primordia—and that of the literary tradition, which is closely linked to it.

In limiting the notion of document to the sources (primarily written sources before archeology became a major player) external to the literary tradition and not present in that tradition (we shall see that the distinction is useful), hypercriticism gave itself the most important role from the outset and made its own task easier, eliminating both eventual difficulties and indispensable nuances. Yet it would have been good method for hypercritics to do more than attract attention to the distinction between monuments the ancients merely mentioned and those they had actually seen. (The hypercritical assumption was that everything the ancients had not seen with their own eyes but had nonetheless commented on could be the result only of falsification. That was the interpretation given commentaries by ancient scholars regarding monuments that had already disappeared in their time.) They ought not to have assumed that what was not cited by the ancients was necessarily unknown to them, thus limiting sources of information to those the ancients explicitly cited as such. Momigliano has shed light on ancient writers' indifference toward documents, which they often did not consult even when they were easily available (there are a few examples from Livy in particular).[25] This lack of interest is to be explained less by the rarity of the documents than by the conception the ancients had of history. The writing of history was an oratory pursuit par excellence, *opus oratorium maxime,* as Cicero wrote, and hence the enemy of detail. Voltaire would later call such details "the vermin that kills great books." More generally, as we have already suggested regarding the successive destructions and reconstructions carried out by the ancients in Rome,[26] that indifference can be explained by their fundamentally homogeneous conception of time, which equated past and present. Giving details was precisely the role of the scholarly literature represented by authors ordinarily called antiquarians, which included in the first ranks Varro. And, despite the disappearance of a large part of classical literature, a number of these works have been conserved, at least in the form of fragments, and through them

---

[25] See Momigliano, *Contributa alla storia degli studi classici,* 79ff.
[26] See above, chap. 7.

we possess often precious information on the most ancient practices and institutions of primitive Rome.

Hypercritics did not give the credit to written sources that we grant them today because, without taking proper precautions, they postulated both the nonexistence of a true oral tradition and the absence of authentic ancient written testimony. They could thus criticize the narrative of origins for not making use of more documents and, at the same time, decide, when by chance certain documents were cited or used, that they were falsified.

That was because, for hypercritics, the corpus of texts that spoke of Rome's origins belonged fundamentally to a genre that was in the first place literary in nature, situated in the world of *fiction*. "The narrative is the queen of the tradition," wrote Finley in *Ancient History*, further noting that "the tradition about early Rome is almost entirely a narrative, *histoire événementielle*," which allows him to conclude that "there is massive inconsistency [in] the literary account."[27]

In reality, nothing is less literary and less unitary than the tradition of Rome's origins. Scholarly notes, descriptions of rituals, sometimes the recopied texts of inscriptions, etiological developments based on old names or monuments still known in the classical age, ancient legends adapted to the taste of Hellenistic history, old myths subjected to a rationalizing interpretation, imperatives for continuous narration, all make up what we read as a narrative, but which is actually characterized by infinite diversity. The newly discovered epigraphic documents to which we alluded not only rehabilitate the documents explicitly used by ancient historians, which remain few in number in any case, but also shed light on the very means for transmitting that tradition, the scope of which needs to be measured.

Recently, in a tomb in Osteria dell'Osa, archeologists discovered an inscription in Greek characters that, contrary to all expectation, can only be dated from the eighth century B.C.E.[28] Osteria dell'Osa is located on the site of the ancient city of Gabii, in other words, at the gates of Rome, where, according to legend, Romulus and Remus went to learn "Greek letters." Nonetheless, it was not long ago that historians fixed the beginning of the practice of writing in Latium only in the sixth century B.C.E.

In light of these discoveries, many indications present in the "literary tradition" acquire an unsuspected credibility and density. For example, we read in Livy the description of the very ancient formulary for the Fetiales, priests who, when a treaty was concluded between Rome and another people, had the responsibility of giving it its full religious value. They invoked Jupiter to ensure

---

[27] Finley, *Ancient History*, 17 and 22.
[28] The inscription will be published in the proceedings of the 1989 Congress of Rome, *Anathema—Regime delle offerte ed economia dei santuari nel Mediterraneo antico*, ed. A. M. Bietti-Sestieri, A. de Santis, and A. La Regina. There is an allusion to the inscription in Cristofani, ed., *La grande Roma*, 16.

respect for the clauses recited out loud *ex illis tabulis cerave,* "from the bronze or wax tablets."[29] In commentaries on this expression, philologists habitually speak of "obvious anachronism."[30] The anachronism today would consist in not taking into account the lesson of archeology, which proves the existence of writing in "Romulean" times. Of course, writing was then less a means of communication than a practice situated in the sphere of ritual and the sacred. In the sixth century, for example, the text of the Lapis Niger, written on the four faces of a stele, could not be read entirely by those who saw it.

In considering precisely codified ceremonies or liturgies, whose efficacy depended in the first place on their immutability, historians have often underestimated the role of collegia of priests (*sodalitates,* to use a technical term recently confirmed by a famous archaic inscription of Satricum),[31] which transmitted their immaterial legacy down through the ages, from human memory to human memory. The city of Romulus lived under the gaze of the gods, to such a degree that we cannot radically dissociate the sacred world and the "political" world. Everything we know of the oldest Roman religion represents a source of primary importance for our knowledge of early Rome. Hence a text that has been insufficiently exploited, which dates from the scholarly literature of the Augustan Principate, depicts augurs guarding the secrets, the *arcana* properly speaking, of a certain type of sacrifice. So anxious were they to conserve them, "so that most cannot know them, that they did not even fix them in writing but transmitted them orally from generation to generation."[32]

Dumézil granted a fundamental role to this religious knowledge (and logically so, given his theory of a trifunctional ideology stemming from the Indo-Europeans). For my part, I will not claim to go back so far in time, but I agree that, at least from the moment when these religious brotherhoods existed more or less as we know them today, that is, from the time Rome was founded, the path of memory that passed through them could have crossed the few centuries that separated the era of the foundation from that when the "literary tradition" took shape (fourth or third century B.C.E.). In Rome, through rites assured by the priests of the Roman state, the past once more became present, the present repeated the past, and from that reciprocal conjunction was born a kind of eternity in process.

The Augustan scholar cited above speaks elsewhere of "funerary hymns in honor of the deceased sung at funerals."[33] Certain historians proposed to see this

---

[29] "Tabulis cerave" is usually translated by a hendiadys, based on the conviction that the entire expression results from an interpolation.

[30] For example, R. M. Ogilvie, *A Commentary on Livy, Books 1–5* (Oxford, 1965), 111.

[31] Published and commented on in *Lapis Satricanus,* ed. C. M. Stibbe (1980).

[32] Festus 15: "Adeo remotum a notitia vulgari, ut ne litteris quidem mandetur, sed per memoriam successorum celebretur."

[33] The scholar in question is Verrius Flaccus, since Festus was only his compiler. The text reads:

as possible support for a minimal oral tradition, before the hypercritical steam-roller annihilated that sort of evidence in the second half of the nineteenth century. Nonetheless, when we discern silhouettes of hired mourners on the sides of a hut-urn found near Castel Gandolfo and dating from the beginning of Latial civilization, how can we not think of those funeral chants?[34]

The same "literary tradition" so often condemned on the basis of narrowly philological considerations appears increasingly dense and trustworthy, owing to the contributions of archeology. Recall that, at the beginning of the nineteenth century, the historian and philologist Niebuhr proposed the revalorization of the narrative of origins as part of a theory of the so-called *carmina convivalia* (banquet chants).[35] A few sparse indications in texts note praises of famous men that were habitually sung during banquets, in the ancient times of Rome, in accordance with a practice that had already disappeared by Cato's time, from whom we get (indirectly) this information. Niebuhr himself limited the application of that theory to the period following the Gallic invasion, whose importance and destructive character he did not call into question. Nonetheless, the theory was still keenly disputed, even by the most fervent admirers of the great historian (Schwegler, for example), and was rapidly abandoned. At the same time, we find in Dionysius of Halicarnassus, in the book devoted to Roman antiquities, that is, to the origins of Rome, a mention of traditions about Romulus and Remus that represent them as "children of royal blood who supposedly had a divine origin, as the Romans still sing today in their ancestral hymns."[36] Even more than the texts concerning the *carmina convivalia,* that indication by Dionysius, an author universally disparaged and today held in particular suspicion by many, did not find a favorable echo in modern criticism for very long. But how can we not think of what happened in Zancle, and in other colonies of Sicily, where, according to a text by Callimachus, banquets were celebrated every year in honor of the founders, whose names were shouted by way of invitation?

And what do recent excavations show, those undertaken, for example, on the site of Ficana? What does the site of Rome show in the Forum itself? In Ficana, archeologists have discovered an entire banquet service, dating from the seventh century B.C.E.;[37] in Rome a few years ago,[38] the archeologist Giovanni

---

"Nenia est carmen, quod in funere laudandi gratia cantatur ad tibiam" (155). On the composition of the Verrius/Festus treatise, which has elicited numerous studies, see my "Les mots et les choses: La composition du 'De verborum significatu,'" *Revue des Etudes Latines,*1991.

[34] Mentioned by G. Colonna in *Storia di Roma,* ed. A. Schiavone (1989), 2: 293 n. 10.

[35] On this question, in addition to the famous article by Momigliano (1957), now in *Roma arcaica,* 449–65, see N. Zorzetti, "The Carmina Convivalia," in *Sympotica: A Symposium on the Symposium,* ed. O. Murray (New York, 1990). In general, for the problem of the oral tradition in Rome's beginnings, see J. von Ungern-Sternberg and D. Timpe's essay in *Colloquium Rauricum: Vergangenheit in mündlicher Überlieferung* (Tübingen, 1988), 1: 237–86, and bibliography.

[36] Dion. Hal. *Ant. rom.* 1.79. For Zancle, see Heurgon, *Rome et la Méditerranée occidentale,* 374.

[37] A. Rathje, "A Banquet Service from the Latin City of Ficana," *Analecta Romana* 12 (1983): 7ff.

[38] G. Colonna, "Un tripode fittile geometrico dal Foro Romano," *Mélanges de l'Ecole Française*

Colonna attracted attention to a stand for banquet vases, conforming to a model found only in Latium and the land of the Faliscans, excluding Etruria. It dates from the end of the eighth or the beginning of the seventh century B.C.E. These new elements offer the long-missing proof that members of the oldest Roman society gathered together for banquets (symposia), and not only to eat, to display, and to revel. The fact that this was a Greek practice can no longer be a reason to declare it impossible. After all, the oldest text of Greek literature comes from the soil of Italy: two lines in hexameter found in Ischia on a goblet dating from the eighth century B.C.E..[39] Clearly, as soon as the first colonies of Magna Graecia were founded, first, on the island of Pithecusae (Ischia) in about 770 B.C.E., and then in Cumae in about 740 B.C.E., they exerted a considerable influence, as the inscription of Gabii shows. In Gabii, in addition, a more "recent" tomb, dating from the end of the seventh century B.C.E., has provided a rich banquet service, including a goblet bearing a "convivial" inscription analogous to what was practiced in the Greek world at the same time.[40] A few years earlier and elsewhere in Lavinium, an inscription from the sixth century B.C.E. bearing the name of the Dioscuri had already given startling testimony of the importance and great age of that Greek influence.[41]

But although the communities of Latium and Rome adopted the practice of the banquet, they also obviously adapted it to their own memories, singing the exploits of their own heroes or founders, such as Romulus in Rome, but giving them as companions the great figures of Greek myth:[42] Odysseus, Herakles, and, most important, Aeneas, the very hero who, in the canonical account of the origins of the city, became first the father of Romulus, and then, in a version better adjusted to the chronology of the Trojan War, his distant ancestor.

Every time the hypercritical philology of the last century encountered names from the Greek legend, or from Roman traditions presented by a Greek author, it immediately decided they were falsified, late additions, or imaginitive inventions. And if an ancient text,[43] Hesiod, for example, mentioned a character

---

de Rome (1977): 471–91. The presence a century later throughout Latium of decorative terracotta representing banquet scenes demonstrates the diffusion of this Greek lifestyle. The *carmina convivalia* are thus a path of memory practiced by the aristocracy and not a vehicle for plebeian culture as Niebuhr thought.

[39] See Heurgon, *Rome et la Méditerranée occidentale*, 148.

[40] See Cristofani, ed., *La grande Roma*, 16 and 100. Pasquali's analyses before World War II concerning the importance of the Greek influence in archaic Rome deserve to be reread in the light of this sort of discovery. See G. Pasquali, *Preistoria della poesia romana* (reprint, Rome, 1981), published with a study by S. Timpanaro.

[41] See Cristofani, ed., *La grande Roma*, 190. An important colloquium was devoted to this problem of the Greek presence in Latium. See the issue of the journal *La Parola del Passato* (1977 and 1980) entitled *Lazio arcaico e mondo greco*. See also C. Ampolo's survey "Roma e il mondo greco dal secolo VIII agl'inizi del III a. C." in the collective volume *Roma e l'Italia: Radices imperii* (Milan, 1990), 583–626.

[42] For all these figures, see P. Grimal, *Dictionnaire de la mythologie grecque et romaine*.

[43] Hes. *Theog.* 1012–17.

from the Latin legend (Latinus, king of the aborigines, whom Virgil shows us allied with the Trojans of Aeneas to form the new "Latin" people), it immediately saw it as the result of an interpolation. More gravely, the Roman legend itself could only be a Greek fabrication, according to hypercriticism. Hence the presence of "Boreignonoi" in the Greek poet Lycophron's writings (no doubt inspired by the Greek historian Timaeus) "proved" that the aborigines of the Latin tradition were only the copy of a Hellenic fable. And the presence in Plutarch of a narrative of origins (attributed to "a certain Promathion, author of a history of Italy") that combined in surprising ways elements from the legend of the twin founders of Rome and other legends that were Etruscan in coloration (one Tarchetios appears, closely suggesting the Tarquins, kings of Rome), or that depicted the founders in contact with Servius Tullius, was considered one of the most obvious signs of the artificial character of the tradition of origins.[44]

But today, archeological documents favor a schema of transmission that is exactly the reverse, and the study of literary data suggests that, far from being secondary, the "aborigine" form was primary.[45] If there was any copying done, it was on the Greek side.

As for Plutarch's Promathion, he is the very exemplum of the impasse to which a method grounded in the criteria of hypercritical philology leads.[46] What are the goals of that method, in fact? To identify in each text its source, its author, its date, and the literary genre to which it belongs. It is time to recognize, at a moment when archeological documents lead us to revalorize the entire tradition concerning the primordia, that never were criteria less well adapted to the study of the ancient legends! By definition, a legend has no author, no date either, inasmuch as it remains alive, that is, recounted, over the long term, and the fundamental elements that compose it lend themselves to every adaptation, every metamorphosis, and to the most diverse literary genres. In other words, the application of that method to the interpretation of the narrative of Rome's origins could lead only to the condemnation formulated by hypercriticism. Just because moderns discover the first mention of a Latin legend in a Greek author does not compel us to conclude that its origin is Greek. For the Romans, the memory of the foundation of Rome was alive and present, even before the Greeks, attracted by the growing power of the city on the banks of the Tiber, took an interest in its legends. In the transmission of these legends, theatrical traditions must also be taken into account. When the poet Naevius writes a tragedy entitled *Romulus* in the third century B.C.E., or when Laberius, an author of pantomimes and a contemporary of Caesar, writes

---

[44] See Plut. *Rom.* 11.

[45] See my "Le roi Latinus: Analyse d'une figure légendaire," in *Comptes rendus de l'Académie des Inscriptions et Belles-Lettres*, 1988, 481–97; and D. Briquel's essay in *Mélanges de l'Ecole Française de Rome*, 1989, 97–111.

[46] In fact, a long list of hypotheses regarding identification and dates (from the sixth to the fourth century B.C.E.) have been proposed for this text.

a play with the title *Twins* (*Gemelli*), it is probable, as has recently been suggested,[47] that they had predecessors, and that they were themselves writing as part of a preexisting tradition.

We increasingly realize that, far from being a neutral, objective, and demonstrable fact, the idea of Greek primacy in the narrative of the origins of the *urbs*, and of the almost total absence of a Latin and Roman legendary content, was nothing other than a postulate, or more exactly, a methodological prejudice, born of an exclusively philological approach to the sources. And that prejudice informed a type of research that could lead only to negative conclusions.

In reality, not only was Hellenism present in Latium and Rome much earlier that was once thought, but it encountered peoples already endowed with a legendary, mythic, and religious legacy of exceptional richness. Under such conditions, there is no point in asking, following an approach implicitly grounded in the notion—which is literary and anachronistic in this case—of authorship, who precisely lay at the *origin* of the legend of Aeneas, from what Etruscan city in Lavinium he came, and how he passed through Rome. If the numerous studies carried out on the basis of those questions have led to any result, it is to show the diversity and great age of the presence here or there of the legend.[48] Considered as a whole, the particular conclusions of these studies in favor of one provenance or another (Etruscan, Roman, or Greek), and of one date or another, contradict and obliterate one another. What they point out in spite of themselves is that when the very first Greek navigators trod the banks of Italy, they brought with them heroes or demigods—Aeneas, Diomedes, Odysseus, and Herakles—who were to be subsequently, and throughout the entire peninsula, the great ambassadors of Hellenism.[49] From there, a figure such as Aeneas, belonging to a non-Greek people but present in the prestigious Homeric epic, provided the Romans, already faithful to the memory of their founder, a particularly attractive means to increase the prestige and influence of their national legends. Conversely, the Greek arrivals considered the legend an irresistible argument for reconciliation and rapprochement with the "indigenous" peoples. In modern terms, we can say that through that legend and the arrangements of all kinds it allowed (from one end of the Italian coast to the other, Aeneas formed an alliance with a number of local peoples), each people affirmed in a single movement both its otherness and its identity, its resemblance and its difference. That is why the welcome given in Latium and Rome to the legend of Aeneas

---

[47] T. P. Wiseman in *Journal of Roman Studies* 79 (1989): 129–37 (regarding J. N. Bremmer and N. M. Horsfall, *Roman Myth and Mythography* [1987]).

[48] The very numerous modern studies on the subject (by J. Perret, K. Galinsky, and Alföldi) are indicated by A. Momigliano in "Come riconciliare greci e troiani," in *Roma arcaica*, 325–45.

[49] On the early diffusion of Hellenism in Italy, see P. Grimal, *Le siècle des Scipions*, 2d ed. (Paris, 1975), 56. The legend of Aeneas developed in places whose layout might have suggested that of Troy to the ancients, according to D. Musti, "Una città simile a Troia: Città troiane da Siri a Lavinio," *Archeologia Classica* 33 (1981).

tells us even more about the Romans than it does about the Greeks. It tells us about their openness to the world and their capacity for assimilation, which was, as we now know,[50] one of the major characteristics of their city in the archaic era and was reflected in their tradition by indications regarding the diversity of origins among Romulus's companions.

As a result of the exceptional Archimedean lever that archeology brings to the knowledge of the *primordia Romana,* "the literary tradition" concerning Rome's origins, in losing its so-called unity and deceptive simplicity, acquires a documentary value that, needless to say, must be evaluated case by case, apart from any systematic conception. That value can no longer be denied, however, quite simply because, even in the very recent past, it was not even suspected.

And that value is all the greater in that it cannot be confined to the definition of document given by hypercriticism, at least in its ultimate expressions, for example, in Finley, when he seeks to clarify ancient history's view of its sources. Compared to Niebuhr, Schwegler, and even Pais, Finley's definition is infinitely more restrictive. He no longer even includes etiology, to which the others granted a large place (too large almost) and which, by way of toponymy and topography especially, was one of the principal contributions of the narrative of origins. "The most ancient history of Rome originated in the shadow of the sacristies," wrote Pais. It is true, however, that he was writing from within a historiographical context not characterized by all the serenity and objectivity we might desire on this matter . . . But for Finley, that all disappears, and although he mentions topography at one point, alluding to the work of Filippo Coarelli without naming him,[51] he immediately asserts that "the tradition about early Rome is almost entirely a narrative, *histoire événementielle.*" In fact, the final words tell us less about the ancient tradition of Rome's origins—which is not a narrative, that is, a pure product of fiction, but a *putting into narrative form* of diverse and complex elements, which is a different matter—than about the conception of history at the foundation of hypercriticism pushed to the extreme, no doubt for the needs of the polemic. "*Evénementielle*" is the key word here.

Let us admit that we will never know very much about the "events" of the early centuries of Rome, even though what we can know about them goes beyond anything we might have imagined in the past. But who would seriously maintain today that history can be reduced to "events," to the chronology of battles and reigns?

Livy—and apparently some of his modern readers—was the first to be astonished by everything that the names of the most ancient buildings of the Forum, their surroundings, and their layout on the terrain could provide. Such a

---

[50] Thanks especially to the writings of C. Ampolo. See, for example, "Roma arcaica fra Latini ed Etruschi: Aspetti politici e sociali," in *Etruria e Lazio arcaico* (Rome, 1987), 75–87.

[51] Except in a note. See Finley, *Ancient History,* 112 n. 48. The passage cited is from p. 22.

history is not strictly that of events, institutions, or "realities"; it is also a history of mentalities. No, I am not so sure he was astonished after all, since he had read Varro, who already took pleasure in seeking out the traces of the most ancient history of Rome in its names. In the same way, simply in the names of the hills of the city of Romulus, modern research can decipher the mark of a very ancient state of civilization:[52] Mount Caelian was still "Oak Hill" (Querquetulanus); the goddess Pales, a deity belonging to the world of pastoral life, was honored on the Palatine; the Fagutal was covered with beech trees (*fagus* in Latin), and the Viminal with osier beds; the Esquiline remained outside the primitive community (the word is a composite of *ex*, "outside," and *colere*, "to cultivate," "to live"); and, on the other side of the river, the Janiculum still marked the site of a *passage* to foreign lands, placed as such under the aegis of the god Janus.[53] In all these cases, how do we know of these names, and many others as well, if not through "the literary tradition"? Tacitus gave the old name of the Caelian, and the "literary tradition" allowed Finley to give a name—Satricum—to a site explored by recent archeological research, which he considered a "cul-de-sac." Although that last city appears in the sources only with the fifth century B.C.E., this is no doubt because before that, according to an appealing hypothesis that the English historian himself mentions but rejects in a note,[54] it bore the name Pometia, given, again, by "the literary tradition."

If there is a mirage of origins, it lies in the modern vision of a unitary and, as a result, artificial literary tradition. The tradition is certainly literary when Dionysius or Plutarch wonders about Romulus's psychology, but not when it provides the structural elements of the legend that, beginning with the very name of Romulus, preexisted the tradition and imposed themselves on it. We must stop speaking of *a* tradition, as hypercriticism does, and seek to measure in all its diversity, age, and authenticity certain of the data transmitted to us, but not invented, by tradition. This does not mean that what was declared "false" in the past is now "true." We have seen throughout this book that a Manichean analysis of that kind is inappropriate. The tradition deserves to be taken completely seriously on every occasion, without being judged a priori a deliberate forgery.

Why, finally, was the nineteenth-century historical criticism of the primordia a hypercriticism? Because it began with a narrow definition of the document and, more fundamentally, because it rested on a conception of history where priority was granted to political and chronological questions, to events, in accordance with a point of view that can no longer be our own. For that history, a document was finally only what offered itself as such from the

---

[52] See, for example, S. Mazzarino, *Il pensiero storico clasico* (Bari, 1965; reprint, 1983), 1: 193.
[53] P. Grimal, "Le dieu Janus et les origines de Rome," *Lettres d'Humanité*, 1945, 15–121 (esp. 41–43).
[54] Finley, *Ancient History*, 112 n. 52.

beginning: primarily, archives and inscriptions (at least when they were contemporary with the "events").

We now know that everything is history, that everything is a document, and that the definition set in place by hypercriticism is not only restrictive but increasingly incomplete and inexact.

That is why the new territories recently conquered by history must lead to a broader and deeper conception of the notion of document. We now know that there can be a history without events or, more exactly, that the events are not the essential part of history (even when we know what those events are). In the same way, how can we act as if the identification of sources has to remain the principal objective of the analysis of "the literary tradition"? To a history without events there must correspond a philology without authors,[55] and the study of legend must no longer depend on an exegesis grounded exclusively in the notion of source. Parallel to calling into question the concept of event, history must move toward a reading of the narrative of origins stripped of the primacy granted to categories that are in great part inadequate. That reading will be more concerned with identifying the great currents of the traditions rather than the falsifiers, preferably Greek, supposed to be "responsible" for one legend or another. Since we now know from archeology that the Greeks were in contact with Rome and Latium much earlier than was once thought, it has become very difficult to maintain that they invented what they reported. Philologists of the last century, unable to identify precisely ancient historians' sources, refused to trust what Fabius Pictor, Timaeus, Diodorus, and Polybius said about Rome's origins. But the risk is not that these ancient writers invented false legends, but rather that they suppressed a certain number of them, in their dual concern for rationalization and plausibility. This is implied in their choice to address a broader public in Greek, respecting the rules of Greek historiography, whose methods were grounded precisely in those two criteria. No one could have known the old national legends better than Fabius, a member of the Roman aristocracy, or Timaeus, who probably went personally to Lavinium to seek out information, and who took care in his writings to note typically Roman ceremonies such as the sacrifice of the October Horse.[56]

---

[55] That need for methodological revision is not limited to antiquity, as the example of L. Cerquiglini's analyses of medieval philology shows. Cerquiglini discusses lais attributed to an author who was given the name Marie de France by an "authoritarian" literary criticism anxious to reduce the proliferation of variants to individual unity. See L. Cerquiglini, *Eloge de la variante* (Paris, 1989).

[56] The priests of Lavinium told Timaeus of the "chapel to which inhabitants of Lavinium forbid access to foreigners, because they consider it sacred." Dionysius of Halicarnassus, from whom we get this information (*Ant. rom.* 1.57) later explains that "the historian Timaeus declares that the sacred objects found in the secret chamber of Lavinium are caducei in iron and bronze and Trojan pottery, and that he personally obtained that information from the indigenous peoples" (1.67). It is wrong to doubt these comments. The example of Paestum, in my view, allows us to form a very precise idea of the reality they refer to, if we understand that legend called Trojan whatever

We shall not conclude, therefore, that Romulus (and Latinus) were more or less late Greek creations, on the pretext that their names are found for the first time in Greek texts.[57] The issue is no longer to establish the principles of fabrication for a tradition considered a priori as a gigantic enterprise of falsification. The obsession concerning fakes that pervades the nineteenth century is quite obviously the obligatory corollary of its restrictive conception of the document. On this point and many others, archeology, in showing the reality of the foundation of Rome in the eighth century B.C.E., has so thoroughly revived the legend of Rome's origins that it is now urgent to inquire into the circumstances that allowed for the legend's early development, the modes of transmission of the data it conveyed, and the very reasons for that transmission. A legend remains alive only as long as it serves a purpose, and such explanations belong to history through and through.

In fact, for a legendary figure such as Romulus, who was rooted solely in the city of Rome (and even in the particular site of the Palatine), to the exclusion of other sites, the archeological discoveries of recent decades and their implications, which are still often unrecognized, not only oblige us to review the too strict definition of the document given by hypercriticism, but also lead us to broaden and deepen the notion of event. If we understand by that word an act known with precision, down to the year, the day, or even the hour, accomplished by characters who are all identifiable, then yes, the history of archaic Rome is in great part a history without events. Pushed to its extreme, that conception of history, characteristic of hypercriticism, led to the conclusion that there is no history possible for archaic Rome.

But if we understand by "event" a change in a situation that can be reconstituted through its effects more than through its actual occurrence, a change to which we can assign a place in time with a reasonable margin of error, but with-

---

was old and related in one way or another to the Greek world, and attributed it to Aeneas. In Paestum, along the *via Sacra*, modern archeologists have uncovered a small buried structure, made to be "completely hidden from view and inaccessible." Once offerings had been placed inside this "chapel" (as Dionysius said), "it was covered and as a result made invisible" (P. C. Sestieri, *Paestum* [Rome, 1968], 28). Hence we now know what these famous "sacred objects" look like. These objects, supposedly brought by Aeneas, sparked the imagination of many earlier generations of scholars. The offerings of Paestum were discovered intact and can now be seen in the magnificent museum built near the site. They consist of eight bronze vases (six hydriae and two amphorae), which, when discovered, were still filled with honey. Near them was "a large and very beautiful Attic amphora with black figures" (Sestieri), which Dionysius (and Timaeus) would no doubt have called Trojan pottery.

57 The age and authenticity of the Romulean legend have been demonstrated by T. J. Cornell, "Aeneas and the Twins: The Development of the Roman Foundation Legend," *Proceedings of the Cambridge Philological Society*, 1977; and by D. Briquel, from an Indo-European perspective. See D. Briquel, "Trois études sur Romulus," in *Recherches sur les religions de l'antiquité classique*, ed. R. Bloch (Geneva, 1980), 267–346; and id., "La triple fondation de Rome," *Revue d'Histoire des Religions* 189 (1976). See also B. Liou-Gille, *Cultes "héroïques" romains: Les fondateurs* (Paris, 1980).

out being able to identify the actors, then the legend of Rome's origins acquires a density of "eventness" that has constantly been denied it until now. The history of the beginnings of the city may well be a shadow play, where characters who were in fact historical advanced wearing the mask of myth; nonetheless, certain silhouettes, certain "primordial" scenes, are illuminated by an unexpected light.

What is more legendary and less historical, for example, than the story of the ravishing of the Sabine women, and more generally, than the Sabine episode as a whole, which constitutes the obligatory complement to the tradition of the foundation of Rome? Anthropology has sought to save what history abandoned to it, and has analyzed the conduct of Romulus's companions toward the Sabine women as the mythical justification of marriage by abduction. Indisputably, there are elements in the legend that can be explained in terms of the real details of Roman marriage: for example, a young Sabine woman is led to the home of one Thalassius, whose name closely suggests the cry "Thalassio" heard in Rome at every nuptial procession. Thus this type of explanation appears pertinent on at least certain points. We must not forget, however, that the reality of marriage by abduction in the oldest Roman society has not been demonstrated. Even if it were, the anthropological schema leaves unexplained what may be the essential part of the legend, that is, that the women raped by the companions of Romulus were depicted as being of Sabine origin. It was with the Sabines, and with them alone, that the Romans made an alliance, making Rome a city shored up by the union of two peoples and two kingdoms into a single entity, *geminata urbs*.

Certain indexes seem to suggest there was a dual organization in primitive Rome: in particular, the existence of *two* collegia of Luperci, *two* collegia of Salii, and *two* gods called Lares Praestites, guardians of the city,[58] not to mention, of course, the *two* founders. Despite that, however, modern research, having abandoned any archeological basis for that Romano-Sabine duality (which is, however, consistently asserted in the literary sources), generally posits the totally *legendary* character of the legend, seeing it as one of the most obvious signs of the nonhistoricity of the narrative of origins. At most, here and there a few prudent efforts at rehabilitation have been made, grounded in general considerations of "geopolitical" plausibility and, perhaps even more, in the reluctance to reject totally such an important part of the primordial narrative.

It is thus not astonishing that the Sabine episode provided Dumézil with the opportunity for one of his most famous analyses, in which he placed the rivalry and subsequent reconciliation between the Romans of Romulus and the Sabines of Titus Tatius side by side with an analogous Scandinavian myth opposing the Aiser gods and the Vanir gods.[59] Note that, in accordance with an approach commonly used by Dumézil, the interpretation adopted as its starting point a conclusion elaborated by nineteenth-century hypercriticism, in this case by

---

[58] See Cornell, "Aeneas and the Twins."
[59] See, for example, Dumézil, *La religion romaine archaïque*, 82–88.

Mommsen, for whom the role of the Sabines of Titus Tatius in Rome's origins was only the transposition of the part taken by the Sabines in the history of the *urbs* in the third century B.C.E. Beginning from the same principle of explanation, other critics proposed different dates: fourth century B.C.E. (Benedictus Niese), fifth century B.C.E. (Pais), and, recently, the end of the sixth century B.C.E. (Poucet). In 1967, in fact, Poucet devoted a fundamental study to the legend as a whole.[60]

It seems to me, however, that a fundamental misunderstanding is concealed behind the generally favorable reception reserved for Dumézil's exegesis. If its purpose was to point out what in the Sabine legend stemmed from general anthropological schemata, then, indisputably, Dumézil's analysis has contributed to our understanding of the narrative of origins. But his exclusively Indo-European and trifunctional interpretation of the Romano-Sabine myth appears significantly more fragile. The learned ethnologist Marshall Sahlins, in a study devoted to the myths of the Fiji Islands, found Dumézil's reflections on the Sabines an occasion for a suggestive comparison.[61] But that is only because the main lines of the myth indicated by Dumézil are not in any way limited to the Indo-European horizon, still less to trifunctional theory, but rather stem from mechanisms of the imagination at work in all "primitive" civilizations. From one end of the planet to the other, from the Hawaiian or Fiji Islands to Scandinavia, and including Rome, we find myths recounting the opposition between two peoples, followed by their reconciliation and their fusion into a new unity.

It is not generally recognized that the very success of Dumézil's analyses among certain ethnologists implies a need to abandon the Indo-European and trifunctional aspects of his theory. Contrary to first appearances, the diffusion of that theory is not necessarily the sign of its success.

More precisely, between the Romano-Sabine myth and the Scandinavian myth there is what seems to be a significant difference, which prevents us from reducing one to the other. The women in Rome who were at the center of the rivalry between the Romans and the Sabines, since their rape was at the origin of the war, were absent in the struggle that opposed the Asiers and the Vanirs.[62]

Does that mean we must now leave legend in the mists? Perhaps not. In spite of everything, we possess an instrument for approaching it that may allow us, if not to provide definitive answers to the difficulties elicited by the tradition, then at least to ask a few questions of it.

In an extremely dense book devoted to the temples of republican Rome,[63] a Polish scholar, Adam Ziolkowski, reveals with particular clarity a phenome-

---

[60] Poucet, *Recherches sur la légende sabine*; id., *Origines de Rome*.

[61] M. Sahlins, *Islands of History* (Chicago, 1985), 77–78.

[62] See Momigliano, "G. Dumézil e l'approccio trifunzionale alla civiltà romana," in *Saggi di storia*, 45–66, esp. 59.

[63] Forthcoming in English (Rome). I summarize the conclusions presented by the author in a lecture given 23 May 1990 in John Scheid's seminar at the Ecole Pratique des Hautes Etudes.

non that has long been known but that has remained somewhat in the shadows. Studying one by one, and in relation to all the available sources, the locations of every sanctuary identified in republican Rome, he points out that they were divided into two large groups, with ten temples in the region called Collina, that is, the Quirinal, and nine in the region called Palatine. In the Palatine region, almost all the buildings are arranged in two groups: in the northeast, on one hand, on the Velia and its surroundings (the temples of the Penates, of Vica Pota, and of the Lares in particular); and in the southwest, on the other, on the Germalus (the temples of Victoria, of Victoria Virgo, of Pales, and of the Magna Mater). Let us add to that list the sanctuary of Tellus, located in the district (*regio*) called Suburana, but closely linked to the Velia. Hence all the temples located in areas that the tradition recognizes as occupied by the Latins of Romulus, that is, the "regions" of the Palatine, the Esquiline, and the Subura, were regrouped within the Palatine-Velia zone, whose importance we have noted several times. Facing them on the other side of the valley of the Forum, all the temples of the "Collina" region were grouped on the Quirinal (leaving the nearby Viminal unoccupied), that is, on the site where tradition places the Sabines.

The fact is all the more striking in that it results from data totally outside the literary tradition (otherwise, we would obviously be falling back into a simple tautology), obtained by an investigation whose initial thesis did not at all concern the period of Rome's origins. Nevertheless, several centuries after the foundation, the sacral topography of the *urbs* revealed between the lines, as a superimposition as it were, an indisputable bipartition of the Roman community.

When we then (but only then) return to the Sabine legend, we can only be struck by the opposition presented between the city (*urbs*) of Romulus and the people (*nomen*) of the Sabines. In that differential definition, which Dumézil interpreted as the mark of an artificial and late opposition, it is now legitimate to detect the confrontation between two societies, one of which, the Roman, had already developed the first forms of urban (or at least preurban) existence, while the other, the Sabine, remained divided into tribes disseminated throughout the mountains and hinterland. The construction of the Forum, an indispensable condition for the effective union of the residents of the Palatine with those of the Quirinal, was undertaken only at the end of the seventh century B.C.E. According to a new interpretation,[64] the vestiges interpreted by Boni and Gjerstad as proof of early occupation of the Forum are finally only debris from nearby hills. This shows once more, if need be, that the "facts" of archeology are no less fragile and disputable than those of history. These first

---

[64] See Ammerman, "On the Origins of the Forum Romanum." The date of Rome as classical city including the Forum is fixed at the end of the seventh century B.C.E. by T. Dohrn, "Des Romulus Gründung Roms," in *M.D.A.I.* (R.), 1964, 1–18. See also G. Fuchs, *Das Datum der Gründung Roms*, in *GWU* (1966).

tribes established around the Romulean Palatine exerted a force of attraction toward neighboring populations, especially those in the interior of the peninsula. In fact, that force must have been translated into conflicts, before the definitive reconciliation and alliances.[65] The tradition indicates nothing less when it attributes the creation of the Forum not to Romulus but to Titus Tatius.[66] Before it was the site of the reconciliation and alliance of the Romans and the Sabines, the Forum, delimited on all sides by the Quirinal and the Palatine, was the place for their confrontation.

And, despite what has been claimed, it is not just the figure of the mysterious god Quirinus,[67] one of the cornerstones of Dumézil's interpretation, that acquires a new coherence in the Sabine myth. Why, in fact, did the classical tradition stubbornly attribute a Sabine origin to that god? To respond to that question, we must first overcome the apparent obstacle raised by trifunctional theory, which wished to see Quirinus as the deity of abundance and fecundity (the "third function"). But, as recent studies—notably those of André Magdelain—have shown,[68] Quirinus was instead the god who managed legal relations between members of the civic community of the Quirites. The etymology of his name refers to the curiae,[69] that is, to citizen associations that together constituted the city of Rome. Far from being artificial and recent, the deification of Romulus into Quirinus appears as a piece of legendary data as logical as it is necessary. There is nothing astonishing in the fact that the founder of the city was assimilated to the god who symbolized the union of citizens who composed the civic body. Having limited Quirinus to a role uncharacteristic of him, trifunctional theory discovered a link between Romulus and Quirinus it no longer knew what to do with, and, to resolve the difficulty, could only declare it of late and literary origin. But once Quirinus is restored to his true sphere of influence, it is clear why tradition presented him as a typically Sabine god. Given his characteristics, he is the god of an enlarged community, which could exist (or "function," as they say) only once populations that were originally outside that community, and were then incorporated under the aegis of shared laws and duties, had made their contribution. When the legend became fixed, these populations were essentially Sabine in origin; therefore, the god who watched over the unity of the civic body, who presided over their integration into the Roman state, was considered to be of Sabine origin.

[65] This interpretation was also proposed in Pallottino, "Le origini di Roma."

[66] See Tac. *Ann.* 12.24: "The Forum Romanum and the Capitol, it is believed, were not included in the city by Romulus but were added by Titus Tatius. After that, the pomerium was enlarged in proportion to the growth of Rome."

[67] On this god, see Dumézil, *La religion romaine archaïque*; and D. Porte's essay in *Aufsteig und Niedergang der römischen Welt* 2 (1981): 300–342.

[68] A. Magdelain, "Quirinus et le droit (spolia opima, jus fetiale, jus Quiritium)," *Mélanges de l'Ecole Française de Rome* 96 (1984): 195–237.

[69] As P. Kretschmer showed in the journal *Glotta* (1920). On the assimilation of Romulus to Quirinus, see Coarelli, *Il foro romano*, 1: 188–99.

In any case, it is certain that in the "bipartition of temples" in Rome, we see a particularly valuable path of memory opened, since it is totally independent of the "literary tradition," which it revitalizes in turn. Until now, that tradition had seemed more "legendary" and less "historical."

The interest that religious memory might present for the knowledge of Rome's protohistory has long been known. Think, for example, of the *favissae,* or votive repositories, that dot the substratum of the city, and which the ancients dug when they wished to get rid of objects (gifts or ornaments) upon building a new temple. These objects cluttered up the old building, but their destruction might have angered the god. For the modern archeologists who discovered them, these votive repositories were truly "stores of memory," rich in lessons of all sorts about the periods to which their contents belonged.

The archeological exploration of the temples of Rome allows us to reconsider from a new angle the old question of the Annales Maximi, one of the sources for the first historians.[70] Certain excavations, for example at the temple of the Castores in the Forum,[71] confirm the inauguration date given by Livy. The only possible conclusion is that the data used by the historian or his predecessors, which go back in the last instance to the Annales Maximi written by the Pontifex Maximus, provided precise and exact information on this point at least.

Thus the paths of memory outside "the literary tradition," which substantially confirm that tradition, or more exactly, which show it was not based on nothing, turn out to be much more numerous than a superficial examination might have led us to believe.

As we know from Alföldi's writings in particular, however literary the tradition might be, it sometimes conveys data that come to it from the outside. Thus the great Hungarian scholar identified in Dionysius of Halicarnassus (was there ever a more "literary" author?) passages coming from the local chronicle of the city of Cumae, which had early and continuous relations with Rome.[72]

There are also some true documents that can be used as such. As we know from one of Mommsen's most remarkable discoveries, the Roman calendar, known through numerous inscriptions (called Fasti), can be read as the outline of the calendar of the archaic city, conserved and incorporated into calendars reworked in the following eras. In certain ways, this archaic calendar conserved features from immediately prior periods, that is, from preurban periods. Thus a *document* of the first order has come to us on Rome's origins.

[70] On this question, see the collection entitled *Römische Geschichtsschreibung,* ed. V. Pöschl (Darmstadt, 1969).

[71] See I. Nielsen, "The Temple of Castor and Pollux on the Forum Romanum: A Preliminary Report on the Scandinavian Excavations, 1983–1987," *Acta Archaeologia,* 1988, 1–14; id., "The Forum Paving and the Temple of Castor and Pollux," *Analecta Rom. Inst. Danici* 19 (1990): 89–104. See also Dion. Hal. *Ant. rom.* 1.73: "Although the Romans do not have a single ancient historian or logographer, they nonetheless each composed their writings by drawing something from the classical accounts conserved on sacred tablets."

[72] See Alföldi, *Early Rome and the Latins,* chap. 2.

It is also possible that old myths, such as that of the brigand Cacus, or ancient practices, such as that of using only milk and not wine in certain sacrifices, go back to the times before the foundation of Rome, where, on the site of the future city and throughout all of Latium, populations dedicated to pastoral activities were living.

That is why, having retraced these paths of memory of Rome, we hesitate to reject as purely fictive the concordant indications given by a tradition that, on so many points, emerges more solid (even though, to say it one more time, it is not a matter of deciding whether it is "true" or "false") as a result of its confrontation with the archeological discoveries.

What are we to think in particular of the date assigned by the tradition to the foundation of Rome? Despite sometimes notable variations, it is striking that the ancients fixed it by almost unanimous accord at about the midpoint of the eighth century B.C.E.[73] The only real exception was the Sicilian Timaeus, who placed it in 814 B.C.E., a date analogous to that of the legendary foundation of Carthage, the great rival of Rome, but perhaps still its ally when this synchronism was established. And the midpoint of the eighth century is "precisely," as we recall, the era from which the wall discovered at the foot of the Palatine dates.

The hypercriticism of the last century believed it had found the explanation for the traditional chronology. Since it saw the origins of Rome as the place of a mystery and, at the same time, as the product of a falsification, it had to discover the formula for that fabrication and the key to that mystery.[74] Hypercritics thought they had found them when, with Mommsen, they established that the length of the regal period had been calculated by assigning to each generation, in other words to each reign, an arbitrary length of thirty-five years (customary, they said, in Greek historiography), and then by multiplying that number by seven, that is, by the number of kings the tradition mentioned for Rome, to arrive at 245 years. The date of the foundation of Rome, which Varro places in 754/753 B.C.E., was thus fixed from a reference point provided by the date of the beginning of the Republic, that is, 509 B.C.E., a date whose historicity, owing to the ancient lists of consuls in particular, can be considered certain.

The most extraordinary thing is not that such an ingenious solution has been shown to be false[75] and in contradiction with the tradition itself. As many

---

[73] A convergence underscored in Momigliano, *Roma arcaica*, 23. It is not without interest that the excavations carried out in Carthage seem to validate the "high" date for the foundation of the city, contrary to everything believed until now. See F. Rakob, "Karthago, Die frühe Siedlung: Neue Forschungen," in *Mitteilungen des deutschen archäologischen Instituts* 96 (1989): 155–288ff.

[74] On this, see O. de Cazanove, "La chronographie grecque et la durée de la période royale," forthcoming in *La Rome des premiers siècles: Légende et histoire.*

[75] See M. Piérart, "Les dates de la chute de Troie et de la fondation de Rome: Comput par génération ou compte à rebours?" in *Historia testis: Mélanges offerts à T. Zawadski*, ed. M. Piérart and O. Curty (1989), 7ff.

excellent minds noted early on, the tradition does not assign an identical length of time to each reign, and, in any case, the standard unit of thirty-five years is inadequate. The astonishing thing is rather that its fortunes lasted so long. That is how strong the conviction was that the tradition could only be artificial and that, as a result, the secrets of its fabrication had to be revealed! In reality, that calculation shed little light on the tradition, but a great deal of light on hyper-criticism and its methodological prejudices. In its system, then, the length of the regal period and the date of the foundation of Rome were both considered artificial pieces of data (*calculations,* in the exact sense of the term). The only piece of data considered primary was the list of the seven kings. In reality, it could very well be that that list resulted precisely from the work of transformation effected by the tradition, from its interventions, which it is out of the question to deny. One of the most curious things is that on this essential point, the hypercritical construction rested on a literal reading of the tradition. The texts themselves lead us to suspect that Rome had more than seven kings, since it seems that, without mentioning Titus Tatius or Aulus Vibenna, Porsena (as both Alföldi and Beaufort show) and perhaps Brutus exercised a power that was royal in nature at the beginning of the "Republic."[76]

It is thus much simpler to suppose that the literary sources were unanimous in fixing the length of the regal period at 244 or 245 years, and in situating the date of the foundation of Rome so consistently toward the middle of the eighth century B.C.E., simply because they possessed a preexisting tradition, transmitted by one of the paths of memory we have just explored.[77]

Writing is much older in Latium and Rome than was once believed, and however unusual it might have been, one of its first functions must have been to record changes in reigns and the beginning of all things, that is, the birth of the city. In that sense, a recent study by Colonna, based on archeological documents and their relation to precious "literary" indications, has shown the importance of the role of scribes in the archaic societies of central Italy.[78]

How can we not mention on this point the surprising synchronism revealed by archeology? In Rome, in three distinct sites—the Regia, the Comitium, and Sant'Omobono—and also, it seems, in the southwestern area of the Palatine, excavations have revealed successive constructions, destructions, and reconstructions. And not only are the transformations observable at these four sites exactly contemporary with one another, but their development corresponds in its main lines to the great stages of the monarchy, as the tradition delineates them: the

---

[76] See Heurgon, *Rome et la Méditerranée occidentale,* 227–28.

[77] A hypothesis already suggested by Heurgon, *Rome et la Méditerranée occidentale,* 227. It may be that the name Romulus was mentioned in the victory ceremony (Dion. Hal. *Ant. rom.* 2.34), as were the names of Cossus and Camillus (Livy *Ab urbe condita* 5.49.7). See G. Wille's essay in the collection *Studien zur vorliterarischen Periode in frühen Rome,* ed. G. Vogt-Spira (Tübingen, 1989), 199–225.

[78] G. Colonna, "Scriba sum rege sedens," in *Mélanges Heurgon* (1976), 2: 187–95.

arrival of the Tarquins, the eventful reign of Servius Tullius (framed, it seems, by episodes of violence leading to fires), and the advent of the Republic. In and of themselves, these indexes are sufficient to lead toward a rehabilitation of the traditional account of the origins.[79] Combined with the new discoveries just described, it would be "chancy" to allow "chance" to reign as master over so many "coincidences"!

Should we then attribute to the Greeks (in this case, to Eratosthenes or his imitators) the invention of the chronology of the foundation of the city? That would less solve the problem than displace it, by imputing to the Greeks, in accordance with a principle of explanation dear to hypercriticism, "the invention of Rome," of its chronology and its legends. But from whom did the Greeks get these legends, this date of the foundation, if not from the Romans themselves? And can we suppose, after all we have seen regarding the paths of memory of Rome and the early date of the Greek presence, that it was not until the very end of the fifth century B.C.E., after the Tarquins, after Servius Tullius, after the establishment of the Republic, that the city of Romulus began to concern itself with its origin, its traditions, and their place in human time?

Of course, within the length of the regal period delimited in that way, manipulations and camouflage of all kinds were not lacking. Owing to a critical remark by Dionysius of Halicarnassus regarding his distant predecessor Fabius Pictor,[80] we have proof, for example, that the chronology of the Etruscan kings in Rome had been manipulated, perhaps in the second century B.C.E., in order to synchronize it with events of Greek, and particularly Corinthian, history. But the correction proposed by Dionysius is hardly convincing, as Pierre Bayle excellently pointed out in this regard: "The historian succeeded better at refuting his predecessors than at avoiding his own mistakes."[81] In the last century, hypercriticism, always rightly attentive to the slightest variations in the literary sources, showed that this synchrony was artificial,[82] since the data transmitted by Fabius turn out to be incompatible with it. Furthermore, the accepted chronology, which adds an intermediate generation[83]—that of Servius Tullius—between the two Tarquins, is only the result of a work of reelaboration, as has recently been shown,[84] based precisely on this synchrony with the history of Corinth.

---

[79] See the final pages ("Rome au VIᵉ s.") of the Paris exhibition catalog *Naissance de Rome* (Paris, 1977). See also Coarelli, *Il foro romano*, 1: 137. The traces of fire in the Regia evoke the charred vestiges dating from August 1792, which Parisian archeologists found in the Tuileries when the Grand Louvre was renovated.

[80] Dion. Hal. *Ant. rom.* 4.7.

[81] P. Bayle, *Dictionnaire historique et critique* (Paris, 1820), s.v. "Tanaquil."

[82] "The appearances are deceiving," said Schwegler in *Römische Geschichte*, 1: 676 (see also pp. 48, 49, and 677–80).

[83] See Schachermayr in *RE* 4A (1932), 2351–52, s.v. "Tarquini." Servius Tullius was inserted through the creation of a second Tarquinia.

[84] O. de Cazanove, "La chronologie des Bacchiades et celle des rois étrusques de Rome,"

In short, one of the most interesting things about the whole matter is that Fabius Pictor, far from being the falsifier Beaufort and Alföldi considered him, now appears as the witness to a first tradition, which was manipulated and "falsified" only after him.

Hypercriticism and, before it, the historical Pyrrhonism following in the footsteps of Bayle and Lorenzo Valla (who in 1442 devoted a famous dissertation to the question, thus marking the beginning of philological and historical criticism on Rome's origins) concluded from these chronological "contradictions" or "impossibilities" that the tradition had to be condemned as a whole, in the name of a history reduced to chronology. Yet we no longer believe that the figure of Servius Tullius, so atypical, so "abnormal," was a late invention, but rather that his reign, or more exactly, his power in Rome (for in many aspects, he does not seem to have been a king like the others, and Virgil says nothing about him)[85] was then subjected by the tradition to considerable retouching and normalization, which, however, could not totally efface the color of the original.

As for falsifications introduced into the tradition, as the ancients claimed, on the initiative of the great families (*gentes*) of republican Rome, we can reduce them to their true measure by noting (with de Sanctis) that these great families play almost no role in the narrative of origins. In other words, the successive transformations brought about in the tradition do not authorize us to reject it without further ado. Regarding the length of time assigned to each reign in particular, the account of the regal period continued to evolve, but from original elements that are still recognizable, beginning with the names of the kings themselves.[86] For example, the relations between Corinth and Etruria, attested to in abundance by archeology, suggest that the synchrony established secondarily between the reign of the Tarquins and the history of the Hellenic metropolis was favored by a tradition, this one authentic, that linked Tarquinius Priscus to the Greek city in one way or another.

Thus I shall speak not of "falsification" (a word dear to hypercriticism), but of the evolution of a tradition that, at each of its stages and expressions, must not be condemned as false testimony but must be analyzed historically.

In the data constituted during the regal period, the additions, suppressions, transfers, and rearrangements have certainly not been lacking. Nevertheless, the tradition of a foundation of Rome in the eighth century B.C.E. had to be strong

---

*Mélanges de l'Ecole Française de Rome,*1988, 615–48.

[85] In book 6 of the *Aeneid*, where Virgil has the (future) kings and great men of Rome parade before Aeneas; they come from the underworld to consult his father, Anchises, concerning the future (line 817).

[86] See T. Köves-Zulauf, "Die Herrschaftsdauer der römischen Könige," *Acta Antiqua Academiae Scientiarum Hungaricae* 30 (1982–84): 192–203. Köves-Zulauf shows that the better the "image" of the king in question, the longer the reign attributed to him by the tradition. In addition, the numerical correspondence between the reigns reveals artificial elaborations.

enough that, even when the desire to link the origins of the *urbs* to the great Trojan saga made Romulus a contemporary of Aeneas, the tradition had to imagine a second Romulus, situated "fifteen generations" later.[87] Whatever embellishments were introduced on the façade, the building rests on a foundation that is none other than the date of the foundation of Rome.

And yet, despite the paths of memory we have just traveled, how are we to believe in a tradition that contains so many legends, so many implausibilities of all kinds? What serious historian would dream of according faith, even with infinite goodwill, to all these lovely stories that seem so far from history? How are we to believe in a legend in which the Romans themselves did not believe?[88]

Can Servius Tullius, about whom the sources have accumulated so many tales, have been a truly historical character?

To these questions, as old as the research on Rome's origins, the response seems to be given in advance. And of course, in asking them once more, we would doubtless obtain the same result.

What we have to change, in fact, is not the response but the questions. "Belief," "faith," and "plausibility" are instruments of evaluation that, at least from this point of view, only prolong a mode of exegesis already present among the ancients, when they sought to account for the myth of the she-wolf who suckled Romulus and Remus by recalling that the word *lupa* was also applied to the prostitutes who frequented Subura (the district of ill repute in imperial Rome).

But it is also possible to say that, after all, the tradition claiming there were two Tarquins reigning in Rome is not in itself as implausible as the history of France, during which one Napoleon succeeded another after an interval of a generation (this argument comes from the historian P. de Francisci). We might therefore resolve to reduce the study of the primordial legends to the history of their reception and diffusion, following a prudent method that has often led to significant results.

But for a myth such as that of Romulus, for example, reception and diffusion are not the essential thing, and the response ought to be situated on another plane. It is clear that, behind these questions, there is nothing other than a conception of history that is constantly encountered in hypercriticism and entirely grounded in the notions of "facts" and "events."

Viewed from this perspective, the history of the beginnings of Rome remains in great part the obscure void it was for hypercriticism. But as soon as one considers it with different instruments, that void is filled by elements that had escaped observation and that appear more clearly every day in an analysis stripped of inadequate criteria.

---

[87] See Dion. Hal. *Ant. rom.* 1.73. In this version, the founder of the first Rome was also called Romos.

[88] For the question of the "reception" of ancient legends, see P. Veyne, *Les Grecs ont-ils cru à leurs mythes?* (Paris, 1983).

Nothing shows this better than the figure of King Servius Tullius, whom legend depicts as bearing so many similarities to Romulus. In fact, Romulus has often been interpreted by hypercriticism as merely a copy of that king. But since Servius Tullius himself appeared to hypercriticism as a nonhistorical character, hypercriticism led to a problematic and mysterious jostling of phantoms. The easiest thing was then to decide that these legends as a whole were invented very late, in the first century B.C.E., by some *imperator* anxious to create predecessors for himself. A century after the first excavations by Boni, the archeological data revealed over the years have dissipated these "modern legends" (to use Massimo Pallottino's expression).[89] But even though the traditions concerning Romulus and Servius Tullius are quite different, and one is not simply the doublet of the other, it is true that they display undeniable similarities.[90] Both kings are closely related to the god Volcanus; their births were both placed under the sign of Vesta; both were victorious over the Etruscans of Veii; both had the same comrade in arms (Caeles Vibenna); both played a role in the organization of the comitia in Rome; and, in general, both were depicted by the tradition as founders of the city.

These analogies are neither fortuitous nor "secondary." In my view, they open the door to elucidating the very mysterious legend of the Roma Quadrata, linked to Romulus by the sources, but also to Servius Tullius. More generally, they illuminate the nature of that legendary history of early Rome, which has so often been misunderstood.

Most of the time, the apparent wavering by the tradition between the two kings was explained as one of the signs of a tendency among ancient historians to relate everything to Romulus.[91] This phenomenon was well known to Dionysius of Halicarnassus, for example, who intentionally stripped the Etruscan reigns of their content and attributed that content to Romulus, who was presented as the almost Greek founder of a Greek city.[92] Beaufort writes: "As for Dionysius of Halicarnassus, everything he says must be suspect. Once he resolves to give a Greek origin to the Romans, he never loses sight of that object."[93]

Of course, regarding Servius Tullius, whose Etruscan origin is far from certain, the link with Romulus is not at all restricted to the author of *Antiquitates romanae*; it largely transcends what can be noted for the other kings of Rome. An interesting element for the interpretation of the relations between the legend of the Romulean foundation and the gesture of King Servius Tullius has

[89] See M. Pallottino, "Fatti e leggende (moderne) sulla più antica storia di Roma," *Studi Etruschi* 31 (1963): 3–37.

[90] See Coarelli, *Il foro romano*, 1: 197–99.

[91] This is what Poucet calls "the phenomenon of Romulization"; see *Origines de Rome*, 200–217.

[92] On this matter, see D. Musti, *Tendenze nella storiografia romana e greca su Roma arcaica* (Rome, 1970).

[93] L. de Beaufort, *La République romaine ou plan général de l'ancien gouvernement de Rome* (1766), vol. 1, chap. 1.

been provided by the archeological exploration of the Comitium. There, in addition to the famous Lapis Niger, traces have been found of a structure on the site dating from the sixth century B.C.E., and the contents of a votive repository (*favissa*) stemming from between the second quarter of the sixth century and the first century B.C.E. Included among the animal bones identified with the votive objects are the remains of a sacrificed vulture,[94] that is, the auspicious bird that, according to tradition, was sent by the gods to Romulus to indicate that he had been chosen the founder of Rome. Does that mean that these bones belonged to one of the vultures seen, as the tradition says, by Romulus from Palatine Hill? No, of course not. But, to schematize, I would say that if they were not seen by the man we are calling Romulus, it is possible they were seen by the man called Servius Tullius in Rome.

In other words, these remains suggest that in the sixth century B.C.E., the Comitium was a "Romulean" place, just like the *casa Romuli* on the Palatine, about which we discover, and this is certainly no accident, the same legendary hesitation, this time between Faustulus and Romulus. On the Palatine and at the Comitium, we find two "memory sites" where the recollection of the foundation of Rome was commemorated, and where the Romulean legend found two of its privileged vehicles for celebration and transmission. The successive renovations of these symbolic sites can no doubt be read as successive stages, which can be discerned in the elaboration of the "literary" legend. The construction of the Comitium in the sixth century B.C.E. corresponds to a legend attributed by Plutarch to one Promathion, which gives the legend of Romulus the features of the Servius Tullius legend. The equivalence posited by that legend must be reversed. In other words, it shows that Servius Tullius claimed to be a new Romulus, as an examination of the different phases of the Comitium also demonstrates.

The preceding considerations also allow us to illuminate the tradition of the *Roma Quadrata,* so charged with obscurity and mystery that it has become a veritable myth of modern scholarship.[95]

In fact, the tradition locates the Roma Quadrata, that is, the Rome traced according to the rituals of augur divination, sometimes exclusively on the Palatine Hill, and sometimes in a much larger area, including the Forum in particular. Most of the time, the classical sources associate it with Romulus, but sometimes with Servius Tullius. Another difficulty: even when confined to the Palatine, the expression "Roma Quadrata" seems to designate at times a small building, at others the hill as a whole. In my view, archeology provides the

---

[94] See Cristofani, ed., *La grande Roma,* 55 and 58.
[95] See D. Musti, "Varrone nell'insieme delle tradizioni su Roma quadrata," in the proceedings of the congress, *Gli storiografi latini tramandati in frammenti* (1974), 297–318. All references to the ancient and modern texts on the question can be found in this work. In the pages that follow, I summarize the conclusions of a forthcoming study of my own.

explanation for this last apparent imprecision. Used to refer to a stone rectangle located in front of the temple of Apollo (in other words, near the House of Augustus), the expression designates an *auguraculum,* that is, one of the augur terraces that the excavations of Marzabotto, Bantia, and Cosa have taught us to recognize. That was where the augur and king stood to trace the sacred limits of his foundation, and it was thus through metonymic slippage that the expression came to designate the Palatine Hill as a whole, which was part of the space thus defined. Rome then extended toward the Forum, which in turn saw itself endowed with all the signs of sovereignty that had been the privilege of the Palatine. Thus, when Plutarch mentioned a Roma Quadrata centered on the Forum, it was not, as has often been said, a confusion or error on his part. That location and that name can be explained as a use of the founding legend by Servius Tullius, creator of an enlarged and regularized Rome, the Rome of the four regions, and promoter of a thorough social reorganization, the famous "Servian constitution."[96] Because that extension and the reform that accompanied it constituted a new foundation, Servius Tullius was a new Romulus and the city he redefined a new Roma Quadrata, no longer confined to the Palatine alone, but extending to the Forum, which had become the center of the city.

From the exclusively philological perspective of hypercriticism, "the literary tradition" was thus only a great cadaver—lifeless, motionless, without history. Its vision of the written sources, arranged along the shelves of the scholarly libraries of *Altertumswissenschaft,* was stripped of relief and depth. Interpreting changes in the legend in terms of variants between authors, the imagination of falsifiers, or scholarly errors, it saw a recent and fabricated "literary tradition" where we increasingly see, imprinted in the materials of buildings endlessly renovated, the fossilized traces of ancient and historically significant interventions.

Hypercriticism came into being during a century that institutionalized rights of authorship, if it did not invent them outright. For hypercritics, legend was in the first place a literary and philological fact. The goal in studying "the literary tradition" was thus to identify the authors, determine *the* date of each text, and, if possible, return to its sources (*Quellenforschung*), in short, to discover, for each of the legends of the primordial "account," the guilty party (that is, the supposed author) and the motive for the crime (that is, the reason for the falsification supposedly represented by every legend). All these pursuits were grounded in the conviction that people invent legends the way they write novels (recall Michelet's definition of Roman legend as a "novel of origins"), and that writing is in the first place a process of individual invention and creation. Why, however, should what was true for the century of Hugo and Chateaubriand have been so for an archaic civilization where writing was first of all a phenomenon on the collective order, whether as instrument in a rite or as a mode of memory? Thus a legend

---

[96] See J.-C. Richard, "L'oeuvre de Servius Tullius," *Revue des Etudes Latines* 60 (1982): 30–36.

attested to only late can have an ancient origin, as in the example of Greek myths found only among Byzantine authors, but illustrated on vases from the seventh century B.C.E. The analysis of legends thus reveals a diachronic complexity, a stratification that is not necessarily that of the "sources," since, to borrow the very image suggested by a word dear to hypercriticism, we know that "resurgences" can appear very far from the original source. In the legendary landscape of the primordia, a text such as the *Origo gentis romanae* today enjoys renewed attention on the part of specialists,[97] even though it is anonymous and late, two characteristics that, for hypercriticism, meant it literally did not exist.

It is thus because they were the site of living memory transmitted from generation to generation that the Comitium, the *casa Romuli,* and many other monuments as well continued to be maintained, renovated, and transformed. Toward the end of the fourth century B.C.E., the Comitium underwent important renovations, as did the site of the *aedes Romuli,* where it seems that a kind of "heroon" was built, a sanctuary dedicated to a founding hero.[98]

During the same period, when Rome was asserting its domination over Latium as a whole, an old tomb from the seventh century B.C.E. was also transformed into a heroon in Lavinium. The study of the literary sources shows that the legend of Aeneas—which, in a certain way, had always been available to everyone—received a decisive push following an intervention that it would be difficult to attribute to anyone but the Romans. The structural analysis of the myth of Aeneas,[99] as it was attested to in Lavinium, and of Latinus, another legendary figure of the city of Laurentum, demonstrates, through the numerous similarities it brings to light, that one hero came to replace the other at a time we can fix in the fourth century B.C.E., when Rome asserted its domination over the whole of Latium. Hence myths live and are transformed over the centuries by the circumstances and interests of those who use them.[100]

The Romans also situated the seat of their Penates (gods of the origin par excellence) in Lavinium. Because they were the gods of *before,* they could be only *elsewhere* (than Rome).[101] In that way, a journey through space was also a journey through time, and every year Rome discovered, on the occasion of a solemn sacrifice to the Penates,[102] the place of its origin and the consciousness of its own destiny. There is certainly a "narrative" of origins according to which Rome, daughter of Alba, and, so to speak, granddaughter of Lavinium, maintained the memory of a past where it continued to read its future. Indisputably,

---

[97] As a result particularly of J.-C. Richard's edition (Paris, 1983).

[98] See P. Pensabene in *La grande Roma,* ed. Cristofani, 90.

[99] See my "Le roi Latinus."

[100] These considerations lead us to relativize the polemics on the "exact" date of the text attributed to Promathion by Plutarch.

[101] Here I follow the illuminating demonstration in Y. Thomas, "L'institution de l'origine: Sacra Principiorum Populi Romani" in *Tracés de fondation,* ed. M. Détienne (1990).

[102] See A. Dubourdieu, *Les origines et le développement du culte des Pénates à Rome* (1989).

this narrative was fabricated, or rather imagined, since as we have seen, the Lavinium-Alba-Rome succession on which the narrative was founded has no archeological reality. But that arrangement has a meaning and a function that are properly historical, whereas the choice of these two sites as "metropolises" can be explained only by the most ancient past of Latium and Rome.

In the history of these paths of memory—that is, of legends—in Lavinium and in Rome, other stages followed. Near the beginning of the Common Era, the narrative of the primordia took the definitive shape that we know today. But just because the Comitium, the temple of Vesta, and so many memory sites were restored or rebuilt in the first century B.C.E., we would hardly lend credence to an archeologist who wanted to date their origin from that moment. Yet hypercritical philology did nothing else when it dated one or another legend of origins at a particular time as a function of the author who first attested to it.

One of the major achievements of the archeological science of this century was the discovery of the importance of stratigraphy.[103] Texts are no less complex than stones, and it is time to apply the principles of a diachronic stratigraphy to their interpretation. The legend of Romulus was not invented by Servius Tullius but was used by him, which is a very different matter, historically rich in implications.

How, under these conditions, are we to understand that assimilation, which was not late and after the fact, but contemporary to the reign of Servius and no doubt intentional? Certainly not by appealing to the interpretive grid provided by the chronological history of past events, since all the "facts" provided us by legend would pass through the grid without even being noticed.

That is why we must abandon the accepted opposition between history and legend and must finally understand that legend is historical, just as history is legendary. On this point, the methods of anthropology—but an anthropology no longer conceived as the antithesis of history—indicate the path to take.

In an excellent book, Marshall Sahlins analyzes how the arrival and then the death of Captain James Cook in the Hawaiian Islands in 1779 were experienced by the indigenous peoples of the archipelago. In "reality," if we can call it that (since, as the saying goes, the real is mythic, and the mythic real), the Hawaiians considered Cook an incarnation of the god-king Lono, "the dying god" (the expression used by Frazer in reference to him), who died every year and was reborn the next. To his misfortune, Cook, whose ship had been damaged, unexpectedly went aground at the time of the ritual death of Lono. Thus, according to Sahlins, "everything transpired as if . . . the historical event were the metaphor of a mythical reality."[104] Cook was killed in an assassination that was in fact a sacrifice.

---

[103] The excavations of G. Boni in the Forum and on the Palatine had decisive importance for this discovery.

[104] Sahlins, *Islands of History*, 4.

At least in the archaic era, the Romans also "thought that the future was behind them." History realized myth, and myth announced history. Servius Tullius was a new Romulus, and, like Romulus before him, he was "a myth before he was an event, since the myth was the frame by which his appearance was interpreted."[105]

Will it be said once more that it is not "plausible" that Romulus was the son of Mars? But that filiation has no less "historical" interest and value than that which makes the emperor of Japan the child of the Sun!

Hence the foundation of Rome, commemorated and celebrated over time, was not a myth that could never have been real, or an event that much later became a myth. It was an "event" that, with the advent of Rome, was conceived as a myth, a history that was, at the time of its occurrence, a legend, a beginning that was already a celebration and a new beginning.

---

[105] Ibid., 73. Similarly, I do not think that the relation between Servius Tullius and the legendary figure of Herakles is necessarily the result of a late addition. After all, in Athens, Peisistratus magnificently exploited "mythistory" when he arranged to be accompanied by a young girl disguised as Athena as he carried out the coup d'état that brought him to power.

CONCLUSION

ENCE IT ALL began and ended with the foundation. When, on the banks of the Tiber, the ancient organization of leagues gave way to the inaugurated city, there emerged with it a new universe and a new era.

A unique moment, perpetually remembered, a primordial break and a principle of eternity, a mythic history and a historical myth, the foundation of Rome, where space and time met, had the value of the creation of the world. That is why, in the end, the best proof for the historical existence of the Romulean foundation is its mythical character. Because there was only one Rome, there will never be another Romulus, another foundation, anywhere else. After more than a century of comparative research, it remains without known equivalents or parallels.[1]

In a famous passage,[2] Dumézil opposes the Romans and the East Indians and delineates point by point the differences in their conception of the world, despite the fundamental identity supposed by their shared Indo-European origin. Nothing is more accurate or better observed than the description given of what used to be called the Roman genius.[3] But if the Romans thought "historically" and the Indians "fabulously", the Romans "nationally" and the Indians "cosmically," if Romans "were interested in a story only if it had some relation to Rome," if their reflections were oriented "practically" and not "philosophically," "relatively, empirically," and not "absolutely, dogmatically," "politically" and not "morally," if "the life of Rome" was for them "a constantly posed problem," this was not the result of some metaphysical and transhistorical frame of mind. It was because they continued to read the beginning of all things in the foundation of Rome that had brought them into their own. The explanation for that perception of the world is not theological but historical.

---

[1] "For the Romans, Romulus was above all the founder of Rome. His gesture was centered on that essential event for which the imagined parallels provide no true equivalent" (D. Briquel, "La mort de Rémus ou la cité comme rupture," in *Tracés de fondation*, 171–79). See also, in the same collection, C. Malamoud, "Sans lieu ni date: Note sur l'absence de fondation dans l'Inde Védique," 183–91. Malamoud writes that "Vedic India is silent about foundations" (p. 183).

[2] Dumézil, *La religion romaine archaïque*, 129–30.

[3] See A. Grenier, *Le génie romain dans la religion, la pensée et l'art* (1925).

Constantly tested by numerous archeological discoveries, the tradition, or rather the complex set of texts designated by that name, appears increasingly to be an "unavoidable" basis of interpretation. While all the great systems of exegesis believed able to substitute for it have disintegrated one by one, the tradition is more than ever the place from which any analysis must begin and then return, to test its hypotheses and its conclusions each time. On many questions, the proof has been given during recent decades that such a method is still the most effective and "economical" approach, compared to reconstructions that required destroying half the edifice before being able to reinforce the other half.

Under such conditions, must we simply return to Dante's "Livy, who does not err"? No, of course not. "True" even when it turns out to be "false" ("Romulus" was not the son of Mars), "false" even when it turns out to be "true" (the Palatine is not the place where it all began), the tradition continues to escape the equally simplistic readings of hypercriticism ("everything is false") and fideism ("everything is true").

"Truth," "error," "myth," "history," and "legend"—in the end, it is much less a matter of calling into question the *distribution* of the different elements composing the tradition into these different categories than the categories themselves. Therein lies one of the major lessons of the study of the *primordia Romana*. It shows that, because of the fragmented approach they entail, the antinomies that ground our modern "human sciences" by opposing politics to religion, the written to the oral, anthropology to history, history to legend, the true to the false—antinomies constituted by the Cartesian project to elaborate a knowledge of each question that is "precise and different from all the others"[4]—are powerless to account for a world where everything is very complex because very simple. Hence the contemporary quality of Vico's message. What history, sociology, and anthropology bring to modern human beings, thus allowing them to understand the universe in which they live and the past belonging to them, myth and legend brought to the Romans of archaic times. But what to us is distinction (in the Cartesian sense of the term), description, and analysis was for them totality, analogy, ritual, and remembrance.

Hypercriticism treated legend as the eternally accused, who had to prove his innocence before the tribunal of history. But the ingenuity and cunning of the accuser inevitably doomed him to failure. We know, however, that by all rights, it is not guilt that is presumed, but innocence, and the burden of proof falls upon the accuser, not the accused.

The evaluation of the legend of Rome's origins thus requires a reelaboration of our own criteria for evaluation. Scientistic positivism, of which hypercriticism was the expression in the field of the *primordia Romana*, made science the

---

[4] "I call distinct . . . knowledge, that which is so precise and different from all the others that it includes within itself only what appears self-evident to anyone who considers it as he should" (R. Descartes, *Des principes de la connaissance humaine,* 1: 45).

absolute antithesis of uncertainty, setting them up against each other as fullness to emptiness, being to nothingness. Today, a configuration of uncertainties appears, but a configuration that is endlessly in motion and where, in a perpetual play of mirrors and reflections, knowledge may be no more than a particularly elaborated form of uncertainty, and ignorance may be the final stage of knowledge.

In the future, we can be certain that, in the dual discovery of this knowledge of uncertainty and the uncertainty of that knowledge, we will still have much to learn from the continued and ever renewed exploration of Rome's origins.

APPENDICES

CHRONOLOGIES

1. Traditional Chronology

753	Foundation of Rome (according to Varro)
753–715	Romulus
715–672	Numa Pompilius
672–640	Tullus Hostilius
640–616	Ancus Marcius
616–578	Tarquinius Piscus
579–534	Servius Tullius
534–509	Tarquinius Superbus
509	Beginning of the Republican regime and dedication of the temple of Jupiter Capitoline (509/507)
390	Sack of Rome by the Gauls

2. Archeology

Period I	About 1000–900 (Late Bronze Age)
II A	900–830 (Iron Age)
II B	830–770
III	770–730
IV A	730–630 (Early and Middle Orientalizing)
IV B	630–570 (Late Orientalizing)

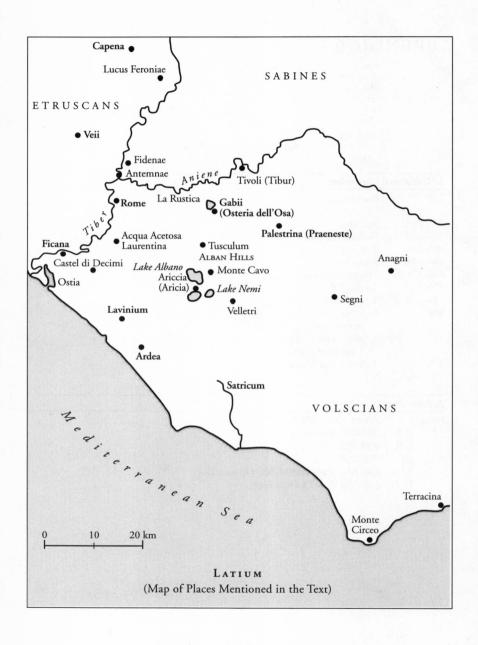

LATIUM
(Map of Places Mentioned in the Text)

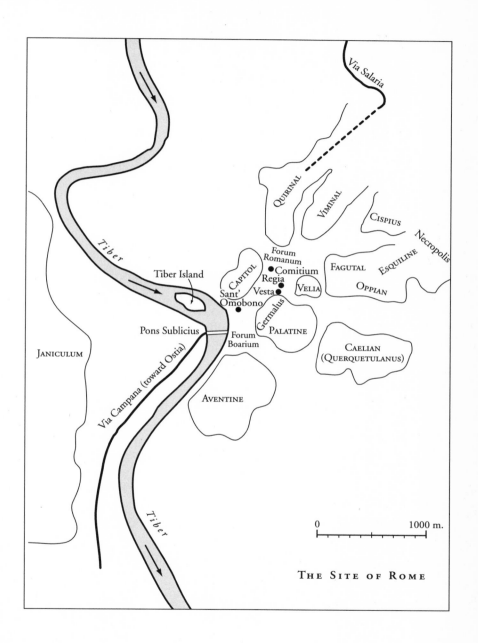

THE SITE OF ROME

BIBLIOGRAPHY

1. SOURCES OF EXTENSIVE BIBLIOGRAPHIES

The Cambridge Ancient History. Vol. 7, no. 2. 2d ed. Cambridge, 1989.

Cristofani, M., ed. *La grande Roma dei Tarquini.* Catalog of the Rome exhibition (June–September 1990). Rome, 1990.

Heurgon, Jacques. *Rome et la Méditerranée occidentale jusqu'aux guerres puniques.* Paris, 1969; rev. ed. 1980.

Poucet, Jacques. *Les origines de Rome: Tradition et histoire.* Brussels, 1985.

2. PRINCIPAL LITERARY SOURCES

Dionysius of Halicarnassus. *Antiquitates romanae.* For commentary, see *Actes du Colloque Denys d'Halicarnasse (Dijon, 16–17 juin 1988),* in *Mélanges de l'Ecole Française de Rome* 101 (1989).

Livy. *Ab urbe condita libri,* book 1. For commentary, see R. M. Ogilvie, *A Commentary on Livy Books 1–5.* Oxford, 1965.

Plutarch. *Vitae. Romulus* and *Numa.* For commentary, see C. Ampolo, ed., *Le vite di Teseo e di Romolo.* Milan, 1988.

3. WORKS IN THE FIELD OF THE HISTORY OF MODERN HISTORIOGRAPHY

Erasmus, H. J. *The Origins of Rome in the Historiography from Petrarch to Perizonius.* Leiden, 1962.

Grandazzi, Alexandre. "L'avenir du passé: De l'histoire de l'historiographie à l'historiologie." *Diogène* 151 (1990): 56–78.

Momigliani, Arnaldo. *Contributi alla storia degli studi clasici e del mondo antico.* Rome, 1955–87.

———. *Roma arcaica.* Florence, 1989.

Richard, J.-C. *Les origines de la plèbe romaine.* Paris, 1978.

4. WORKS IN THE FIELDS OF ARCHEOLOGY AND HISTORY

a.

Archeologia Laziale (Quaderni del Centro di Studio per l'Archeologia Etrusco-italica) (1978–).

Carandini, Andrea. "Palatino, pendici settentrionali: Campagne di scavo 1985—88." *Bollettino di Archeologia* 2 (1990).

———. *Schiavi in Italia.* Rome, 1988.

*Notizie degli Scavi di Antichità,*1899, 1900, and 1903. Preliminary reports on the excavations of Giacomo Boni.
See also a forthcoming publication by R. T. Scott, who has undertaken an exhaustive exploration of the temple of Vesta.

b.

Anzidei, A. P., A. M. Bietti-Sestieri, and A. de Santis. *Roma ed il Lazio dall'età della pietra alla formazione della città.* Rome, 1985.
Bloch, Raymond. *Tite-Live et les premiers siècles de Rome.* Paris, 1965.
Briquel, Dominique. *Les Pélasges en Italie.* Paris, 1984.
Briquel, Dominique, and François Hinard. *Histoire de Rome.* Forthcoming.
Coarelli, Filippo. *Il foro boario.* Rome, 1988.
———. *Il foro romano.* Vol. 1: *Periodo arcaico.* Rome, 1983.
Colonna, Giovanni. "I Latini e gli altri popoli del Lazio." In *Italia, omnium terrarum alumna,* 411–528. Milan, 1988.
———. "Preistoria e protostoria di Roma e del Lazio." In *Popoli et civiltà dell'Italia antica* 2 (1974).
Dialoghi di Archeologia, 1980 (2 vols.). Proceedings of the colloquium "La formazione della città nel Lazio."
Dubourdieu, A. *Les origines de le développement du culte des Pénates à Rome.* Paris, 1989.
Dumézil, Georges. *Mythe et épopée.* Vols. 1 and 3. Paris, 1968 and 1973.
———. *La religion romaine archaïque.* 2d ed. Paris, 1974.
Gjerstad, Einar. *Early Rome.* Lund, 1953–73.
    Vol. 1: *Stratigraphical Researches in the Forum Romanum and along the Sacra Via.* 1953.
    Vol. 2: *The Tombs.* 1956.
    Vol. 3: *Fortifications, Domestic Architecture, Sanctuaries, Stratigraphical Excavations.* 1960.
    Vol. 4: *Synthesis of Archeological Evidence.* 1966.
    Vol. 5: *The Written Sources.* 1973.
    Vol. 6: *Historical Survey.* 1973.
Magdelain, André. *Jus, Imperium, Auctoritas: Etudes de droit romain.* Paris, 1990.
Meyer, J. C. *Pre-Republican Rome.* Odense, 1983.
Momigliano, Arnaldo. *Roma arcaica.* Florence, 1989.
Momigliano, Arnaldo, and A. Schiavone, eds. *Storia di Roma.* Vol. 1: *Roma in Italia.* Turin, 1988.
Müller-Karpe, Heinrich. *Von Anfang Roms.* Heidelberg, 1959.
———. *Zur Stadtwerdung Roms.* Heidelberg, 1962.
Pallottino, Massimo. *Saggi di antichità.* Vol. 1. Rome, 1979.
La Parola del Passato, 1977 and 1980. Proceedings of the 1977 colloquium in Rome "Lazio arcaico e mondo greco."
Poucet, Jacques. "Le Latium protohistorique et archaïque à la lumière des découvertes archéologiques récentes." *Antiquité Classique,* 1978–79.
———. "La Rome archaïque—Quelques nouveautés archéologiques: S. Omobono, le Comitium, la Regia." *Antiquité Classique,* 1980.
Quilici, L. *Roma primitiva e le origini della civiltà laziale.* Rome, 1979.
Torelli, Mario. *Lavinio e Roma.* Rome, 1984.

c. Exhibitions and Exhibition Catalogs

Civiltà del Lazio primitivo. Rome, 1976.

Naissance de Rome. Paris, 1977. Abridged French version of the preceding entry, marking the arrival of the exhibition at the Petit Palais in Paris.

Enea nel Lazio: Archeologia e mito. Rome, 1981.

Il viver quotidiano in Roma arcaica. Rome, 1989.

La grande Roma dei Tarquini. Rome, 1990.

La Rome des premiers siècles: Légende et histoire. Actes de la Table Ronde en l'Honneur de Massimo Pallottino (Paris, 3–4 mai 1990). Florence, 1992.

An exhibition is in preparation in Rome dealing with reports on the *urbs* and on Veii in the archaic era.

In Rome for several years, there have been discussions about the creation of a large museum devoted exclusively to the *primordia urbis*. Its eventual configuration has begun to take shape with the various exhibitions. We can obviously only hope that such a project is realized.

INDEX